Walking on Thin Water:
A Memoir

by Cindy Lou Bechtold

Acknowledgements . . .

Thanks go to all those wonderful people who spiced up my life, specifically my husband, Carl, who has been my strength for forty six years. I want to thank my family, especially my mother, the one that always says I do the best I can. Thanks to my writing group for hours of sharing and helping. P.S. Some of the names inside have been changed to protect the guilty.

Walking on Thin Water: A Memoir
by Cindy Lou Bechtold

Published by the author
Cover art original collage by the author
Book design by Carl Bechtold

To Toni —
Written by one of
your best fans —
Enjoy a read up
Cindy B.

Gigi

Table of Contents

Taking the Long Route

My husband, Carl, has always called them "Cindy-isms." The rest of the family pretty much ignores them, but not my man, the English/psychology major.

"They're usually mixed metaphors," he explains. "Everybody slips once in a while. Short circuits in the neurons," he analyzes. "The thoughts are just getting too crowded in your brain, and ideas just sort of arc from one to the other."

Oh great. It's a tumor.

"Lovely, and it's only going to get worse," I reply.

"Dang!" he says. "I was always going to write down the good ones. We could publish a book."

Perfect Cindyisms, like the time I was really irritated at him and proclaimed, "Buddy, you're walking on thin water!" It didn't have the desired effect. Then there was the time I was relating how a friend was taking her life in a bad direction, and I explained, "She's jumping from the frying pan into the pot." (It's become something of a family slogan.)

And recently I was explaining the talent of one of my young cousins, Ben. "He's a master of the cello. One of these days he'll be playing in the Philharmonica Orchestra."

And this one scared me into thoughts of dementia. I was at the nursery looking for plant fertilizer. "Do you have any Miralax?"

"Maybe you have that mixed up with Miracid, ma'am," a curly-headed young clerk responded.

Oh boy, pretend you know what you're doing.

Probably the best one ever uttered was due to my athletic prowess. I had been playing softball for several summers. (They kept me on the team even though I ran the wrong way once in a sticky situation.) I decided to try out racquetball. It sounded fun and would be a different motion for my shoulder, which grinded like two bricks rubbing against one another. I think people could hear it when I raised my hand to answer questions at church.

But, the new sport didn't help. As a matter of fact, it got worse. Some mornings I could barely lift my arm high enough to poof out my hair. This was getting serious. We tried ice. We tried heat.

I went to the doctor.

He listened to the crunching and suggested I go see an orthopedic specialist in the nearby "big city."

We couldn't both go, with no one left to mind the shop, so I headed to Billings, Montana early one morning. Late that afternoon I drove back home and arrived a bit after the shop had closed. Carl was waiting for me. "So what did the doctor say?"

"He said I should quit playing sports for several weeks, take Ibuprofen every day, and alternate hot and cold packs."

"And what if that doesn't help?"

"He said I may have to have procto-scopic surgery."

Silence.

For a while, there was only the furrowed brow. Then he deadpanned. "Sounds like a long route to take to get to a shoulder."

"Cindy-isms." He never wrote the book, so I did.

Here it is. *Walking on Thin Water.*

"The Look," over the generations... Though it comes in varieties from funny to frown, the eyebrow thing has long been a feature of "The Look" that follows my best-mixed metaphors. Notice grand daughter Celie has inherited the ability to keep me in line, even if Carl goes deaf.

Biting Hoof and Nail

Ah—to bathe, perhaps to soak.

I drew the bathwater, chose a relaxing mix from my essential oils and dribbled a few drops under the spigot. Water churned citrus and mint leaf smells. I needed a good soak. Work had been frustrating and evening meetings long.

I slipped out of my clothes, anticipation building as the water rose. I turned off the water, steam seeping into my cells, smells knocking down stress like a toddler toppling wooden blocks. My big toe figure-eighted the water, testing the temperature before I buried myself up to my neck.

Eyes closed, I slid deeper, wetting my hair, feeling for the shampoo bottle. I sunk further into tranquility, staying prone several minutes, listening to the sweet sound of nothing much. Rubbing my eyes, I reluctantly gathered the resolve to come back to the world. As I focused first on the water, then my knees, my gaze caught sight of something on the opposite edge of the tub. It took a minute to register the mess under the bunched up shower curtain. Sitting straight up, I leaned closer, flipping the tip of my pointer finger through the pile. It really was.

Nail clippings.

His toenails mixed in with a couple of fingernails. I recognized the curve of his big toe…nail.

Carl had apparently beat me to the tub that evening, soaked his nails, and ripped them off one by one, piling them in a heap. What does one do with someone else's nail clippings? How rude. Other pet peeves surfaced as I jumped out, dried off and pondered how to pick up the pile. Okay, I've cleaned toilets bare-handed, I'll just scoop them together, slide them into my palm and toss them in the garbage—the same thing he should have done with his grooming remnants.

And that reminds me, he's got three days of socks lying at various angles around the clothes hamper. He missed every toss. AND how hard is it to use nail clippers, anyway? Clip, place in garbage. Clip, place in garbage. We don't argue about sticking wooden-handled knives into the dishwasher anymore. I just followed his suggestion not to. Now, I was going to give him one of my suggestions.

"Did you actually tear off your toenails and stack them on the edge of the tub?" I asked him as he got into bed.

No answer.

"Why don't you use the clippers? It's much more—should I say, couth?"

"Love me, love my toenails," he said. His smile the same one he used for justifications.

I'm going to kill him. "Do you know a pile of toenail ends are gross?" I said instead.

"I'll try to remember that. I bet they're scratchy," he muttered.

I grumbled a goodnight and lay awake, tension plugging all the cells I had tried to unclog.

The next Saturday after a day of yard work, I was tired. A good soak in the tub is what I need, I thought, as I finished the supper dishes and headed back to the bedroom to pick out a book. When I reached the tub, thoughts of scratchy toenails surfaced. Surely he wouldn't do that again. I pulled up the shower curtain to be certain and once again it took a minute for what I saw to register.

My husband had been trimming and shoeing our horse that day and had left me a surprise. Lined up in brown crescent moons, sliced horse hooves fanned the tub edge, their jagged largeness a reminder of how bad things really could get. Laughing, I found him outside in the corral, the hoof clippers jutting from his back pocket.

"You are so bad," I said. Laughing, I reached my arms around him in a squeeze. "That's too funny."

"Love me, love my horse." He pulled out the horse clippers and feigned clipping his thumbnail.

"I love you," I said. "But it's your horse, your chore. Please just gallop in there and collect your souvenirs."

Mud Ball Prayers

Crocus pushed through the earth. Rhubarb twisted green shoots like instruments tuning for a spring concert. Our horses pawed the pasture as if to awaken what lie beneath. High under the eaves of the house, a brown spot was growing on the wood. A bird nest! Oh, baby birds to sing accompaniment to spring.

Within days the tune changed. Those weren't baby birds; they were full grown barn swallows. They didn't sing, they screeched. The flock constructed mud homes for a whole community. Birds spit nests as big as giant tea cups on the eaves. The romantic tales of the swallows returning to Capistrano morphed into swallow bird-horror.

The irrigation ditch bordering the pasture was the cause. Swallows need a mud source; gooey enough to attach nests, close enough for easy access to the manufacturing site. One or two builders were cute; hundreds were hideous.

As the nests increased, so did the screeching.

I got out the hose.

Spraying off their dwellings would surely send the homeless flappers back to Capistrano, or at least over to the neighbor's house. Because our home was on a hill, garage underneath, the hose I dragged from the backyard was not nearly adequate. Aiming it skyward, spray fell short of the nests and back on my face.

No ladder on the place would extend high enough, so our old camper-special pickup would have to do. Backing that truck down the sloping driveway was no easy feat. Finally parked, I climbed on the hood, shimmied up the window and stood on the camper shell, hose in hand.

With the nozzle on "jet," I pulled the trigger. The connection leaked, but there was enough force to reach the first nest. Water broke through the mud shells. Chunks began sliding down the siding; water had long since been sliding down my sleeves. Chunks oozed into blobs as mud plopped onto the driveway, rendering the spitters homeless.

I wielded my weapon like a machine gun, spraying water until my arms ached, every inch of clothing soaked. "Take that, you invader, you home wrecker, you…rat…I mean birdie," I yelled. Every nest was gone, only brown rings remained, outlines of swallow house plans.

Drenched, sore and not looking forward to cleaning the mud pies splattered on the cement, I nonetheless claimed victory.

Even before I made a dent in the cleanup, the nasty grinding squeal I knew so well was back. I marched into the house. "You've got to help me get rid of these birds," I told Carl.

"If we can't drown them out, we'll shock them out," he said.

The next day he told me the plan.

"Don't spray any water near those birds. I'm going to string a piece of electric fence wire across the eaves where they're building. They're sure to trip it."

Barbequed bird feathers didn't appeal to me, but the thought of ridding my life of the pests made me want to sing again, no matter how crazy his scheme sounded.

Later, I took a huge breath and went to check it out. The noise was electrifying. The wire wasn't. Birds were spitting and flying, dive bombing into the ditch, heading back to the house, totally ambivalent to the trap. Hubby joined me. I think I heard what he was thinking. *No flock of butt-feathered, mud-slinging swallows is going to get away with this.*

I heard noise on the roof. Carl was dragging up another set of wires. "I've got 110 this time," he yelled down. "They'll land on one wire and touch their butt feathers to the other. This will work."

It didn't.

Not one of those swallows connected with the force. In fact, they seemed to be growing in population.

"Turn the juice off," I said. "I'm getting out the water." Beyond reasoning, I returned to my position and began obliterating newly-rising nests. My glasses needed windshield wipers, my arms were sunburned clear to my armpits and water dripped into my sandals, but I was on a mission.

As the sun set I took a reprieve. The next morning I peeked out the front door, reconnoitering. Beautiful rays fell inside the entry but a movement above my head uglied the scene. An insistent swallow flew out of a nest glued above the door frame.

I ran to wake my sons. "Boys, I know I've told you how I feel about killing living things."

"Huh," Dustin, our oldest son moaned as he rose on one elbow.

"This is an exception. Dad told me last night that sometimes a dead comrade hung by the colony will scare away the others. Get out your ammo."

"We get to use our guns?" Jonathan, his brother, asked.

"This one time, I'll let you use your BB guns to kill one or two birds. I'm desperate."

"The last time we used them you said, 'No more guns until you're thirty'."

"Last time, as I recall, you had a couple of shot guns out there blasting Jack O Lantern faces into a pumpkin on the fence post. Dad also mentioned a while back something about gallon ketchup cans in the shed, apparently waiting to be targets. Be careful and use your heads. I have a couple of errands. I'll be back before lunch." I worried the whole time I was gone. I returned before schedule, gritting my teeth as I neared the house. Had the squatters left the premises? I spotted the martyred birds before I reached the driveway. Swinging from pieces of string hanging from the edge of the roof, two swallow bodies twirled in the wind. Their fellow builders continued spitting mud all around them, not even pausing to mourn.

Birds swarmed like gnats, building more and more nests. Dropping my purse, I retained my weapon of choice. I intended to outlast the squad of mud-blobbers.

I didn't.

I climbed down, dripped across the kitchen floor and reached for the phone book. Someone must know how to rid a home of unwanted mud slingers. I called the Game and Fish Office.

"Hello, I'm hoping you can suggest ways to discourage barn swallows from building nests in the eaves of our house."

"The first thing you must know is they're protected under the migratory bird act. You are not allowed to kill them."

Protected? There was enough nesting around my house to wallpaper the Grand Canyon. How many does one country need? But visions of my two sons dressed in matching stripes, eating bread and water at the county jail was too much. "Okay, we'll do some more searching," I replied. "Thanks."

I called the boys. "You'll have to bring down the bodies. Killing those birds is illegal. Give them a proper burial. Quick."

I thought about my brother, Jay Anthony, and the time he accidentally killed a pheasant out of season. When he realized his goof, he went into the Game and Fish Station to confess.

"Thanks for being an honest citizen, but what are *we* going to do with it? Go home and cook it up. You're off the hook."

Those two birds would have tasted like mud. I didn't even ask where the boys had buried them.

That night Carl took out his binoculars to get a closer look at the situation. "Those boys used my shotgun," he said. "The end of the beam is riddled with holes."

I felt my resolve shrink. Mud *and* holes were an omen. "They win."

When the birds flew away for the winter, I drove the camper in for one final shot. Mud plopped off as before, ring lines still intact—reminders through the winter that they might come again.

Moving wasn't an option, spraying poison too unhealthy, diversion ineffective. I prayed nightly that the swallows would bypass our house next spring. Some heavenly force needed to send them to a birdwatcher's home. After a few months, birds flew out of my nightmares and sweet dreams returned.

One day after a wet snow I felt cooped up and tired of winter. Walking around the yard, I saw signs of spring. Crocus spears edged through a melting crust. A fat robin lit long enough for me to exclaim, "Pretty bird."

Bird? Oh, no—mud-spittin' beak heads.

As the days passed there were no sign of swallows. Maybe they had stayed in Capistrano. Maybe they thought more of their fallen comrades than they had let on. Weeks went by and I was elated. The only contact I foresaw with the eaves would be a paint brush.

My flower gardens soon needed water. "When are they going to let out the ditch water?" I asked Carl.

"There's a big cave-in down a couple of miles. It might be a month or more before it's repaired."

No water, no mud. "That's why those ignorant birds aren't back!"

"Guess we should be careful what we pray for," Carl said, flapping his arms.

The barn swallows did not return. One day I had an urge to sit in the sandy loam in the bottom of the dry ditch. Watching ants and bugs brought to mind the wonders of nature—and birds. I pondered the mystery of ways prayers can be answered.

Disabling an irrigation ditch was not one I had ever considered.

Listen to Me!

I can remember as a toddler, sitting on a stair leading to the basement, eating a cube of butter. Toddlers don't have much experience, and butter is really pretty good. When my mother took it away, I threw the biggest tantrum known to man (and her).

When I was old enough to ride my tricycle to the neighbor's she called me home.

Too soon for my timeline.

I screamed my lungs out. I wouldn't leave, and thus the punishment of dragging my own tricycle home was implemented, all the while getting a switching on my legs with a branch.

That's the first time I remember her repeating a nursery rhyme she used throughout the years:

There was a little girl
who had a little curl
right in the middle of her forehead.
And when she was good, she was very, very, good
and when she was bad, she was horrid.

The not-ready-to come-home- fit was not the last one. I kept promising myself I was through being bad. When I was busy in my happy world, I wanted to stay there. Someone would say "no" and I found myself on the floor again. I knew I was old enough to make my own decisions. Why was I always told what to do? Each episode I let it out, then comforted myself with my thumb.

"I'll be good now, can I get up?" I asked.

"Yes. Run and play and try to be happy."

Her reminders annoyed me. I did not try to be unhappy.

But sometimes I was. I hated being sick. Mother was the one who took me to the doctor with high fever convulsions. She was the one who sat by my hospital bed and brought me Huey and Louie coloring books. I always got those shaky body things from asthma medicine and she would tell me over and over that I was going to be all right.

Maybe it was those convulsion's fault. Maybe shaky medicine made me throw a fit.

But, I forgot all about that stress when I went outside. I ran barefoot through the grass to the welded- pipe fence surrounding our yard. Grabbing the pipe, swinging onto the imaginary platform high above the crowd, I walked the tight rope. Balancing with arms straight out, levering my wings, I waved to the crowd. Off-kilter I jumped to the ground with a thud. I was big on "overs." The act never ended until I had walked clear around the perimeter without falling once, long after the audience had departed.

Family movie reels show a happy little girl. The black and white silent movie camera pans in on toys surrounded by grass, floating in a plastic swimming pool. I'm sampling the water, a cup in one hand waving to the camera with the other. The film flickers, goes dark and resumes spliced footage at Grandma's house riding the hay forks on Grandpa's Ford tractor, playing croquet or picking gooseberries.

Grandma always made iced tea. I looked forward to the crackling and a tall glass of tea. I wasn't supposed to drink tea, but Grandma didn't believe in any of that Mormon stuff anyway. She let me have all the tea and sugar I wanted.

Horrid tea, bad girl.

In those days, I compared myself to my peers. I didn't measure up.

My hair was a disappointment. Thin strands wouldn't hold the fat braids I longed for. Mother would give me Toni permanents. Adorable waves pictured on the box transformed to fried frizz on my head.

I was stuck with hand-me-downs: a clumsy blue bicycle. My newspaper-stuffed ice skates three sizes too big flopped, not floated over the ice. Clothes from my aunt were six years behind the style.

I longed for more.

A symbol of my unfulfilled hopes was our Christmas tree. A smattering of decorations clutched the branches as tinsel scrambled over the boughs, having been tossed haphazardly by my impatient siblings. The tree seemed half dressed—like a molting chicken. Rightfully, the tree should have worn glittery colored balls, while perfectly placed tinsel embraced each light.

I felt inferior in style and creativity. Every February the popular kids made paper valentines, speared with red heart suckers. My frugal mother bought the plain boxes of cards. No frills for her.

But I was a model student and good grades became who I was. Although at home my highs and lows were labeled good and bad, I was always good at school. Conforming and following the rules, my behavior was consistently marked superior on the white report card, my grades straight A's.

Proof that I was acceptable.

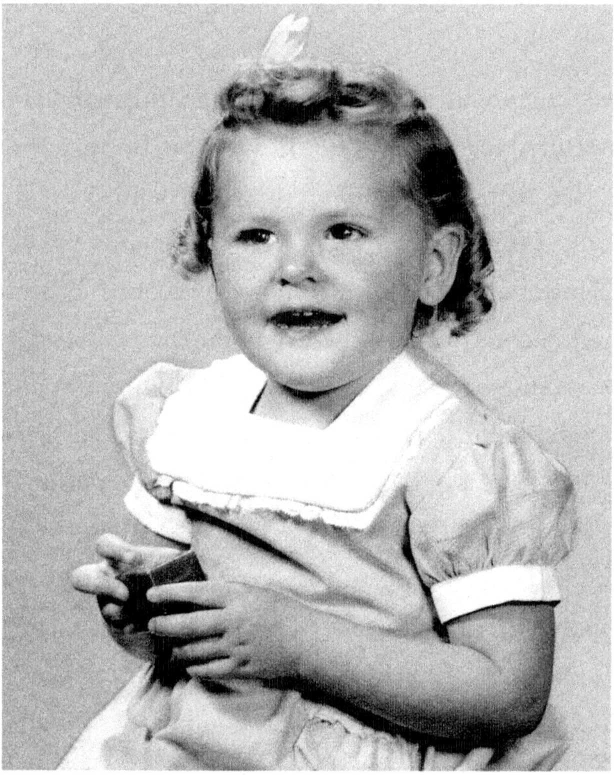

I did have little curls.

Maybe she did Shut the Drawer

In a town not far from Lovell, Wyoming, Dad's father had spent his life managing an old, cold hotel while black-smithing and repairing autos to keep up. This farm spot caught tumbleweeds and poor people. Grandpa Dub was his own collection agency, driving to the customers' houses with a loaded pistol in the glove compartment. Working and cussing harder than most men, he earned his reputation—tough, but fair, strong enough to squeeze a misshapen piece of raw, hot iron into submission.

I was born in Lovell (county 9) and lived on an adjacent farm next to my other grandfather's homestead in an old converted chicken coop. I assume it had been swept and painted. Not having enough money to purchase a crib, Mother pulled out one of the dresser drawers and stuck me in there to sleep. Carl says that's why the back of my head is flat—continually squished into a board. It's so pat-able—flat on top, flat on the back, square cornered.

He insists Mother shut the drawer.

When I was four, we moved to the place I would label home for the next sixteen years. Powell, Wyoming, a city of barely 5,000, sat in the middle of the basin under the Big Horn Mountains, a farming community where bean mills stored the fall harvests year after year.

Folks like Nellie, our ancient Avon lady, lived there. Straddling the centerline she putt-putted down the highway in her old Dodge, her makeup sacks piled high on the passenger's side. Drivers waited to pass until she moseyed over onto her side of the road. Crawling combines and farm equipment were part of everyday traffic.

Politics involved big fishes in little ponds, splashing occasionally at election time, city budget hearings, and discussions over adding another stop light on Main Street.

Successful people, like the owner of the drugstore, were pillars of the community, holding the town together. After lunch every school day, we walked to Moyer's Drug for candy. The display cases were arranged like stadium seats, tiered in rows that reached the highest-priced items on top—the twenty-five cent Pez dispensers. One-cent bubble gum, butterscotch twists and candy cigarettes held down the bottom. Yep, I bought the cigarettes and "smoked," twirling the end around and around in my lips until I sucked it into a sharp point. I might have pretended to puff out some smoke. They were so crunchy and I can still taste the mint hotness.

The jewelry store stood for forty years, the same owner sporting his jeweler's loupe attached to his glasses. I longed for the day when I could purchase my own jewelry worthy of him twisting the loupe over his glasses to check for flaws. He stood behind the counter, always dressed in a suit, wearing a ring the size of the Pope's, showing generations his line of identification bracelets worthy of engraving.

The newspaper editor directed the town, his word swaying opinions like a scale bouncing up and down. Doris, the society columnist, could imbue a wedding dress with royal dripping detail, down to the pearl buttons and princess neckline. She only printed polite words about tea parties, family dinners and such.

The hushed Peyton Place retakes were ignored. A rumor of audacious couples swapping partners, and a high school actor being "one of those" was quelled before the children heard.

Farmers were respected. They took out loans every spring and paid them back every fall. The local bank commissioned a statue built to immortalize these men, the roots of the economy. The bronze farmer, frozen by the front doors, posed in an irrigating stance—shovel resting on his shoulder, rubber boot tops open, metal clasps in mid-snap.

Contrasting incomes existed in quiet recognition. Old Man Essex, a wrinkled geezer with a jungled beard and greasy clothes, owned a few sets of clapboard tenements on the south side of town. The city mostly overlooked the squalor, closing an eye to any code. At least the shacks gave the poor folk shelter from the weather.

Somewhere in the middle of the social structure, my dad labored in the oil fields, a welder by trade. He wore green work shirts, riddled with pinpoints of burn holes, splayed by his welding torch. The

Dad.

bigger holes were patched with fabric from an older shirt, a shade off. We were taught from an early age that the black under his fingernails and pungent oily musk meant security for our family.

Mother kept us together. Frugal, faithful, and stubborn, she moved us through our childhoods, allowing us to roam our pasture, poke sticks in the ditch, pull tin cans out of the garbage barrels to play store, but all after we had offered our morning family prayer.

My little brother, Tony, two years younger than I, was soon to have three younger sisters, Cheri, Christie, and Cathy. Of necessity he was quiet, but sneaky. One of his infamous stunts, only a few knew, was to coax a couple of the girls to climb on the roof of the horse shed and then he instructed them to jump. The winner was the one who could hold their legs the straightest.

He was put in charge one day while Mother ran errands. Wrapping a towel around Cheri's eyes, he spun her around and around and instructed her to walk to the door. She was so dizzy, she split her head open on the wall. Blood spurting down her face, he rewrapped her with another towel that didn't staunch the bleeding. "Now, don't you tell Mom," he warned her.

I started working at fifteen.

Dad always told me, "You don't have to work—you *get* to work and always give the boss an extra five minutes on the time clock."

Dad passed away at age fifty two of heart failure. I rushed to his hospital bedside and he was laying there with his boots still on. "I can't decide whether to die with my boots on or off."

"Oh, Dad. You're too tough to die," I replied.

But, he wasn't.

Mother is in her eighty-seventh year. She lived in the same country home for sixty years. Up until her move to assisted living, she plugged in the car's head bolt heater in the winter and limped out with the broom to brush snow and scrape ice from the windshield.

Just a few years ago, she was my charge as she recuperated from major surgery. She fought me about pulling out a nice little cot for her to sleep on, insisting she would sleep on the love seat, which was about a foot too short for her. She fought me when I tried to get her to drink more than half a glass of water a day, She wanted to go shopping and to the movies three days after the operation.

I drove her to the hospital in Salt Lake City to have her last checkup before heading back to Wyoming. She fought me about being pushed in a wheelchair. The doctor called me in to say she hadn't been following some of the instructions for faster recovery. Grrrrrr.

Once back in the car, my nerves bolted out by mouth, "Mother, why are you so stubborn? Why can't you listen to anyone? Blah, Blah, BLAH. Of course I felt like a bad little girl and immediately apologized.

Her response? "Oh Cindy, You *have* been a trial."

Pickled Eyeballs

The morning heat beat on my face as I watched the top of the Ferris wheel circle the sky. I breathed in odors of lube grease, popcorn and cotton candy—warmed pillows of spun sugar. The dusty breeze stirred all the smells together inside the gates of the county fair.

I was nine and I belonged.

My home-sewn gingham skirt tacked to the wall in the 4-H building was proof. Snicker doodle cookies, my other entry, were displayed under glass on paper plates. Both had won blue ribbons.

The electrical wires I stepped across every few yards connected a magical place. Thrill riders' screams spun freely as gravity pushed them against the seats. Carneys leaned further from their stalls, their bold tattoos making me feel somehow weird, their cries insisting, "win a prize every time."

I kept walking, as far from the hawkers as I could get. But as one enticed a crowd of takers, I stopped, calculating the odds of winning a stiff teddy bear or at least a cheap pink-feathered kewpie doll.

I held onto my tickets and strolled through the games, rounding the corner to another world. A huge rat, his pointy teeth sparkling like a toothpaste ad, covered a board behind the ticket taker. The sign read: "Amazing Live Rat Inside. Eats Animals Three Times Its Size."

My stomach lurched and a warning signal beeped in my brain. I should leave the sideshows and go back to the midway. Glancing around, I saw no one I knew. What harm could there be in reading the signs. I wouldn't spend even one ticket looking at an overgrown rat.

The next tent featured a bearded lady. The sign, smaller than the fat rat, was just as tacky: "Man or Woman? World's Hairiest." I didn't read further.

About to turn back, a long line two booths down caught my attention. Holding my breath and squeezing both arms at my sides, I wished myself invisible. Darting between two tall men at the front of the line, I peeked from under their armpits and saw a gallon jar on a table by the entrance. Something floated inside. I looked away before identifying the blob.

I backed out and leaned far enough through the line to read the sign. It was more scientific: "Two-headed Calf. Survived Two Years After Birth." It was fifty cents to enter.

I wondered if the calf would be in a pen eating hay with both its mouths. Maybe one head was dead and the other was busy mooing. Whatever was in there was something extraordinary and I wanted to see it.

Sprinting away from the crowd, I ran to find my mother. She had told me to meet her in the garden and flower building.

Out of breath, coughing from the dust, I found her. "Mother, have you ever seen a two-headed calf? There's one back there and it's only fifty cents to see it."

She kept strolling along the flower entries, stopping to smell a bouquet of white roses. "It's not real. Were you over at the sideshows?

"You should have seen the people trying to get inside," I said.

We entered the next room and Mother turned over a purple-ribbon afghan. "Those guys just want to take your money. It's dangerous to walk into that area." She continued. "Mrs. Bunnion is still in charge of the handwork in here. Her husband owns the pool hall you know."

"But I REALLY want to see a two-headed calf. How can that happen? Did God do it?"

"It's some kind of a trick."

"I still want to see it," I said and turned from her in a huff.

Mother bent down to look at the grand champion quilt, read me the artist's name—another person she knew, and stood. "I've got to go get some work done at home."

"But, I have two more tickets," I said, my voice ascending to a whinny pitch. "And I have to see that calf. It will never come here again."

"You have to give them money at those sideshows, tickets only work on the rides. You couldn't have gone in there anyway. I have to go to town later this afternoon and I'll drop you off for an hour to use your tickets, if you won't mention that calf or whatever it is, again."

"Okay." Immediately I dropped the pout and obediently followed her out of the building. "Did you see the size of that corn-on-the-cob in those wash tubs? I asked. When is the tractor pull? I wonder if there'll be a magician this year." I chatted, formulating a devious plan.

When we got home I ran to my bedroom. The dollar bill Grandma gave me for my birthday was sitting on my dresser. I would duck out if I saw even one person from church close to that tent. I agreed not to mention the calf; I hadn't agreed not to check it out. Mother would never know.

I wasn't going to miss a once-in-a-lifetime chance and I just had to get closer to that jar, even though I was afraid it might be only a floating eyeball, or four.

Later that afternoon I was back with the fair smells and sights. It was easy to find the two-headed calf tent again. I scoured the area like a bobble head doll checking for spies—grownups that would know I was disobeying my mother.

Once in line, I edged behind a teenager in front of me for cover. My insides quivered, worse than when I had to give a talk at church, but the calf waited and I was committed.

"We're wasting our money," a man behind me told a blonde woman with dangly earrings.

"It's just for fun," she replied. "It's worth a dollar for a couple of minutes inside that tent. I bet those calves are sewn together."

That run away feeling was at me again, but I advanced with the line, only feet from the entrance. If I left, I'd look even more suspicious. I sucked in some stale air, put my hand over my thumping heart, my dollar clenched in my other hand.

Standing at the edge of the tent, I considered closing my eyes and blindly walking through following the sweaty odor running out of the kid in front of me.

I didn't have to fake being blind, the darkness inside shut down my vision for several seconds. As my eyes adjusted, I still couldn't see anything but shoulders and backs. Finally, weak lights swinging over several jars brought my focus to a surreal display. There was no living calf chomping in a pen, no hay, no mooing, just a floating blob in the first jar.

It looked like guts ripped out of the chickens my mother killed. My stomach jerked and I belched up cotton candy spit. I looked for a way to escape, but bodies hedged me on all sides. I scooted forward, wanting light. Sweat dripped so hard I licked my tongue and it was loaded with salt.

Why hadn't I listened to my mother?

The next jar was big—big as a bushel basket. I couldn't stop staring. Two heads split from one calf neck. Identical white markings blazed the faces. I fixated on the wet fur, wondering if the solution inside the jar was pickled like cucumber brine, or concocted from chemicals mixed from the depths of some scientist's stockpile.

How did they… I mean he… I mean it—die? Their eyeballs, glasslike under long lashes, seemed friendly. Slick fur plastered over two faces revealed four nose holes, just like the two on a regular calf running around grandpa's farm. It, I mean they, were real! The whole display mimicked a martyred Halloween mask. Images arose; slaughtered chicken gizzards nestled among dill stems floating in quart pickle jars.

The next two jars went by in a blur. I wanted to shove the kid in front of me, pushing the whole bunch out the bent tent flaps and into some light.

Finally, I stepped into the sun. If I ran really fast, I could say to myself I was never in there with any pickled innards or heads. I'd merely mingled with the kids by the merry-go-round and the spinning teacups. Maybe I could shed the dark covering I felt pressing me.

Mother was a few minutes late picking me up at the front gate.

"I went to see the two-headed calf," I blurted out the second I got in the car.

Mother looked straight ahead; her fingers gripping the steering wheel tighter. "I told you not to do that."

"I just had to. It was creepy. I'm sorry."

Mother didn't have to think long to come up with a consequence. "You will have to stay home from the 4-H Style Review tonight. I planned to take you and your grandmother."

This time I didn't argue. I thought maybe she'd change her mind by evening, but the car rolled out of the driveway without me.

The poem she usually uttered when I acted out, remained unsaid, but it crept into my mind and buried itself levels deeper.

I Didn't Know We Were Poor Too

I didn't know about social status or popularity until I entered grade school. In first grade I met a girl with hair so light it was white. She sat on the playground blacktop, her back leaning against a brick wall, holding a notebook against her folded legs.

"What's your name?" I asked, overcoming the stomach jitters.

"Tencil" she said, still moving her pencil over the surface of the paper.

Fascinated by the motion, I asked, "What are you doing?"

Tencil hesitated too many minutes, but finally replied, "Drawing."

It took some talking to get her to turn around the notebook. When she finally relaxed her legs to show the picture, I was captivated. A horse stood on a flowered hill, one front hoof in mid-air, his mane flowing across his neck. The tail was equally as majestic, each detail of the mane blowing in a warm breeze that I thought I might actually feel coming from the page.

"I never knew anyone who could draw like that," I said. "Can I watch you?"

She nodded and placed the pencil on its side, coloring with the edge of the lead. Holding the tool in her other hand, she smeared the graphite in controlled directions, creating shading that gave the stallion life. Her dress and fingers were stained with lead. I could have watched her all day.

Because her wrinkled clothes hung around her skinny bones, and because her hair matted, brittle-like over her slumping shoulders, I guessed she was from a poor family. The tips of her protruding shoes were scuffed until the navy blue was down to dirty leather. Envisioning her breakfast a crust of bread, I asked, "What did you have for dinner last night."

"Spaghetti." The word came out flatly.

"Do you like meatballs?" I asked.

"We only have venison once in a while. Last night it was plain."

That cinched it.

Right after school I stepped off the bus and sprang into a run. I found my mother in the kitchen. "There's a girl at school that's really poor. She can draw."

Standing the iron in its cradle, she left the ironing board to check on my baby sister, fussing in the other room. I followed. As Mother leaned over the crib, she asked, "So, you have a new friend?" She picked Cheri up, patting her gently on the back and went on, "How do you know she's poor?"

I told her what I knew. "She dresses real bad and her hair's a mess and her shoes have holes in them." Not hardly taking a breath, I went on, "I asked her what she ate and she said, 'plain spaghetti.'"

"I'm sure someone at school will help her."

"I want to help her. We could give her a couple of my dresses and maybe some food." I compared my longings to being on the front lines of the Red Cross. I wanted to fix her situation—to be the first grade good girl rescuing Tencil from her fate.

"Ok, I'll put together a few things."

The next morning, I pulled a perfectly ironed cotton dress, stiff with starch, from the closet and slipped too easily into my polished shoes. They were only a little too big. Mother had packed a paper sack filled to the brim with clothes, a pair of shoes, and bottled jars. A homemade loaf of bread, wrapped in aluminum foil, perched on top.

I hoisted the sack, both arms bearing the weight as my fingers laced underneath. I couldn't wait to get to school and to Tencil.

When the heavy bag started to slip, I hefted it to my hip, like shifting a baby to security, and walked toward the waiting bus. Turning back to see if my mother was watching, I saw her wave from the porch.

I glanced at the scruffy brown buffalo board covering our house, for a brief moment wondering when we would get real siding.

I didn't catch Tencil on the playground before the first bell rang. She was in the other class. I just hoped she was there today. I fidgeted in my seat until recess and shot out of my chair at the sound of the bell. Racing to my coat hook, I ignored my jacket, too excited to bother with it. On the shelf below my jacket, the burgeoning sack remained intact. Wrapping my arms around the middle, I carried it to the playground and found Tencil in her usual spot.

I put the sack down, leaving enough space to sit next to her. For a few minutes we sat in silence—she drawing—me folding my arms over my knees to huddle against the chill. Tencil didn't have a jacket either.

"I brought you some things from my house," I said, almost in a whisper.

Tencil kept drawing. She didn't speak.

Reaching for the sack, I scooted it over in front of us.

She still didn't speak. I tried to make small talk. "My mom made the bread. It wasn't much trouble. She makes it all the time anyway."

Finally she replied, "My mom doesn't make bread."

I knew the conversation was over. The sack sat like an intruder, shutting off the tentative progress I had made.

When the bell rang, she picked up the gift and headed for class. I never saw Tencil wear one of my dresses. She returned to the same spot every recess, unpolished shoes poking out of her tattered dress hem, her spiral notebook poised to create drawings over the lined sheets. She wore her poverty unobtrusively as she hid behind her pencil and leaned on that wall.

Before Christmas, Tencil had dropped out of school and I had to be content with the scanty answers gleaned from my continual questioning. I asked the kids in my class, the teacher, my mother. Mother always read the local newspapers and one day she told me that Tencil's brothers kept getting into trouble and one of them was in the penitentiary. That led to a whole new set of questions and a curiosity that stuck. One day we drove by her house and Dad said, "That's where that convict lives." When I found out it was Tencil's house, every time we'd drive by, I'd imagine Tencil inside eating spaghetti. Old cars, junk, and dead trees held down the yard. Maybe one of those old cars was stolen. Maybe the broken windows were from Tencil trying to escape. Would she remember the paper sack that sat between her and me that day on the playground?

Tencil's Departure, Donald's Arrival

With no exposure to the arts during recess, I looked to fill the gap left by Tencil's departure.

Along came Donald.

I hadn't thought much about boys before this year. My brother, Tony, was a boy, but just family. I played with him when I was in the mood and tried to be his protector, consoling him when thunderstorms sent him scurrying under the kitchen table.

Donald wasn't afraid of anything.

One day at recess, he followed me. "Hop on my back and I'll give you a piggy back ride," he said, his grin curving from cheek to cheek.

"You'll drop me," I said, embarrassed, but still curious about the intentions of this would be play-horse.

Donald walked toward the fence separating the foursquare ball markings on our playground from the grass that graced the junior high lawn. "Stand on this fence post and I'll get in front of you."

It sounded weird and kind of naughty, but I was bored and Donald seemed quite confident. "Ok, but don't drop me."

I stood on the post, about the right height for me to descend onto the back of a wavy-haired boy, bent over in a weed-pulling stance. He took off, but soon wobbled back and forth as he tried to balance my weight, walking even faster as if the speed would straighten his load. He stopped once to boost me higher, but I slipped and one foot dragged on the pavement, my wrinkled anklet wadded into my shoe. I felt my dress billowing and air breezing around my other leg, as he dropped me onto the ground in a heap.

"That hurt," I said pouting, getting up, wiping my dress—smoothing out the indignities.

Donald was not one to easily admit defeat. "Let me try it again. I know what to do now."

I climbed back on the same post. This time I tried counting before I slid onto his back, but before I got past two, I saw the playground monitor heading our way. "You kids can't do that. Someone's going to get hurt." My heart raced and that spidery feeling crawled around in my chest. I never wanted to get into trouble at school.

"You two go play with your own groups."

Her reprimand forever ended my contact sports on the playground.

With a first-grader's instinct, I knew that Donald was different. His ratty hair and slower sentences gave away his social position at school. I began to see how poverty and certain differences weren't characteristic of popular kids. Popular kids fit the mold, tightly like a newly worked puzzle. Awakened to this truth, I began to explore the ways of both, realizing more after a telling conversation.

Soon after the horseplay incident, Betsy, a girl who sat behind me, whispered to her friend across the aisle, "We already did this counting stuff in kindergarten."

"It's so boring," Kay replied, twirling her braid around her pointer finger. "At least we got snacks last year."

Betsy sighed and listed more evidence. "We all know the alphabet and the books Mrs. Sering reads to us are for babies."

I kept quiet, not even knowing what kindergarten was. All day I rolled around the secret in my head, imagining the worst possible reason why these kids had counted and been read to in a place called kindergarten and I was left out. There must have been something wrong with me and my parents just didn't want to tell me.

I was probably adopted.

That afternoon I dashed off the bus to find my mother. She was raking some dead weeds from around the woodpile. I upended a log and sat down, lowering my books to the ground. The smoke from burning leaves funneled over the stack, and settled in my hair and clothes. I sat in silence as Mother heaped more weeds onto the fire and came back to work. Maybe I wasn't supposed to know all the other kids already knew their alphabet and numbers, but I had to ask.

"Mother, what's kindergarten?" I began, pointing my toes together, sucking on my thumbnail.

"It's a class you can go to before first grade," she said, scraping little pebbles as she raked down to dirt.

"Who goes to it?" I kept my eyes down, afraid of the answer.

Mother walked to the now smoldering pile and lifted the bottom layers with the rake to stir the fire. I noticed she was wearing dad's old work gloves.

"Kids go when they're five."

"But I'm six and I never went."

"You have to pay money for kindergarten," she said simply. She did not look at me as she spoke.

I couldn't comprehend that money was a reason not to go. "Why didn't you just write a check?"

Mother put down the rake and walked toward the shed to get a bucket. I trailed along behind. "We didn't have the money. We knew you could catch up."

Suddenly, I felt naked, exposed to the cold.

I was different. I was poor.

The next day in class I secretly took my own poll, asking some of the friendlier kids, "Who was in your kindergarten class last year?" To my best count, all but three in the entire class had been in kindergarten.

They weren't popular.

Don't Do It

Multitasking is on the rise. I'm acquainted with secretaries who can jockey five incoming calls, tidy their desks, and flirt with a salesman in the opposite cube. I've seen a guy in tech support attend to a customer, assure his wife via cell phone the dog *will* come back, and load the printer at the same time. Some women carry a baby on one hip, stir soup, and dry dishes in sync.

Others slip behind the steering wheel, joining multitasking-wannabes who all think the highway gives them some extra time to get 'er all done.

Over the years, I'll admit, I thought I was one of the talented few. I've dialed the cell phone, smoothed my blush and changed everything in the audio world; from eight track tapes to CDs, but my crash record is clean. I did get a lecture from grandson, Kade, however. One car-pool afternoon I tugged my sunflower seed package open with my teeth and began spitting seeds into the garbage sack attached to the drink carrier.

"Grandma, my teacher said to tell any adult who is multi-tasking while driving they are putting me in danger."

"Sunflower spitting has kept me awake on many a road trip," I said. Reach, pop, savor, split—spit.

"Please don't do it. Teacher said."

I put the sunflower seed package away.

During my next few trips I took a survey. I counted drivers yakking on their cell phones—five within one block and only six cars passed. On the interstate I noticed a guy in suit and tie shaving, another eating a burger while driving with his elbow, and wiping the special sauce from his chin with the back of his other hand.

I began to drive more defensively.

Thinking back, I remember seeing a woman apply her mascara, women dabbing on lip gloss, smacking their lips at the rearview mirror. I don't think they were watching their backside.

I've heard stories of women driving in the fast lane, their eyelash curler clamped on their eyelid. What if someone was skidding toward their blind side?

I'm going to keep my eyes on the road, my hands on the wheel.

My survey list grew: embracing lovers, dogs riding on a driver's shoulder, cats lounging on the dashboard.

It's dangerous out there.

The other day I saw a phenomenon that clinched my new-found commitment to non-multitasking. As I slowed to stop at a red light, a yellow-haired woman in a Mercedes turned in front of me on the green arrow, some object suspended in midair in front of her face. Was it a book, a box of corn flakes, some kind of new battery-powered skin exfoliator?

I could not believe my eyes. A powder-blue Cockatiel sat on her pointer finger. I thought it must be stuffed. Rigid enough to be out of some aviary's diorama, it suddenly flapped its wings as the woman kissed the critter on its beak. It was a totally new take on a "bird's eye view."

Multitasking has not proven to be a talent worth working for. I've recommitted to keeping it in check while driving. I skipped the "55 Alive" driving course, but it's never too late. Information on the internet mentions part of the course includes minimizing driving distractions—cell phone usage, smoking, eating. I wonder if I had attended the classes, would we have received further instruction on avoiding problems with those who adore cats on their laps, dogs in their chops, and overly affectionate birds.

Abundance

My body hovered above the mattress, hung up on the rumpled covers tossed aside by sweating feet and hands.

"Daddy Claus says it's time to fill the stockings," Carl said.

"I can't do it. I just can't," I mumbled.

"Come on. Just a few more little Christmas chores and you can rest."

Strings of duty yanked, and I wobbled to my feet. "Just give me a minute to drag all the stuff out."

He whistled and hummed a "Ho! Ho! Ho!" The sound pierced my nerves, severing the final Christmas connection.

Weeks of overtime at the office, hours of shopping, wrapping, candy thermometers, and minutes upon minutes of mentally repeating wish lists had won.

Reaching to the top of the closet, bags avalanched and bounced off my head. Stocking stuffers fell on my feet.

"Did you get plenty for all of them?" he asked.

In the middle of a kneel, my body slid to the carpet, oblivious to jabs from black boots, red heels, and a raggedy pair of slippers.

Scooting little soaps, card games, chocolates, ribboned sugar, and piles of one dollar bills out of the closet was the last effort. The loot pointed in the right direction. Let an elf come fill each stocking, so lovingly stitched in sequins and felt.

"Come on. You can't quit me now," Carl implored. "Just separate the piles and I'll finish."

One- two- three—one- two-three—one-two- three—equality.

And more stuff and Ho! Ho! Ho!

I didn't hear all three kids sneak quietly beside the bed at 5:00 a.m. The hours of stress, wrapping, and lists running constantly through my head vanished as I became aware. Rattling Carl awake, I said, "Don't quit me now. Merry Christmas."

And I meant it.

Pink Poodle Skirt

Even though poodle skirts had gone out of style in that fall of 1959, I wore mine so much the poodle's nose was only a tiny patch of pink fuzz where once had been a pert round ball. I was ten years old, keen to acceptable styles, but Aunt Janet's hand-me-down skirt graced my wardrobe with as much pizzazz as the latest fad.

I loved the way the wool skirt flared when I spun around. When I sat, my finger automatically traced the length of the ribbon leash looping from the poodle's collar. I wore it everywhere.

During the weekly children's' church meeting one February, our teacher pulled out paper, glue, and glitter, to make invitations to the upcoming daddy-daughter date that weekend. I ran out to meet my dad as I heard his welding truck crunch into the driveway. Before he was completely out of the truck, I rattled, "We get to go to dinner. All the dads can come. Do you have to work that night?"

Setting his metal lunch box on the gravel, he took the invitation from my outstretched hand. His fingers printed the edges as he held the paper with his oily fingers. "What is this?" he asked with a twinkle dimpling his smeared face. "I'm not too good at meetings."

"This isn't a meeting, it's a dinner, and you just have to come." I envisioned every other girl laughing with her dad, while my teacher sat in the chair designated for my absent father.

"I think I can come." He leaned over and put his arm around me. I savored the greasy aroma permeating his work clothes. "They wouldn't call me to the field when I have a date with my girl."

Locking my arm under his, I skipped to the house, jolting my dad's step with every hop. The rest of the week I basked in the anticipation of my first date, counting off the days. I would wear the poodle skirt for sure. It came with an Angora sweater that tied around my neck, designed to allow two feathery balls on the end of the ties to bounce.

Sitting beside him the evening of the Daddy Daughter Date was everything I had imagined. "They're not going to make me give a speech are they?" Dad asked with mock fear.

"No, we girls are going to say a poem about our dad's though." There might be a short talk too. I watched for his reaction, knowing he didn't go to church much, hoping he wouldn't make us leave early.

Dad raised an eyebrow at me. "I think I can handle that much."

That evening Dad came in and went directly to the shower. He was going to come! I could envision him reaching to the top of the medicine cabinet to grab his comb. Even though it was missing a couple of teeth—it was his. Watch out if he couldn't find it. All three of us girls had caught onto where he hid it. I think Tony knew too. There were never any combs around.

Dad wore his plaid flannel shirt, the green and brown one. He smelled good and his hair looked nice. We rode to dinner in the Chevy station wagon, even though Mother had hauled a few sheep home in the back the week before.

As we came into the gym, all the men gathered around Dad to welcome him. He liked to gab, but not necessarily in this location. He preferred a couple of good rounds of pinochle down at the pool hall. He couldn't sneak away though, we had a date.

Some of the leaders and older girls began to serve dinner. I had to look twice at the paper plate presentation. I had dreamed of china on my first date, not disposable plates. I thought meat loaf a common choice too, but perked up a little when I noticed our slices had baked ketchup glazing the top.

"What's the right way to cut this up?" Dad teased as he cut a piece of the meat and stabbed it. I didn't care if he didn't even use his napkin. He was there. Placing my napkin in my lap, I painstakingly patterned the proper manners in my mind before I took one bite.

"Why is this potato wrapped in tinfoil? Your mother doesn't do that."

I unrolled the tin foil as the potato clunked onto the plate and lay like an impenetrable lump. Studying the plate, I chose to taste the meatloaf first. It looked more accessible.

Dad was busy buttering his potato.

Rolling the potato closer to the edge of my plate, I tipped my knife into the brown skin. With all the finagling, the plate had crossed the edge of the table and hung just a few inches above my poodle skirt. So intent on remembering the proper ways to eat it, I didn't notice the shift. As I sawed through the potato, pressure flipped my plate over, the contents landing in my lap.

Before I could even exhale, Dad grabbed the food and put it back in its place. It didn't hurt his hand a bit. He was calloused from oil field work.

"I can't believe it." I said, as embarrassment coiled around my body in neon red.

"That was a close one." He smiled "Pretend like it never happened,"

My skirt shed like a plastic bib, leaving only a dab of butter on the tip of the poodle's tail. I loved that skirt even more after that. It not only flared when I twirled, it repelled food, leaving most of my dignity intact.

P.S. The invitations were made out of yellow construction paper.

That Didn't Hurt a Bit

A few weeks after the daddy-daughter-date, I had an argument with Mother. Not finding her in the house, I checked the next logical place, her plentiful garden.

She was bent over the plants, gently pulling ripened Super Sioux tomatoes from the vines. She wore one of my Dad's oldest green welding shirts, riveted with burn holes and mismatched patches. It hung past her knees, her polyester pants flaring to her muddy shoes. I stood at the edge of the garden, unwilling to track through the mud to ask my question.

"Can I spend the night with Grandma? I can ride her bus home after school."

Mother placed a plump tomato on top of the others in a bushel basket. "I need you home to help with the kids. I'll be sorting tomatoes and getting them ready for people."

"Tony can watch them."

"No, I want you around for Saturday too. I have orders for beans and tomatoes."

Mother's tone had a finality that killed my hope.

"Why can't I go?"

"I told you, I've got too much to do." I gritted my teeth and turned away so she couldn't see my uninvited tears.

I had looked forward to shopping on Saturday with Grandma. I loved how she called it "trading," the word conjuring pictures of old country store shelves loaded with tins of baking powder, barrels of flour, and pickles. I imagined a bonneted woman unloading her basket of eggs in exchange for dry goods.

My Gramma, Maggie Lou Sheets. I was her first grandchild, and I adored her.

Grandma really wore a hair net and paid for her goods with a check. The times we traded, I got to pick what we would have for supper, pushing the grocery cart around the aisles, filling it to the brim with taco ingredients, round paper tubs of ice cream and six packs of Coke.

Mother didn't buy pop except on special occasions.

Later, Grandma and I would play games and she would let me stay up late until the end of Perry Mason when the television would go fuzzy, snowed with lines crossing the screen.

We didn't even own a television set.

I shut my ears to my mother's voice and formed a plan. I would show her that I could run my own life.

I didn't want to be there when those people pulled up in their station wagons and pickup trucks to buy produce from Mother's garden anyway. I knew she'd be wearing the same old patched shirt and muddy shoes. I feared she would pull out the bathroom scales again, straight from their place beside the toilet stool. She would fill her plastic ice cream buckets with everything from tomatoes to green beans, weighing them on those bathroom scales. The bucket would sit on the black rubber indentations where two feet were supposed to stand.

I sniffed and turned back to ask, "Why don't we have real garden scales."

"The bathroom ones work fine," she replied.

"Those scales are for weighing people, not food," I said. I didn't mention the toe germs surely wiggling over the metal sides.

"I'm not spending money on something we don't need."

Little hairs prickled across the back of my neck with the finality of that often used phrase and I lashed out, "Other people don't use bathroom scales to weigh stuff from the garden. It makes us look stupid."

She placed more tomatoes in the basket, handling them like babies in a bassinet.

I gave up, stomped my foot and did an about face to the house, my frustration thinking about revenge. I would go to the farm, whether Mother wanted me to or not.

I boarded the school bus the next morning and chuckled to myself about not riding it back home. All day, even at recesses, my conscience tweaked at my intentions but when the last bell rang, I draped my jacket over my arm, stacked my homework and headed for the bus lot. I couldn't back out now, could I? Passing my own bus, my knees buckled and a chill whooshed through my stomach.

"I'm going to my grandma's house." I told the bus driver as I climbed the steps. He nodded. The bus smelled different from mine, like week-old gym socks. I faked a comfortable stroll as I made my way down the aisle.

"Why are you on this bus?" some kid asked as I bumped his arm.

"I'm going to my grandma's," I said. I spotted a vacant place next to a high school girl. She sighed as I sat down on the squeaky seat. The bus crawled out of the lot. My eyes felt big and my skin felt prickly and I promised myself I would call Mother the minute I got to Grandma's.

I hadn't remembered all those stops the other times I had ridden that bus. On those other trips time was lost. I had engaged in solving the what-are-those-people-like riddle as each bunch of kids headed for their homes. Had their mothers made a platter full of after school cookies? How old did a kid have to be to milk the cows I gawked at, their green-manured rumps surrounding the mangers? Did girls have to slosh around in those corrals?

However, this trip was unending. All I could think about was telling my mother the truth.

Finally the bus stopped and the doors unfolded a few yards from the familiar cattle guard piped across my grandparents' lane. I didn't even stop to worry about falling through as I bounded down the dirt road, not slowing to jump the potholes.

"I didn't know you were coming tonight," Grandma said as she heard her front door open.

"Mother said I couldn't come and I came anyway. I have to call her."

I finished my sentence as I dialed my number, still panting from the sprint to the house. There was some old ladies having a conversation. I was ready to jump out of my skin. I put down the receiver and picked it up—down and up. The last time I picked it up one of those old gals said, "It looks like somebody's in a mighty big hurry. I'll call you back."

The ring finally went through. "I'm at Grandma's," I said, before she finished saying hello. "I rode her bus."

"You were not supposed to go there. I want you to come home." Her voice was hard as burnt candy.

I realized I wanted to go home too. Any fun I could have had on the farm had been dampened by guilt. Grandma had already put on her flannel jacket and was buttoning the pearl buttons. I didn't want to talk about anything even though she chatted the entire eight-mile distance to my house.

She dropped me at the front door and waved, pretending it was like any other time she had given me a ride home. When I reached the kitchen, I could hear Mother rattling dishes into the drainer. She turned and looked right in my eyes. "You were very disobedient. I'm going to have to tell your dad."

Why did he have to be brought into this I thought, as memories of the few times he had been mad at me flashed in my face. When he yelled, I would squeeze my eyes shut hard enough to shut off my ears. It never worked. I would rather have a whipping than hear him holler.

When Dad got home from work that night, I hid around the kitchen corner, dreading what my mother would report.

She was wiping down the counter when he clomped into the kitchen. "I told Cindy she couldn't go to Mother's house tonight after school," Mother began.

"Good, she can stay away from there this weekend.

Mother wiped her wet hands down the sides of her brown pants.

"She went anyway."

"Did you give her a note to ride that bus?" Dad asked.

"She's ridden out there enough times. The bus driver knows her." Mother's voice remained calm, but I could tell I was going to get it.

"I'll have to have a talk with her when she gets home."

"She's here. She called me when she got out there and I told her to come home."

"Oh, boy. I guess I'll have to get out my belt."

I scooted to my bedroom, wishing I had a lock on my door.

When I swept my skirt under my legs to sit on the bed, the familiar feeling of the felt reminded me of the night Dad and I had dined on glazed meatloaf at our daddy daughter date. The ketchup stains were gone, but the memory of my gallant rescue from the food-flop was still clear. He wouldn't spank me after escorting me on that date?

"You had your mother worried when you didn't come home from school." He walked toward me, a serious look on his face.

"I felt awful on that bus ride to Grandma's house," I said, winding the poodle's tail on my skirt around like the prop on a rubber-banded plane. "I'm sorry."

He brought the belt from behind his back but didn't look at it. He was studying my poodle skirt. "That was some good meat loaf that night."

I was saved. I recognized the smile. He wasn't yelling—he was thinking about my skirt and the baked potato and ketchuped meatloaf sitting in my lap.

"Turn over. You have to get a couple swats for being naughty."

I played along with his assignment, protesting loud enough for Mother to hear, "No, Dad, I won't be bad anymore."

He pelted my backside with his folded leather belt a couple of times. I heard the belt but didn't feel it. My favorite skirt cushioned the impact area, repelling the swats meant to straighten me up. I wanted to laugh, but didn't want my mother to know that it didn't hurt one bit. Dad took my elbow and turned me over, winking to seal our secret pact.

That was the last spanking I ever got.

Aunt Beverly at Thanksgiving Dinner

Aunt Beverly had always been there. We grew up with her blathering voices talking out of turn, her abrupt fancies, and her food obsessions. She made her own dresses—flowering cotton kingdoms of colors and gathering stitches—her short-sleeved creations gapping to expose hairy armpits. We kids tried to never look under there.

Cleanliness was not next to Godliness in her realm. God wasn't even invited.

Aunt Beverly's musty body groaned from her weight. Her unwashed hair parted in oily rivulets down her scalp. She was afraid of water.

Every Thanksgiving was spent at Grandma's house. She gathered us for dinner, saving the end chair for Aunt Beverly.

Aunt Beverly never had to be called. She surfaced from her bedroom in her rumpled dress, chanting, "It's over, it's done. The matter's closed from coast to coast." All the way down the hall her voices argued with themselves.

The adults ignored her when she thundered through the room. The kids mostly sighed.

My brother, Tony, hid.

Grandma whispered when she heard Aunt Beverly, "She's coming. Don't worry, I hid the gizzard."

Several members of the family favored the gizzard, including our aunt. "Um, I'm hungry." Beverly pulled out the chair and plopped down with another mutter. "Where's the gizzard?"

Thanksgiving dinner was one of the few meals started with prayer at Grandma's house. Because she went to church, Mother was usually asked to say it. Aunt Beverly never closed her eyes—my brother and I peeked. She just mumbled and picked up her turkey leg, shredding the meat with her teeth.

We said amen and passed the potatoes.

One year, when I was about nine, we took turns around the table telling everyone what we were thankful for. When it was Aunt Beverly's turn she blurted, "I don't participate in that sort of thing," and wiped her arm across her mouth, removing the gravy off her lips. I accidentally looked at her armpit and there was still hair in there.

Grandma always got the turkey wing. My Uncle Buzz sat at the card table next to the TV. Grandma slipped him the gizzard on one of her return trips from the kitchen. I pushed little pearl onions through the cream sauce on my plate, slurping up the liquid and leaving the

Aunt Beverly and me at Thanksgiving dinner.

onions. Beverly got seconds. "I really shouldn't—um, but this is so good," she repeated, each time she scooped more food onto her plate.

We all left the table before Aunt Beverly finished. I went behind the recliner and craned my neck to spy on her. Whipped cream coated her fingers and cranberry sauce dribbled down her chin. Her hairy kneecaps touched both table legs. Her anklets folded above her old-lady-shoes—the kind with soles like cushions and laces crossing eyelet to eyelet.

I wished she could get some help. I wanted to know what she really was like without that company in her head.

Aunt Beverly pushed herself from the table, stuck her little finger in her ear and frantically scratched. "I really shouldn't, but where's the pumpkin pie?"

Birds in the Room

Aunt Beverly harrumphed, pushed her chair from the table, and complimented her voices on the way back to her room. "Um, that was delicious. I really shouldn't have eaten so much," she said. And then arguing with one voice, she defended her actions. "Fat is back, kill the suspect." She slammed her bedroom door.

As much as I wanted to, I was too scared to ever sneak into that room, afraid she would catch me, lose herself in the game in her head and think I was one of those others. She might grab me and tie my arms behind my back and rope me to her bed.

Once when she was out irrigating with Granddad, she left the door ajar and I peeked in, pushing the glass doorknob forward just a little as I looked back over my shoulder to make sure no one saw. The sound of my thumping heart filled my chest. My breath was too loud.

Inside, an iron birdcage sat on a tall wooden stool. The caged birds twittered in a frenzy, announcing my intrusion. They were so pretty, so out of place, perched above soggy newspapers, white droppings splattered over last month's news. The windowsill mounded in their mess, like hills of coal-speckled snow. A smell of sweaty armpits mixed with rotten apples gave the room a fermented stench. Other smells stirred the mixture, reminding me of aged farts, but I never said that word aloud.

I knew she let the birds fly around in there. They had escaped a couple of times and Grandma cussed the parakeet poop that spurted from their frightened flight. I felt a little guilty goggling at Aunt Beverly's privacy—like the naughty feeling that summer at the carnival when I sneaked into the sideshow to see the two-headed calf sideshow—but curiosity won.

Rows of paperback mysteries formed a barrier around the bed. Dozens of green Coke bottles stood in formation behind the books. My conscience told me to leave, to get out before I got caught, but the book titles titillated my urge to feel fear.

Suddenly, I heard the front door open. Backing across the hall into the bedroom where I slept when I visited, I messed with the blankets on the cot, pretending to straighten the covers. Granddad's voice bounced down the hall. "Maggie, where's my work coat?" I heard him rattling around in the closet, mumbling something about "winter coming on," and then thump out the door, Grandma mumbling about being bothered for some old coat.

My bravery almost depleted, I snuck back to the forbidden door for one last look at old magazines that tiled the wooden floor and candy wrappers that had missed the garbage can. Blankets hung over the edge of the bed and a dented gray pillow smeared with hair oil bore the shape of Aunt Beverly's head. There were no sheets on the bare mattress.

Alert to the possibility of being grabbed from behind, I readied to run, but stood, riveted to the spookiness. I wanted a closer look at the closet in the corner of her room, a cave-like hole with heaps of junk. One of her dresses crookedly hung from the hanger, a slovenly ghost in the darkened hole. Halloween horror pricked my nerves as I imagined bunion-molded old lady shoes dancing under the dress that came to life when trespassers peeked. There must be a bogeyman in that closet. If not there, then they didn't live anywhere.

A shiver scratched my spine and I did an about face and ran into the kitchen, to the safety of Grandma's domain.

Even though I didn't like to think about it, I secretly wondered if my desire to sneak into Aunt Beverly's room, to scare the birds and read the titles of her murder mysteries, was part of my horrid little girl side, the side I wanted to hide. But that didn't stop me from wanting to ask questions.

"Grandma, why doesn't Aunt Beverly take a bath?"

"I can't figure that one out myself."

"Why does she talk to herself?"

Lifting a metal kettle, Grandma poured boiling water over her ice block for tea, causing the ice to crackle loudly.

"Who is she talking to?" I asked.

Grandma turned her back, dipping the dishrag into the steaming dishwater to scrub a bread pan. "She's got problems."

"Can't anyone help her?" My mind raced with whys and how comes, seeking a solution. "Was she always like that?"

"She started this when she was in junior high. Something just went wrong."

"Was she pretty then?"

"I've got to get these dishes done. When we're finished we can play crazy eights." Grandma's elbows pumped up and down over the sink, steadily moving soapy dishes under the rinse water. I wanted to ask many more questions, but I could tell she didn't want to discuss her middle daughter.

I had to be content with my own answers to my aunt's odd and stinky state. I knew Mother wouldn't tell me much more about her sister. It seemed like they were all embarrassed and a little scared of Aunt Beverly.

Years later I convinced my mother to talk to me about Aunt Beverly. She said Beverly was fine until she reached junior high age and then began to act strangely and not keep herself clean.

"Was she really dumb?" I asked.

"No, she just didn't study and quit school, but she'd check algebra and science books from the library and actually work through the problems.

Granddad found her once sitting against the chicken house door with a big, bloody cut across her wrist. She had sliced the wrong direction to commit suicide and only managed a few stitches. She was in her twenties. Granddad sent her to a sanitarium in Denver. The doctor asked her a question to see how smart she was, "What does 'People who live in glass houses should not throw stones' mean?" She answered with a perfect interpretation.

Two days later she called Grandpa to come get her. He did.

Many years later I heard the word schizophrenia and asked again and again why she didn't have medicine to help. No one would answer except saying, "she wouldn't take medicine."

Aunt Beverly went willingly to the nursing home. Her first roommate asked to be moved because Aunt Beverly talked to herself so loudly every night before bed. When mother asked her what she was talking about, Aunt Beverly said, "I like to discuss the events of the day with myself."

Her new roommate was a comatose lady who never uttered a word. Curled up in a little ball in her bed, she wasn't aware of Aunt Beverly or anything else. Aunt Beverly painted, practiced the piano and was the happiest she had been in her life. She had plenty of food, help at her command, and could lay in bed with her HBO channel blaring down the hall.

She died in her seventies holding my youngest sister, Cathy's, hand.

Coast to coast the matter's closed.

And so, it is.

Curiosity and Grasshopper Guts

Before I knew we were poor, I had loved receiving over-flowing sacks of hand-me-downs from my Aunt Janet. As I modeled through the house wearing her clothes, I felt as grown-up and beautiful as she. I was oblivious to the fact that, by the time I grew into the outfits, fashions had changed.

But with my new awareness of rich and poor, came a fixation on what was in style. I was now vividly aware of the length of my skirt. Usually longer than current styles, I felt flooded from the waist down, my hem drooping like an old lady's housedress.

Summer vacation came as a respite from social structure. I dressed in shorts, sun tops, and my favorite footwear—thongs. For days I suffered with a new pair as the tender skin between my toes callused. I flip flopped around until I wore them in—finished with practical shoes for a few months.

Free to roam and play within the boundaries of our ten acres, my brother and I cobbled structures out of stuff. We played store in a patch of trampled alfalfa, floored with the wool blanket from the back seat of our Chevy wagon. Merchandise was stocked from the garbage barrel—snatched before the flames from the daily burning scorched the boxes and blackened the tin cans. We pilfered dry macaroni from the kitchen cupboard, added water, and stirred in pieces of green peppers and carrots from the garden.

Macaroni Delight was served in pie plates.

We built forts using barrels for turrets, boxes for walls. Old pieces of iron from the scrap pile served for everything from dungeons to draw bridges. One day Tony led me around the barn to a homemade portable camping stove. Dad had welded half of a small barrel to four skinny pipe legs. A now-rusted pipe rose out of the end of a smooth plate of iron—the cooking surface. The apparatus had been sitting in the summer sun. Tony didn't need to start a blaze inside the stove to make use of it.

"I dare you to eat a grasshopper," he said, coming closer.

"Yuck. No," I quickly responded, not waiting to hear his whole plan.

He walked a few feet, stooped down and deftly grabbed a jumping grasshopper clicking through the milkweeds. "The stove is hot enough to make him sizzle," he said, holding the spindly insect by one leg.

I considered myself quite tough in the wilds of the weeds and didn't want him to think I was too girly. "I'll do it if you pull off the legs." I wondered if that would drain the "tobaccy juice"—the brown pooh that oozed onto your palm when you closed a hand around one.

I shut my eyes real tight when he started removing the appendages. I was thinking about that poor grasshopper and about poor me. I couldn't back out, so I had to decide if I was going to chew or just swallow. I didn't think that stove was hot enough to cook him crispy, so I decided on whole.

Tony plopped the hopper onto the stove, flipping him over several times with a stick he'd found.

The squiggly legs were gone, but I wasn't certain the thing was dead. I'd seen natives in the Tarzan movies eating bugs, and enjoying them, so I knew it wouldn't poison me. However, his daunting body length caused a gag reflex and I had to turn my back so my brother couldn't see how much I didn't want to swallow that grasshopper.

It took a lot of will power to keep him in my mouth, but I turned back around and stuck out my grasshoppered tongue to prove I hadn't spit him out.

Grasshopper bodies are rough—like miniature plated armadillos.

I didn't think there was enough spit in ten mouths to swallow him, but after three attempts, I gulped him down. I waited for him to jump around inside my stomach, but there was no movement. Even though I knew that insect had no legs, in my imagination, the grasshopper wanted retaliation.

"Wow," was all my brother said.

I really wanted a bike that summer, but knew I would never get a new one. Although Dad had put a doll and a little red wagon on layaway once when we were really young, that had been for Christmas. The rest of the year it was cash up front. Aunt Janet was getting a new one and Grandma offered me her old one. Even though I knew the other kids would laugh, I was willing to swallow my pride for my own transportation.

I was still too young to bike a mile to town to the swimming pool, but I had ideas of gliding down the long hill in the other direction, crossing the river bridge, and pulling off onto the side rode to picnic. The bike would carry me to new adventures.

That blue bicycle was at least two sizes too big and pedaled like the tin man's rusty joints. I rarely sat on the seat that whole summer—most of the time I was standing, alternating my weight on the pedals, moving those fat tires through our gravel driveway.

The time I did decide to take it easy, I sat on the too-big seat and coasted down the hill, dangling my thongs just above the asphalt. Thinking of something else (probably grasshopper pie), my foot dipped down and the tip of my big toe remained embedded in the road at the bottom of the hill.

Now, that caught my attention. Especially since I had to push my bike back up the aforementioned hill because of the pain. I stayed close to the fort for a few days.

That was the summer I discovered bodies.

Sitting alone on a pile of lumber behind the shed one day, I heard baby kittens crying in the haystack. I followed the sound, hoping to find a new litter. When I located the hideout, a dark rectangle between stacked bales, I pulled out the first squalling, sharp-nailed critter. Holding the fluff close to me, I returned to the woodpile to pet the little guy.

The sun felt cuddly as it wrapped us in contentment. The kitten settled down to sleep and I took in the smell of hay, the slivery feel of the boards under me—slender lengths like pick-up sticks that begged to be straightened. I was too lazy to move.

The kitten started to cry again—probably hungry. I was reminded of how Mother nursed my sister, Cheri. I wondered what breast feeding was like. Did it hurt? I thought it looked disgusting—did it feel disgusting? The bawling accelerated. On a whim, I raised my halter-top and stuck the kitten to my flat breast. I pulled my top back in place and imagined nursing a real baby. In moments, the confined kitty panicked and headed toward my neck, scratching teeny nail tracks the entire way. He dug into my flesh, stopping briefly on my shoulder. The trail of wounds stung, especially when I tried to disconnect the ungrateful critter.

The experiment a failure, I gladly gave the baby back to his mom, now frantically circling my feet.

Not long after that, I was restless one afternoon. My brother was playing with a friend, my sister, Christie, was too little to have much fun with, and so I asked, "Mother, can Lee come play?" She looked up from her bread kneading, a powdering of flour connecting her nose to her chin. "For a little while."

An only child, Lee was a quiet kid. His dad farmed the place two fields behind our ten acres. One of my favorite places to play was in his huge red barn. We climbed the wooden stairs to the hayloft, just like in the movies. The sun streamed in the upstairs shutters, sending shafts of light into the horse stalls. I loved the smell of hay and oats and dusty rafters. But that day I had invited him to my domain.

Lee walked across the adjoining field to meet me on the dirt road that ran parallel to the drain ditch and our alfalfa crop. We sat on the bank of the ditch, our swinging heels mashing down the tall grass that grew in the cattails. It was quiet, except for an occasional twittering magpie and the sound of the water trickling through the ditch.

We were alone.

The thoughts of boy and girl differences surfaced once again. I impulsively challenged my conscience.

"I'll show you my parts if you'll show me yours," I said, straight out.

Lee seemed surprised, but stood without saying anything and began removing the skinny belt cinching his new blue jeans.

My stomach crawled. Was he serious?

I didn't think he would even consider it.

I stood up. No words were exchanged. He unzipped his fly, pushing his pants down as I looked away. I had started a game I didn't want to play. I still hadn't looked at him. Ashamed, I didn't know what to do. Slowly I looked up and peeked. He was definitely plumbed different than a girl. He looked vulnerable standing there with his jeans pooled around his sneakers. My crawling stomach lurched and I plunged into pure guilt as I nervously kicked my right sandal back and forth through the dust, starring as it erased the imprints left by the soles.

This couldn't be real. His parts seemed to meld into an image—a knock-kneed, ghostly-white, stick person—so pale I knew the sun had never touched his lower half. He stood there for what seemed like hours. I was so numb my mouth wouldn't move. I mentally willed him to pull up his britches. I just wanted him to go home.

Something didn't gel. I was still a kid. I had just last winter stopped sucking my thumb. Why was I curious about a dumb boy's private parts?

Neither of us spoke about the encounter on the ditch that day—ever. His image remained with me for several days, like a pesky fly buzzing an open sore. We both acted like it had never happened.

Before that day on the ditch bank, whenever my mother recited the "Good little, bad little" poem, I equated it to my moody ups and downs—a reminder of how my own happiness could instantly twist into rage.

Now, I had tangible evidence that I was a horrid girl. I had told a boy to show me his parts, even if I didn't show him mine.

One more in the Tree

I was too old for dolls. Only *little* girls rocked sleeping baby dolls. My walking doll had vanished long ago—the only doll I remembered. She probably got tossed out with the trash—buried in the dump next to a broken bike frame or some kid's cracked hula-hoop.

I was ten years old, a fifth grader. It was time for a phonograph, 45 records and fuzzy sweaters. But as the Christmas spirit burst out of stored boxes and landed as plastic yard snowmen and tree decorations, I knew I was slipping back. I had seen the perfect doll.

Browsing through the Evening in Paris display at the drug store I spotted her—tucked in a box no bigger than a box of Cracker Jacks. The cellophane wrapping crinkled as I touched perfection. She lay in a tiered wedding dress, white ribbon looping through each layer—the dress so full it folded back on itself. Tiny flowers nestled across the gathers on her wedding veil, greenery barely visible through the poof of netting surrounding her face.

Her hair flipped up around the bottom, like the stylish junior high girls.' Eyes lashed with tiny hairs curled toward her eyelids—opened and closed as I tilted the box. Her eyes met mine and as I read her name on the packaging, I sensed a growing need for Betsy McCall.

Fanned around in perfect symmetry, her outfits filled the inside of smaller boxes. The pink summer dress was my favorite. Tiny black party shoes featured straps to cross her delicate feet. Her bonnet, so small it could ride on top of a roll of upended Lifesavers, completed the outfit.

The next day I asked my four-year-old sister what she wanted for Christmas, within hearing range of my mother. "A baby, a coloring book, and ten candy canes," she said.

"I saw the cutest toys in Moyer's Drug Store the other day. There was a baby doll wrapped in a pink wicker bassinet. They had one named Betsy McCall for older girls. I think I want her for Christmas."

Mother had come into the living room to water her plants. "You girls are making out your Christmas lists a little early aren't you? We just finished Thanksgiving."

"We were talking about dolls, I said. Betsy McCall looks like a real person."

"I think you're a little old for dolls, didn't you want a new sweater?"

Mother, the practical one, finished her watering and returned to the kitchen. I had to explain to my dad. He always listened if I said, "please, please, please." Christmas was the time he made sure there was lots of loot.

Pre-dawn on Christmas morning we woke our parents. The presents sprawled under the tree. Our stockings spilled nuts and ribbon candy on the hearth. We sat in our pajamas tearing the wrapping from multiple sized gifts, but none as small as Betsy's box.

My little sisters each cuddled a brand new doll. New outfits and toys sat in piles by each owner. My brother was building a Lincoln Log house, stopping only to search for cotton balls to make smoke puffs. Our parents, content with their gifts, sat back and basked in Santa's generosity and the spirit of the day.

I had opened a blue sweater, a skirt, and Elvis's hit album, "Blue Hawaii." With fewer and fewer gifts left under the tree, my tears balled into a lump half way up my chest. I must have looked like a waif, my pajamas wrinkled from an anxious sleep, my hair knotted to one side, and disappointment scraping my face in an awkward attempt to fake gratitude.

Down to the last gift, dad asked me, "Did Santa bring everything you wished for?"

I nodded, looking down at my rumpled pajamas.

"I think we're missing something don't you, Mom?" he said, standing to survey the goods. "Nothing left under the tree." He shook his head as he batted his way through several crumpled yards of wrapping paper. "I think Santa must have left one in the tree."

All the kids readied themselves for a dive at the missing gift. "No, everyone, sit down. I think he left it for your big sister."

I experienced hope that Christmas morning. In slow motion, I stood and stretched toward the tree. Gently lifting the bubble lights, I felt inside the tinsel and spread the boughs. The smell of pine wrapped around the moment. Glowing red paper, tied with curly ribbons, covered the perfect sized boxes.

As I ripped into the first box, I knew from the wedding veil, this was the very same doll from the drugstore. As I tilted the box, Betsy's eyes opened on my world. Out of the box, I held her in my hand, moving her jointed hands and knees, in awe of her realness. Three perfect outfits completed her wardrobe—including the pink dress.

She was mine.

Betsy was the last Christmas doll I ever received. I remained too old for dolls until my own daughter got her first baby doll. After that, I collected little dolls for her—ones that reminded me a lot of Betsy and the Christmas Dad said he thought there was one present left in the tree.

Granny Goatskin

It was July 24, celebrated as Pioneer Day in Utah, the day the Saints arrived in the Salt Lake Valley in 1847. Our Tuesday children's church classes had been asked to dress in period clothing for the annual around-the-block children's parade.

My imagination immediately saw the whole outfit—the long skirt, the button-down blouse featuring full mutton sleeves, the matching bonnet that shaded the eyes and the back of the neck. For weeks we had sung pioneer songs about marching—about little children playing, picking flowers as they walked all the way to Zion. I wanted blue material to match the bluebells I was sure had brightened the meadows beside the wagon trail more than 100 years ago.

I conveniently forgot about the badgering I would get from the boys in my class. Although some of the boys would throw some sort of costume together—a bandana around the neck, a tin sheriff's badge, a cheap-feathered headdress and tomahawk—I was sure they would find something to pick on me about.

Their weekly teasing had turned ugly in the past few weeks. The group turned up their noses when I entered the room, mimicked my every word when the teacher wasn't there, even pushed me down in my chair if I dared lash back. After every class I came home with a stomachache.

Sudden thoughts of their teasing erased visions of my beautiful outfit.

"I don't want to dress up," I told my mother. "I don't even want to go."

Mother continued kneading bread dough. The cinnamon container was on the counter so I knew what she was making. It did make me feel a bit better, but then the pioneer thoughts came back.

"You have to go to Primary," she insisted, dumping dough on the floured counter and picking up a rolling pin. "Your teacher will want to see your pioneer outfit."

"I hate Primary."

She turned toward me, pointing the rolling pin my direction. "Your teacher prepares lessons about Jesus every week."

"She can teach the boys. They need it."

I was sick of the whole bunch.

"We'll find you a nice skirt and blouse. Parades are fun."

I did like to play dress-up.

"I'll go if I can have a blue bonnet with the flap in back."

Shaking cinnamon, brown sugar, and raisins over the buttered dough, she said, "Wear that gypsy skirt from Halloween last year and I think there's still some long sleeved blouses in those clothes Janet gave you."

The vision of the perfect fashion faded like clothes hung too long in the sun. This outfit was going to be pieced together. The kids were really going to laugh.

"Mother, that skirt is black. I don't think they had Halloween on the trail. Why can't I ever have anything special?" I asked her. "I always have to wear Janet's stuff. I want a real pioneer dress."

"We'll do the best we can, but I'm not spending money on a costume." Mother rolled the monstrous dough circle up and started cutting cinnamon rolls. "I'll see what I can do for a bonnet."

That week she did find a fabric scrap in the closet to make the sunbonnet. It was a daisy-patterned print—not a bluebell to be found.

I was disappointed and self-conscious about my costume, especially the gathered skirt that accentuated my thick waist.

When the day of the parade arrived, I dressed in my bedroom, finally emerging after hearing my name called several times.

Mother herded us all toward the car. Tony wore his mashed black cowboy hat with the white lacing threading the brim. His toy leather holster set held one gun—the other was lost. I liked his neckerchief, but was still mortified by my clothes.

Pushing in my soft stomach, I told Mother, "This makes me look fat."

"Get your sister," she replied. "You look cute."

I picked up Cheri, my curly-headed baby sister and hugged her softness. She giggled and ran her dimpled fingers over the flap of my bonnet. Her baby loves momentarily curbed my need for assurance. I hoped for the best, thinking maybe this was the day the boys would ignore me.

I knew better.

I saw two of the girls from my class as we crossed the parking lot. One had a brand-new coordinated dress and bonnet—soft pink with rickrack trim. The other wore a flowered skirt with a white ruffled apron.

I was doomed.

The game started the minute I entered the classroom.

"So why you parading around in that long skirt?" Bob asked, his head tilted, eyeballing me up and down. I looked at my cotton skirt, actually feeling my stomach flab over the gathers in the waistband. I wanted to run home and change, but instead I spoke up. "Because it's Pioneer Days, we were supposed to. Are you too good to dress up?"

I looked around, finding Jeanette to be the only girl there. She reverently folded her arms over the drop-waist yellow percale—too fancy for a rocky pioneer trail. Nobody was going to tell her, though. The boys didn't pick on her.

"Black skirts are for Halloween witches and I haven't seen any bonnets with flaps," Steve smirked.

"My mom made them," I defended. "Pioneers wore long skirts and bonnets." One of the mousy-faced misfits in the back row, couldn't stay out of the game. "You're a granny. Where are your spectacles?" He asked, his rippling laughter spreading to the other boys.

The two other girls I had seen in the parking lot came in and sat in the front row. They folded their arms, pointing at me and whispering to one another.

I knew they recognized my gypsy skirt from the Halloween party at school.

"All of you just shut-up and leave me alone." I wanted to cry but wouldn't. The girls just sat with their eyes on their feet. One of them eventually looked up and said, "The teacher is coming. You better quit bothering her."

I felt more alone than ever.

"Cindy Olsen. Cindy Olsen." Knocking his chair over, Bob repeated my name as he recklessly headed to the blackboard—GRANNEE GOATSKYN—he wrote in sloppy, tilting print, messier than most second graders. "That's what your name is now." And he repeated—"Granny Goatskin."

The creep couldn't even spell.

"You can't spell *or* write," I flung back.

A bunch of the others joined in the chorus, chanting my new name, "Granny Goatskin."

I hurtled back, "My name is Cindy, My name is Cindy," until I heard Donna's urgent voice break through.

"Someone really is coming down the hall."

Two of the boys ran to erase the crooked name. On the back row, I sat down, twisting the strings to my bonnet into knots.

Sister Smith, her arms loaded with her toddling son, the roll call folder, and her big canvas bag, entered with a flourish and plopped everything onto the wooden desk in front of the blackboard.

"I'm running so late today," she breathed in huffs. "Little Freddie has to march in the parade with us. I couldn't find a sitter." Once again, she was distracted and I knew she would brush me off if I tried to tell.

She pulled out the roll and read each name in alphabetical order. I cringed when she got to my name. My eyes squeezed into blackness when I heard the jerk in front of me spurt out, "Granny Goatskin is her name now."

Sister Smith continued through the list, ignoring the comment.

"Everyone line up now and get ready for the parade. Let's think about all the sacrifices our pioneers made so we can be free to live our religion."

I didn't think these boys were living the religion I believed in. I knew they were itching to see me cry. They weren't finished with me.

Once outside, we lined up by classes and walked around the block, little red wagons turned prairie schooners, bicycle spokes crepe-papered, handlebars hung with matching streamers. A few cowboys pulled out their cap guns and fired, the smoke irritating my lungs, sending me into coughing fits. I was sweaty and thirsty, and feeling sorry for those poor pioneers.

Whenever the teacher went off chasing Freddie, one of the boys would run up and call me Granny.

At the finish, the last few stragglers marched into the church parking lot. I joined the swell of pioneers heading for the treats. I collected my Popsicle and headed for the front, hoping Mother would be ready to go. She wasn't in the car. It was hot and my Popsicle dripped red splotches on the cement. Lifting my long skirt, I swished it around, fanning my legs.

At that moment Bob ran out of the chapel doors, tripping over his own feet in his excitement to get close enough to bug me. "Why don't you wear your dumb hat?" he chided as he lifted it from my shoulders and swung it around my neck.

I spun around, trying to get away from his dirty fingers. "Don't touch it." I yelled. I wanted to hurt him—to feel my fingernails uproot four parallel peels of skin down his cheek. I chased him onto the lawn, tossing my Popsicle in a bush. He outran me.

A couple more boys saw the commotion and ganged around me in the circle driveway in front of the church, chanting "Granny Goatskin." I deliberately walked to the curb and sat, holding my hands over my ears and praying my mother would come.

They only stopped the name-calling as their rides rolled into the driveway. How could their mothers not know how bratty their own boys were? Did they ever get in trouble?

Mother finally came out the chapel doors and directed Tony and Cheri to the car. I still sat on the curb, wanting her to see my pain. By this time she had started the car and drove around the parking lot, stopping in the circle driveway right beside me. She honked, but I didn't even look up.

Disturbed that I hadn't jumped right in the car, she asked. "Why are you sitting there?" coming around to open the back door.

"I will never go back as long as I live," I sobbed. Tears streamed down my face. I rubbed my nose and wiped it on the gypsy skirt. I was so mad—especially because those greasy-fingered boys had been touching my clothes. I was mad at the teacher for not knowing her own students, and mad at my mother for never listening to me. I wanted action.

"You're just going to have to learn to ignore them," Mother repeated as I told her what had happened.

"I can't."

Mother kept driving. Rounding the next corner, she held her arm out to steady Cheri, standing next to her on the seat. As we straightened out she said, "The more you let them know it bothers you, the more they'll do it."

Dad was no better. When I told him about the teasing, he said, "They probably like you and don't know how to show it." I thought my dad had more sense than that.

I wanted him go find them, conk their heads together—scare them so they wouldn't ever bother me again.

Granny Goatskin be gone.

Bring 'Em On

Tulip tops flopped into their crusty snow covers, spring masked once again in days of sloppy freezing rain and slush. Dustin and Karena's kids drug in their suitcases and stacked them by the closet. They were sneezing and coughing.

Stay back, don't go near the darlings. The germs are compounded by four. You'll never survive. My asthma is worse in the spring with latent leaves and moldy woodpiles and moisture aching to scoot into my lungs.

But, oh the sweetness, the soft necks waiting to be kissed… and then they're running, smack into my arms. One must make up for the hugs via phone lines that never quite feel like skin.

I scooped them up, brushing curls away as I found a cheek, another cheek, the back of a little-boy head and we all tumbled over the rug. I wiped my mouth, sure that some bug had attached. But, a virus must incubate and I must reciprocate.

We went to the museum, colored royal crowns and learned about circles. We scanned groceries kid-style—empty Corn Flake boxes, mac and cheese boxes, plastic broccoli. The Kleenex flowed and I wiped and laughed, kissing their ear lobes.

The following day a familiar burning infused my senses, warning that an enemy had landed. No! Germs surely would avoid a grandma at play. But at the dinner table, I admitted to the oncoming cold. A ball of inflammation formed in the recesses of my throat. "I'm going to sneeze."

The three oldest poked their fingers in their ears in preparation. The sound blasted out into the air, powerful as demolition dynamite.

Another quickly followed, sending me sailing a few inches off the chair. One granddaughter, perfectly on cue, fell to the floor as if shot. Tears ran down my cheeks as I laughed and ran around hugging every one of those germ-infested grandkids.

I was short of breath and coughing like I had whooping cough, but it will be approximately six months before I have to have a kiss fix and wipe four freckled noses all over again.

Dollar Pokes

The most fun a kid could ever have was at Aunt Jan's house. All the cousins adored her. Jay had built an A-frame home at the end of the ten acres Mother and Dad owned. The kids had built a two-story play house, they had a trampoline, a small cement ditch behind the house to splash in, and kid-mobiles a plenty. Jan let them grab snacks from the pantry, go to town for movies, and bottle-feed her baby raccoons she adopted each spring.

In fact, she thought it quite okay when her son, Jacob, would drag the trampoline into the living room. The first time he pulled it off, Jay and Jan were out to dinner for their anniversary and Jacob commandeered his sisters outside to help him tear it down. His record time was thirty minutes and that included setting it back up. Little kids climbed up the spiral staircase and jumped, bouncing on each other. Scared me to death.

We had fireworks displays at their house every Fourth of July. Jay and his older sons, being welders, set huge pipes in the ground beside the lawn and loaded mortars inside, lit, and ran. (Not kidding—they bought them at a "secret" place). One year one of the guys had a mortar the size of a soccer ball.

Half the town would be out there to watch the show from the road. No one was crazy enough to get as close as the family. Jan pulled out the lawn chairs and the blankets so folks could hold them over their bodies in case of flying fire and debris. Smoke clouds rolled over the valley, the acrid smell of fire and powder whooshed clear into town. Every year the culmination was the "burning of the box." All the duds went inside, as well as any fireworks the boys (and the men) wanted to stash. Every year the box got more out of control. One year I went inside to avoid it all and looked out the upstairs window. Across the lawn, one of the huge pine trees was on fire.

Of course Jonathan was always a part.

And so was Jett, the youngest of Jay and Jan's eight children. Fireworks were his favorite thing, next to being carried on the shoulders of his dad. One winter, Grandma, Jan and a bunch of the kids struggled to drive the drifted lane to the house and had to resort to foot travel. Their car would be stuck until the snowplow came. Drifts mounded along the Russian olive tree windbreak and clear into the pasture on the other side. When they struggled around the final corner, cold, windblown, and weary, they ran into Jett, decked out in his snow clothes—sitting under one of the pine trees at the edge of the yard—lighting and throwing firecrackers.

Jett had the dark skin passed on from Dad to Jay; his brown curly hair, a hand down from his great grandmother, Lydia. Loving, absorbing life, quiet, yet he was a spirited little kid.

Jett had a dog named Chippy, a favorite blanket, and a family that adored him.

One day Jan was hefting a load and bent to pick Jett up by one arm. That evening his arm was swollen three times its size. She thought it was her fault. The doctor diagnosed it as "nursemaid elbow" and said it would get better.

It didn't.

On massive doses of Demerol, Jett was in agony. A week later Jan took him back in and came out with the same diagnosis.

"It will get better," the doctor assured.

It didn't.

Another doctor in Cody did surgery and found a large malignant tumor.

He was three years old.

Jay and Jan drove Jett to Primary Children's Hospital in Salt Lake City. When they finally arrived, Jan said, "His little three-year-old arm was the size of mine."

He was diagnosed with Non-Hodgkin's lymphoma and started chemotherapy. As his hair began to fall out, his two best friends, Michael and Caleb shaved their heads to look like their pal.

Jett still zoomed around the neighborhood with his brother, Jacob, on his hotrod go-cart, or took a spin on his own red plastic Big Wheels. Jan let them ride the lawn mower around. (Yes, this is the woman who lets trampolines indoors too.) The boys would get on the thing and to grandmother's house they'd go. It seemed like Jett would ride anything, but his favorite conveyance was still his father's arm. I remember hearing the little guy say to his dad, "I love it when you carry me," as he was swooped off the couch, wrapped in his favorite quilt and carried to the dining room to sit with the family during dinner.

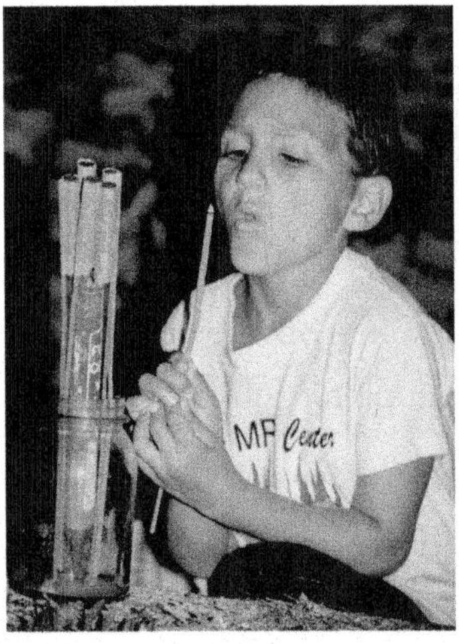

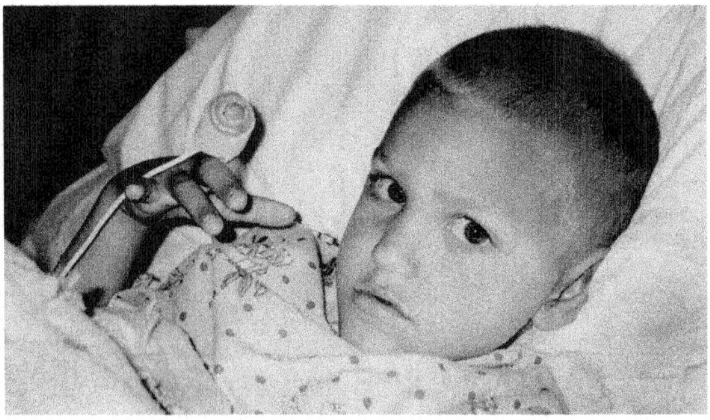

Jett (above) in the beginning stages of chemotherapy and (left) during his last Fourth of July with us.

Within a year Jett had another bout. His scrotum had swelled as wide as his arm had swollen. Once again he was driven to Primary's. The doctor at home thought Jett had a torsion and wanted to do surgery. "Whoa," Jay said. "This guy has cancer."

He was taken back to Primary's. Jan told me, "It was the cancer back, hiding in his testicle. Evil stuff. It has some kind of intelligence if it knew how to hide."

Chemotherapy, pokes, and hospital beds again. But, he was back playing with his toy back hoes and draglines within a couple of weeks. Jett loved to ride our horse, Foxy, the old grey mare. He'd ride with his sisters, up and down the pasture. As soon as he hopped off, he'd be asking me for firecrackers.

Jett started school. The doctors said he would never live long enough to even start. Tough as the metal rods his dad and brothers welded with, he fought. But, the evil monster returned. It was in his legs this time. More chemo, more trips, more needles and hair loss.

In between bouts, were a few months of respite and play on the ditch bank with Chippy and his cousins. Jett played with his cousin, Cammy, the most. She came over on weekends to stay with Grandma, but very quickly, the cousins ended up at Jan's house. Jett would dance with Cammy, sing, and play in the playhouse.

One day Jan called us again and said Jett was in trouble. He was having extreme head pain and was so weak he couldn't walk. Jay carried him into the hospital foyer where Carl and I were waiting. His little bald head stuck out of his quilt. Ashen, frail, and terribly ill, I wondered if he would make it out of the hospital. Jett always assured us, "My mom says we're going to keep fighting."

For additional spiritual and physical help, Jan fasted for twenty four hours every Sunday for two years.

Within an hour, the answer came. Jett came bouncing out the door; Jay and Jan holding hands, the doctor holding Jett's. It was like he had been Lazarus, raised from the dead—med miracles.

Jett really wanted a new bicycle. Jan and Jay decided that the pokes he was getting regularly should really count for something. They assured him that from then on, every poke earned him a dollar. He had now been in cancer combat for over two years, and had collected enough "pokes" to buy a bicycle. (Supplemented a bit of course). His mom and dad took him shopping and he picked out a bike resembling a miniature Harley Hawg. At a local store he tested it out in the narrow aisles. The bike wobbled as Jett overcorrected on a curve, swerved, and bumped into a toy display knocking it over. No one seemed to mind.

Carl and I were in line behind them as Jett walked his bike to the register and reached into his coat to pull out a wad of bills the size of a man's fist. This tiny little bald boy shelled out bill after bill—poke after poke.

The time came when Jett again was fighting the monster, and the only solution the doctors offered was a bone marrow transplant. Jay told the kids, "If Jett can suffer, we can sacrifice a bit and have the tests to see if any of us are a match."

Only one in the family was an exact match, his sister, Cana. She didn't hesitate. While both were in the hospital recovering, Jett played three movies over and over until Cana and he had them all memorized—*Dennis the Menace, Tweety Bird, and Bat Man.*

I got to step in for grandmother's day when he was six because my mother was out of town. Jett was so excited. I asked him what they did in class every day.

"We say the pledge of allegiance to the flag every morning," he said in all seriousness.

"What if I can't remember the words?" I teased.

"I'll help you, Aunt Cindy," he said.

We all stood for the pledge at the beginning of class, just as he said. He glanced at me every sentence to see if I needed any help.

But, in the end, the monster won. We answered the phone in the middle of the night, "Jett has gone home," Jan said. "I finally told him, son, you can go if you want. We'll be okay." Later Jan told me, "He fought it for four years. I'm still working on the trying to be okay part. A lifelong job."

By Hand

Warm days followed his passing
the way a puppy nips at a boy's heels.
Cousins' tears moistened the air
in a space so familiar they resumed play.

Grandma cranked the ice cream.
Aunts wrote the obituary.
Mom reminisced.

Motions clanked over the missing cog.

Dad disappeared to build a casket worthy of his son.
Not a large one, a seven-year-old size—aluminum,
seams welded tight against forces beyond his control.

Jett, a boy who paid for his bicycle with his own dollars,
a dollar a poke as IVs penetrated, needles jabbed.

A boy who loved firecrackers and rides on Dad's
shoulders and writing love notes to Mom.

We felt him at the service, pain-free and strong.
Strong enough to run across fields of flowers.
Strong enough to carry his Dad, in time.

And at the graveside we did not weep.
The family remained as cars pulled away.
Jett's dad lifted shovels off his truck bed, handing
them one by one to each man.

Shovelfuls of dirt pinged the casket.
Men dug in cadence, stopped too soon and let him go,
the work done.

Cousins sat on the mound, flinging fistfuls of dirt into
unfamiliar air, still wanting to play.

~ Cindy Lou Bechtold

Angels and Apples

Dustin had severe allergies as a kid. Mosquito bites by his eyes swelled them shut. Peach fuzz swelled his lips up to five times their size. We were off to Montana again in our Subaru wagon to visit an allergy specialist. Jan, Dustin, and I took off for Billings.

After the visit, Dustin had fiery needle injection sites up and down his back. All he wanted was a nap. He laid down in the back seat and we headed home. I rounded a curve on a two lane highway and saw a fruit stand at the left. Fresh Utah peaches. I still *always* brake for fruit stands. Pulling as close to the yellow line as possible, I waited for oncoming cars before crossing.

One glance in the rear view mirror and I knew we were doomed. A red semi-truck was bearing down on us—I gauged about three feet away. My first thought—Dustin isn't in a seatbelt. My second—we're dead.

I looked again, bracing for the crash as the semi went screaming past on the passenger side, maybe a quarter inch from scraping off the side mirror. I watched him speed off, never slowing, never honking, wondering why he hadn't stopped. It felt like a nightmare—ghost rider in a red truck. He vanished down the highway.

Wait a minute. On the side the truck had barreled through there was no shoulder. The edge dropped off a steep embankment. There was no physical way that semi could have wedged past us.

Jan was talking away, oblivious to what had just happened.

"We were almost killed. Didn't you see that semi-truck? There was no way he could have gotten around."

"I didn't see anything. That can't be true," she said.

"Look at the edge of this highway," I replied. The truck had gone by like a blur and she never looked up.

Dustin stayed sound asleep.

Memory of the drive home is muddled.

When we pulled into Jan's drive-way, Jay ran out to meet us. Illness had kept him home that day, a rare event. "Are you guys alright? I woke up from a nightmare this afternoon in a sweat. I saw a semi bash into the back of your car. Jan was killed." Looking at me he continued, "And you were critically injured. It was so real, I got out of bed and fell on my knees to plead with Heavenly Father to spare your lives."

"What color was the semi?" I asked.

"Red."

Goosebumps spread up both my arms. "What time did this happen?" I asked.

"About three o'clock, I think. I looked at the clock to try and figure out where you would be."

I had checked my watch before deciding to buy fruit. Three o'clock, the exact time we had stopped in the road, my left blinker flashing.

After explaining our exact location, Jay grabbed Jan's arm and escorted her into the house. "What happened today is impossible. That corner is deadly. Some strong angels must have been in the area."

Later that evening at home, my sister, Christie, from Utah called. She rarely called as they were on a tight budget and long distance was expensive. "Are you okay," she asked. "I was thinking about you this afternoon and started worrying."

"What time was this?" I asked.

"The bell was about to ring to dismiss my last class. It must have been around three o'clock."

I told the story again.

On our next trip to Billings, I nervously pulled into the area where the fruit stand had been. Carl walked across the road and stood on the edge, looking down.

"It's impossible for a semi to maneuver through that. It would have rolled."

Sacred moments by a fruit stand.

Felt Hat Flop

Every summer Dad tied the canvas water bag on the grill and loaded us all into the old Chevy wagon to drive the seventy miles to the East Gate of Yellowstone National Park. Paper bags packed with our clothes shifted as we sailed around mountain curves. Dad nudged the shoulder so close we all squealed.

He chuckled.

I knew all the rock formations through Wapiti valley: the old lady and her cabin, laughing pig, chimney rock. When Indian Joe's mummy was discovered in a cave right beside the road, I knew we would be in National Geographic and be famous around the world. I also knew where the best, purest mountain drinking fountain was—beside the road by a big sign and a big pine tree.

We always stopped at Yellowstone Lake and fed bread to the seagulls. Every year we would wade into the lake, thinking somehow it had warmed up. I think snow was still melting off the mountains in June, July, and August. Maybe it was there for eternity. I'd wade in about two feet before rigor mortis set in over my ankles.

In the open grass across the road, birds hitched rides on buffalo with fur looking a lot like shaggy shawls. Pelicans waded through lily pads. We were getting closer to Fishing Bridge, my favorite place on earth. (excluding the bears—brown, black, grizzly, or any other kind).

Dad kept saying we were getting closer to bear country. I begged him not to stop if they were on the road. "Oh, a little bear isn't going to hurt us," he would say.

Bear jams sent cars catawampus across yellow lines, tourists excited to stupidity. Paws climbed the window; Dad cool, me hysterical—visions of teeth ripping me to shreds, swallowed alongside sunglasses and sandwiches. "If they don't get enough sandwiches, they'll chomp garbage at the dumps," Dad said.

I hoped the garbage dumps were clear off in Jackson Hole.

Men in shorts and flowered shirts pointed cameras at any animal they saw. People with binoculars wandered into the woods to see moose and buffalo. I just knew some little kid was going to be charged and I'd be too scared to rescue him. I locked the doors and peeked out.

We got to stop at every pull-off on the road. Where there were parked cars, there were geysers. Warned to stay back from log barriers, I inched closer, mentally measuring bubbling pools under steam. Would good-luck pennies intentionally tossed, rust there or drop clear to China? Mother told me someone jumped into a geyser to rescue her dog and they both boiled. We had a dog named Puppy, but she stayed home.

Back in the car and a million bear jams later, Dad was the first to spot Fishing Bridge.

Loaded from one end to the other, fishermen cast lines in orderly rows, flies bouncing. What kept them from tangling and tumbling into the lake after all those flies?

Pulling into the store and souvenir shop, we all begged for ice cream. Big scoops of vanilla, chocolate, or strawberry.

Heaven.

Huge log doors closed us in with smells of soot, pine slabs, and cedar boxes.

Dad went to rent a cabin and buy pressed logs. How did they get those logs so smooth and so full of those little chips? I hoped our cabin was close to the bathrooms. I was scared of bears walking the paths between those smoky log cabins.

Cots lining the walls and a little wood-burning stove were the only things in the room. I couldn't wait to jump into my sleeping bag and watch dad start the stove with the pressed logs. I didn't have to get up in the morning and light it either. I stayed in bed as the cold bit my nose and my sisters cried a lot.

One trip we had a cabin far from the bathroom. I made it all the way free and clear, but on the way back I glanced back and saw a huge black bear ambling behind me. Never run they said. Why not? I thought as I reached the cabin and shouted, "Bear. Bear. Save yourselves." Itching to see how far from the fangs I was, I peeked around the corner holding unto the doorjamb for backup. I yelled "bear" once again, just as my scaredy-cat siblings inside shut the door—on my fingers. Never mind the pain, I was going to be lunch.

The smells must have filled my mother with generosity. She would let us pick out a souvenir, if it didn't cost too much. Rows of Indian dolls and leather wrapped drums, polished rocks and toy pistols were for sale. The best ever, I found tucked on a shelf between plastic bison and tomahawks. The felt hat had to be mine—a perfect crayon-blue, red feather poked into the side, *Yellowstone Park* stitched in cursive across the brim.

The hat never sat in a bag, but on my head as we traveled loops around the Park. Old Faithful blew on schedule, tourists still hid behind cameras unafraid of twitchy moose. Mother built liverwurst sandwiches on the glove box door.

On the way home we stopped to sip from a stream. Moss floated over stones like hair sprouting from my troll doll. Crouched, water lapping my toes, I had to touch it. Stretching to the threads, a moment of breeze lifted my hat and sent it downstream.

I snagged it a few yards away. Drenched, felting unmolded, it flopped like a kitchen rag, red dye running around the edge. Climbing over the car seat, I dove into the back, mourning stinky stuff, bears, and my hat that would never be the same.

Horse Women

Shetland ponies can be evil. Dinah was a cute little mare—kid-sized, but ornery. Grandpa would lead her out of the barn, give me a hand up, and I'd take off down the lane, bareback. Just around the corner, two huge cottonwood trees grew side by side. One was forked in perfect position for the tree house where my brother and I stored our green apples and grandma's pilfered salt shaker. The other intertwined close enough for Dinah to pass through, but not wide enough for my dangling legs to clear, and she knew it. I hiked my knees as we squeezed through. Her plan to scrape me off never worked.

Resigned to her passenger, Dinah walked in a comfortable gait. Farm smells laced the edges of my nose. I felt my heart lighten and my world wrap me up in contentment on those horseback rides. I checked out the bean fields, the irrigation dishes edged with timothy grass and oats. Pot holes on the road were hardly noticed, riding a horse that skirted them. But, then my stomach started to quiver and my heart ramped up. I had to get her home and I knew what was coming. Turning her around, her pace noticeably picked up. Passing the tree house was her signal.

Taking off at a dead run, there was not a bridle bit on earth that a kid could pull hard enough to stop her. She ran. I held onto her mane and prayed as she abruptly stopped, her nose mere inches from the corral gate.

Ride 'em cowgirl.

I was still on her back.

One of our horses at home, Silky, had a colt. I don't remember his name and I don't even want to. The colt was separated from his mom by putting him in the fenced area around our chicken coup, an area big enough to hold him—big enough for an eleven-year-old to squeeze in and pet him. He was so cute. I pictured myself astride his back, his black mane and forelock so long they broke records, his shiny tail dragging the ground. I slowly walked up and raised my hand to pet him, run my fingers across his velvet nose, and sink my hands into his Rapunzel mane.

Without even a hello, he did one of those side kick numbers, his hoof landing square in my chest. I was offended, out of wind, and mad. I felt for the gate and got out of there, my chest on fire, my air only starting to come back. It's a wonder he didn't stifle my breast development coming soon.

Tony and me standing by Dinah. I think I have an attitude.

Dang it.

Silky was easy enough for a kid to ride. Dad said I could ride her in the August downtown parade. I dragged on my aunt's cowboy boots, but I got to pick out a brand new straw cowboy hat. Lining up in position, Silky behaved quite well as I sat tall in the saddle, proud and important. The procession momentarily stopped and apparently Silky got a whiff of something she didn't like. She danced and kicked up her heels. The fine stallion behind spooked and stood on his hind legs, the rider soon flat on the ground. I thought I was going to get killed by the guy if he could still walk. Several people helped him up and no one said a word to me. I was just a kid.

When I got to the end of the route, Dad asked me what had happened. I really didn't know. "That man's horse bucked."

"That man was Doctor Jones," he said. "Your dentist." I gulped and shivered. I hadn't seen much of his face, as I was looking straight ahead, ignoring the commotion. I felt retaliation coming on. Next time at his office, he'd claim I had twenty five cavities.

One of the last "Happy Trails to You" happened in our pasture behind the barn. My neighbor, Kate, had come over to ride. We led Silky to the iron-piped fence and climbed on. She took a detour under the barn as we ducked our heads, and then she placidly plodded to open ground. Walking was kind of boring so I kicked her into a gentle trot. What was I thinking? Trotting takes a saddle and some practice. Soon we were bouncing like jack-in-the-boxes after the lid pops open. My friend's bouncing scooted me forward and things got a bit out of hand. I pulled on the reins, but lost leverage as I inched up the bottom of Silky's mane and bounced up her neck. Staring through a horse's ear view, I desperately prayed her ears would hold me until she stopped. I know how free floating feels. It's okay, until you hit the ground. I went flying off her neck, Kate went off the other side. Dazed a bit, but mobile, Kate took off to tell her mom.

That would have worried me a lot because her mom could really yell, but I was semi-conscious, lying on a rock—okay, a mini boulder. I finally got my senses back enough to walk to the house, hefting the worst headache know to girls. Mother got a cold rag, the first remedy chosen in similar circumstances. I moaned and moaned. Mother called the doctor and the doctor said, "No more riding, she's landed on her head." I was in bed, the doctor directing light into my eyeballs, checking my limbs. I laid there a good three days before I felt normal.

I didn't get right back on. Years later I did ride Foxy once or twice around the corral. Horses just weren't my thing.

My youngest sister, Cathy, is a real cowgirl. She adores horses. She even got into the rodeo scene a few years back. Cody, Wyoming prides itself on having a rodeo each night during tourist season. Before the bucking starts, Old Glory and flag bearers sponsoring local businesses, circle the ring on gorgeous horses and stop in front of the grandstand. The announcer, in his most patriotic voice, invites all to join for the pledge of allegiance. Then he introduces—usually it's some beautiful cowgirl—high soprano with lots of vibrato, to sing the national anthem. These are proud and heart-felt moments. Cathy just *had* to carry one of those flags.

Of course the horse had to look pretty. Her husband, Brett, washed her Paint—Dash. He groomed and brushed, and then added a product that slicked his hair and made it glow—*Show Sheen.* Cathy and her mount were a beautiful sight. As she got into line and readied to enter the arena, everything was under control. Flags high, heads high, riders prepared, Cathy galloped out and around the corner when suddenly she felt the saddle slipping to the side. She tried to fake it as it inched down her horse's belly. She about made it, until directly in front of the grandstand, in perfect view of the announcer, things got critical. She rode side saddle (for real) for a few seconds and dove into the ground.

"Looks like we have a rider down," the announcer yelled. Concerned oohs and awes undulated over the audience. "Things can happen with these horses, folks," the announcer said in his best rodeo voice.

Her wind knocked out, Cathy watched Dash split the rodeo scene at a dead run, saddle bumping off his side. She stood as quickly as possible, shaking it off.

"She seems to be okay. We never know how these horses are going to act. Let's give the little lady a great big hand."

Cathy waved to the crowd, picked up the flag and held it aloft as she marched out on foot.

She really wanted to hide behind it. Tears already leaking, she silently said, "Just get me out of here."

Brett climbed out of the bleachers and was there to meet her at the gate. Some dude nonchalantly asked him, "What you spread that Paint with?

"Show Sheen," Brett replied.

"Now there's yer problem, partner," he said. "That stuff is so slick it will plumb make a saddle spin."

Actually more truth came out later, as Brett admitted that just before the grand entry, he had helped a young girl cinch her saddle tighter. She had told him her dad would get mad if she had asked him for help. Of course Brett hurried to help her, forgetting to tighten Cathy's.

The saddle didn't stand a chance and neither did Cathy. From the get-go she was doomed. In the entry line up, Dash had shied at a green hose lying on the ground and the saddle started tipping then. She later sighed as she told me, "If it would have slipped off where I was originally positioned in line, I might have been flung into the calf pen, and ridden a calf or two. Now wouldn't that have been pretty?"

Asking further questions, I wanted to know what was happening to the flag during the sinking. The following is her direct quote. "I was thinking, shit, I better hold on to it and then when I was sitting sideways I thought—nope, better not!! It was way awkward, and I was thinking I will never in my right mind do this again!! Amen."

A few yards into the parking lot, another cowboy asked her, "Did you see that poor gal fall from her horse right in front of the grandstand?"

Cathy, discreetly rubbing her sore leg replied, "Wasn't that sad? I heard she was from Australia.

Down Under."

I Finally Got It

Most of you have a story hiding in some worn-out pocket. One that needs a few years of distance between the act and the telling. I'm ready now.

Wyoming is the cowboy state and Carl and I are natives. Cheyenne is the capitol, a mecca for rodeos and western wear—shirts with yokes and snaps, boots broken in through cow pies and dusty trails, personalized cowboy hats branded with no-end of stories. Levi's are preferable, molded tightly around derrieres.

It was 1973. Carl and I drove across the state to take in the rodeo. We had one child, (who we left at grandma's) one on the way, and only one (albeit insufficient) income. Gas was cheap and his sister, Kay, guaranteed us a bed and breakfast.

The next morning we gathered for omelets and family news.

Carl's brother-in-law, Excell, a city guy that landed in Wyoming, talked disco and brother power. Gregarious, and bigger than life, he informed us of his new adventure.

"This state needs some style." He laughed." I'm going to sell elevator cowboy boots."

Ever the jokester, Carl replied, "Pointy-toed boots are made for squishing bugs in corners. Platforms would spoil the plan."

It seemed like Excell's afro grew taller as they bantered. "Hey man, no joke, Richard and I have invested in a store. He'll stock our bag selection.

Richard:

- Status-divorced
- Personality-off beat,

- Occupation-tanning animal hides, making stuff out of them
- Residence- the basement under our feet.

"What's he skinning down there?" I asked. "Please tell me bodies aren't putrefying as we speak."

"You're lucky he's out of town. Last week it was skunk hides."

"Help me, he actually touches skunk?"

"They make good shoulder bags. Black and white."

I caught the humor there. Exell is African American. "What's the name of this store? I want to see it."

Kay laughed and pointed at her husband. "Excell has earned the name. Richard nicknamed him *Gab* years ago, you know his gift of gab. Now it will be an immortalized acronym. The name is....drum roll.... *G G's Boutique*."

We all hopped in our cars. In the lead Excell and Kay drove their black Cadillac sporting red leather seats. Carl and I followed in our brown Plymouth Duster; the color of which Carl constantly argued was green. He's certifiably color blind.

The store was small in footage, big in statement. Leisure suits hung on round racks according to size. Leather jackets and, you guessed it; shoulder bags took up one whole corner of the store.

Artificial boutonnieres in black business suits directed my eye to color and the price tag. Our trailer house payment was penciled on those little tags. Platform boots as tall as the red ones Rick James wore on stage perched like birds on graduated shelving. Wide ties, silk-talking sleek, fanned the tables. Feathered fedoras fine enough for New York street-wear dominated one shelf. I saw no hint of rodeo hats and I'm not just a bird-turding.

"Very interesting," I heard Carl mumble as I passed him in the boxer aisle.

I thought I was in wardrobe for a punk concert. This store just didn't fit the ambience of three to twenty city blocks of lariat logos and bandana red. However, Rick James did wear a bandana, (sure as shootin') around his neck—accessorizing his tiger-skinned jacket tailored to reveal his bare chest. (Maybe Rick could special order a customized skunk bag.)

"We've got some rad leisure suits in your size, Carl. Want to try one?"

Excell selected a three piece sweater-knit suit; patterned in large red and black squares. Yes, the bell-bottomed pants, vest and jacket were all plaid. The feature I liked best was the genuine black leather inserts down the front of the jacket. Keep yokes and snaps on the range, urban had come to Wyoming.

Carl exited the dressing room and turned around in front of the mirror. The suit was tailored for him. He looked….Good. "He must be a *winter,"* I said. "Red and black are winter colors." We girls had been studying which seasonal shades fit our complexions. Dang, he did look handsome.

"It's seriously cool," Carl said. "But out of my budget."

"You look more than groovy in that suit. Think about it." Excell nodded his head up and down.

"Wonder how this would wear on the back of a horse?" Carl teased. "In all seriousness—good luck with your new adventure."

We went home to our daughter, our trailer house (12x64), and our scrimp-and-never save budget. I ached to get that leisure suit for Carl for Christmas. I had four months to save for it.

I called Excell and made it short. Long distance added up quickly. "I really want to get that suit Carl tried on, but I'll have to send you payments."

"He'll look like a brother at those newspaper conventions he goes to. I'll put it aside for you."

After I hung up, a bit of buyers' remorse raised its ugly head (it was wearing a fedora.) He won't really be able to wear it much and it is pretty flamboyant. But he looks so good in it.

You romantic folks out there will identify with this. "The Gift of the Magi" story popped out of some book and lit in front of my imagination—her long hair, cut off without a thought. His watch, sold without regret. I would sacrifice to buy this gift for my beloved, my handsome husband.

I had no part time job, no rich relatives, and no long hair. I'd have to take it out of the grocery budget, keep the lights off, turn down the heat, and.....pray.

That month I started making my own bread, cutting meat into smaller pieces and testing starchy casserole recipes. Women throughout time have saved pennies in canning jars, stuffed dollar bills under the mattress, and buried a bit of savings in the yard.

I had a payment for the next month.

In October, Carl did the shopping and mentioned we hadn't had much meat last month. He spent every grocery cent. I panicked. Nightmares of bell-bottomed, night-stick-carrying policemen stalked my sleep. One night a black hearse drove by my house, *G G's Boutique* engraved on the back. In one dream, I cut my hair for money and had to spend the cash on a cheap five and dime wig to cover my bald head, crusted-in-moles.

Who doesn't blow the budget? What could I have done?

Call my mother.

"Mother, you know how much I love you. Can I have my Christmas present early this year? I have something on layaway for Carl. I need twenty dollars."

She sent the money. I made the payment.

But, November was around the corner and I needed cash. *What can I sell?* My pregnancy was tiring. I had no energy to make crafts or candy. Besides, duh, I needed cash to buy ingredients and supplies. I certainly had no inclination to be listed in the local newspaper under shoplifting. Carl, a journalist at that very newspaper, would have been a bit concerned when he typeset my name.

Forced to be frugal, the previous year we had bought a rocker at the Bargain Box down the street. The upholstery was a goner, but my mother-in-law had given me left over yardage and I had a sewing machine we had purchased out of the back of some traveling salesman's car trunk. Our trailer house furniture was gold and green. This piece would be covered in that swirly lavendery-mauvey textured retro—shabby chic ahead of its time. I was quite proud of my redo.

I had to sell it.

Fitting that chair, a three-year-old and my pregnant self into a two door compact was a bit awkward, but my mind was set. I would have that slick suit and it would be paid for.

Back at the Bargain Box, the old boy gave me $25.00. Not much more than we had paid for it. Didn't he know custom upholstery when he saw it? I took the money and plodded to the car.

Carl didn't even notice the masterpiece was gone. He was too occupied with news stories: hospital and school board meetings, high school sports, obits, and the occasional rodeo.

I squeaked in the November payment. There was only $10.00 left on the bill. I hoped I wouldn't have to cut my hair, beg, or sell anything more, although if there had been an E-Bay I might have resorted to selling a pair of Carl's cowboy boots.

Grandma sent me an early gift of $10.00 to buy myself a Christmas gift. I sent Excell the last payment and waited to intercept UPS.

I secretly wondered if my beloved would sell something to buy me a gift. Would he ponder on the perfect personal present for weeks? I pretty much knew he would. The first year we were married I dreamed of opening something inexpensive, but so personal—a bottle of perfume, a box of my favorite chocolates, a hidden souvenir from our honeymoon.

He got me a Veg-o-Matic.

Chopping celery and carrots wasn't exactly on my agenda for Christmas day. I tried to be happy—honest, but I couldn't hold back the flood. I snuck off to the bedroom and only cried for an hour or so.

It was Christmas morning 1973. A dolly for our little girl sat on the only chair we had left. The tiny tree with tiny tinsel strands glittered between one string of lights. THE box was under the tree, way to the back.

Carl came into the living room, smiling in a nervous sort of way. He would never forget the Veg-o-Matic. I was so excited, the picture of long hair and watch fobs loomed so large, I thought I was walking on cobblestones and could have sworn I smelled chimney soot.

I don't remember many of my Christmas presents throughout the years, except the Veg-o-Matic. I think that year it was a lacey red nightgown. Wasn't the color perfect? I never did want one of those "teddy" things. With my weight it would have been marketed as a "grizzly."

"What kind of a tie did you get me this year?" he asked as I handed him his gift. I've heard that line every Christmas for forty-six years. He ripped off the paper and unfolded white tissue paper. His face was blank. He was REALLY surprised. Carl never has gotten very excited about gifts. I knew he liked it, but I wanted him to rave about the secret, open his arms so I could rush inside, touch my hair to see if I'd gotten it cut.

"How did you get the money? I remember this thing cost as much as our house payment."

"Well, remember the month you whined about not much meat at the dinner table....and....I sold the rocking chair."

"I thought there was something different in here. Where's company going to sit?" He gave me a wink. "You really planned for this one."

Of course I wanted violin music and eternal gratitude, but him being surprised, even astonished was enough.

"It fits well," he said. "I'm a bit worried about what shoes to wear, how about my grey cowboy boots?"

I think I laughed.

"Now, open your Veg-o-Matic."

Real funny.

I did think it funny that he didn't go try on his suit. When I asked he just said, "I know the suit fits fine."

I hung it in the closet. The Wyoming State Press Convention was in Casper in two weeks. I couldn't wait for him to wear his new outfit. It would be one of a kind and everyone would see it because Carl always won awards for photography and editorials. He would receive his ribbons in front of the whole state conclave.

The night of the awards ceremony, he debuted the knit suit. I beamed. Thank goodness the length of the pants was long enough, and the bell bottoms were wide enough, to cover most of those grey cowboy boots.

We were mingling at the cocktail hour. "Nice threads," I heard his boss say. "Kind of loud," another guy mumbled. Of course I was tuning my ears to elephant frequency to gloat on the oohs and awes such a fine outfit deserved. I just stared at my husband, that black and red giving a glow to his complexion, a somewhat different air to his presence.

Back at home the suit mostly sat in the closet as it was special occasion attire. It was a little too sharp to wear to weddings and funerals. If he were assigned special events to report, he sometimes wore the vest, jacket and black pants. I always fell in love all over again.

Fall. 1987. We had moved into an amazing mother-in-law *and* father-in-law basement apartment in our daughters' home. Long story short, we were caring for four of our grandchildren while the daughter with the Christmas dolly finished her undergraduate work and attained a law degree.

The oldest, Kelby, was into retro—big time. I don't think he bought a new outfit for two years. He wore vintage clothes, Salvation army finds—funky junk. He had started a band. He reminded me of Carl's high school stories. Kelby was having a neighborhood gathering to hear his band. His parents had warned the neighbors.

I spilled the beans.

"Kelby, there's an old really, really retro sweater-knit three piece suit in the basement. I bought it at a store named "G G's Boutique" for your granddad one Christmas. There's a story behind it."

I proceeded to tell him.

That suit had been hiding in the closet long enough. Literally. The garment bag had cracked some, but the suit was in great condition. After all, it hadn't been worn much. I told Kelby to sit down and I described the outfit in detail. I reminisced about my sacrifices, Carl's surprise, the grey cowboy boots (which he still had).

I touched my hair.

"Sweet. I've got to see this, Grandma. Can I try it on?"

I dug in the back of the closet and handed him the bag.

"Only if you'll let me see you in it. It's pretty groovy you know. I think you'll actually like it."

"Groovy?"

Fifteen minutes later he walked down the stairs, just as Carl opened the basement door.

"That's my old suit," he said. Be careful with it."

"Oh, honey. Kelby's so handsome. Remember how much you liked that Christmas?"

"I've got to wear this in my band. Grandpa, I'll take care of it. It's awesome."

Carl called me by my nickname, Loucie, (for Cindy Lou) and asked me to sit down. "You remember when we met I was wearing an army jacket from the war surplus store and had two pairs of jeans to my name? Remember how much you hate those cowboy shirts I wear to the rodeo sometimes? Well, I like those shirts and boots and....J.C. Penny's. Think about it. I didn't love the suit. That's the only red and black plaid leisure suit I've ever seen. Sort of like dressing up to be the announcer at the circus—and besides, it didn't match my boots."

Yeah, you should have been wearing elevator shoes instead of those grey boots.

Kelby, our oldest grandson, thought the red plaid suit totally cool.

"Remember how long "G G's Boutique" lasted. Kay still shakes her head about that adventure."

"But you told Excell the suit was COOL!"

"Well, yeah," he said. "What else was I going to say about his finest fashions?

"But you never told me you didn't like the suit."

"I didn't want to hurt your feelings. Didn't you notice I never wore it in OUR town?"

Silence from me.

At least I didn't cut my hair, but that rocking chair was back in style.

"Wait, Kelby. We've got to have a picture of this," Carl said.

After the picture-taking we reminisced about how much we missed Excell and his crazy brother-talk and platforms.

"I was swept away by how good you looked in that suit."

"I should never have tried on anything at G G's Boutique. I would have rather had one of Richard's skunk bags."

Racing Stock

Dad bought a used welding truck in 1967, and I inherited his old red one, a '56 ¾ ton Chevy, my only transportation the summer I was seventeen.

I loved the old beater.

Cracking the wing windows was preferred to cranking open the stiff, dislocated driver's window. The clutch stuck, demanding a tricky toe flip to lift it back into position after every shift. Add braking and accelerating, my driving resembled juggling with feet. Both the clutch and the brake pedals slipped beneath my shoes, the rubber pads long gone.

I was proud of my driving dexterity.

My friend Jean and I alternated transportation between that truck and her tan Beetle Bug. One afternoon I phoned her to go get a Coke. My boyfriend, Ken, had recently dumped me—the bad news penned in a Dear Jane letter, mailed straight from boot camp. I needed soothing.

"Do you want to go get a Coke?" I asked.

"We better hang out tonight. My dad's flying in tomorrow," Jean said. Jean's step dad was on the other end of the work stratum from mine. He owned part of a company and flew around in a private plane.

She and I needed one another in opposite ways. Jean's parents were rarely home, leaving her with a housekeeper, her only sister running with her friends. My mother was always home, oblivious to the wild antics of my brother and three younger sisters. I wanted space—peace, far from my bulging cartoon-house animated with noise and confusion.

The brakes screeched as I pulled up in front of Jean's house.

"Ken's in town," I said. The familiar feeling of rejection stung my ribs, crisscrossing like shoe laces pulled too tightly.

Jean settled into the worn spot denting the tattered bench seat. "I thought he was still at boot camp."

"He's on leave until he's transferred. I gave him back his medals and his letter jacket yesterday." I felt like screaming and clawing, but sunk the clutch and pounced on the accelerator instead, demanding the old truck come to life and lay some rubber.

A utility truck is not built for peeling out.

Jean ruminated and then spoke slowly. "He's a rat fink. You don't want him anyway."

"How could he fall in love with somebody so quickly? He met her at a dance. *We* met at a dance." I squeezed the gearshift knob, wishing it were a hank of Ken's hair.

Jean sat for a few blocks in silence, and as we pulled into an open stall at the A&W, she replied. "He's not worth your time. Lots of boys like you. They don't call you "jugs" for nothing."

I laughed in spite of my misery. "Okay, 'Baldy,'" shortening her middle name, "let's go find some fun." Jean abhorred her middle name, Baldwin, as much as I hated being stacked. We batted nicknames back and forth, razzing each other until we both broke into giggles. "Okay, I'll forget about the jerk. I'm dying for a Coke—make it cherry."

The greasy smell of burgers and French-fry oil somehow helped my pain. I looked around the drive-in lot. "I wonder if that guy I met at the dance last weekend has a girlfriend."

"The one with the new orange mustang?" Jean asked.

"Yeah, he gave me a ride in it. I think he's way cute. Let's go see if he's downtown," I said.

I checked the gas gauge (one of the few things which still worked), noting we could probably cruise for another hour. I fished around in my purse and felt another dollar bill—security to buy enough gas to last for days.

Flipping around the island and heading to Main Street, I tuned into the rattle of the new apparatus corralling the bed of my truck. Dad had just built a pipe stock rack, perfect for hauling a few sheep, but downright embarrassing for me. I didn't need to haul any stock.

I needed a new boyfriend.

We honked at a few cars dragging the strip, passing mostly housewives in station wagons loaded with grocery sacks. About to give up and take Jean home, I spotted a carload of boys in a green Chevette. Checking the license plate, a big number 9 covered the corner reserved for the county designation. Our school had a nickname for the small town twenty miles away. The town's only landmark—a giant brick sugar factory that stunk up the state.

"It's a 9-er! Did you recognize any of them?" I asked Jean.

"No, but I hope they're not the boyfriends of those girls we met last weekend."

"Wait. I do hope they're the ones," I said "Let's retaliate. You and me, Baldy, those threats those 9-er girls sprung on us last weekend were totally uncool."

The weekend before we had decided to cruise on over to Lovell and check it out. We got to take the good car—Dad's tan dodge, sporting fins the size of sharks.' After dragging main a few times, a carload of teetering girls, shellacked with Dippety Dew, had jumped out at an intersection and run toward our car waving a bottle of liquor. Surrounded, Jean and I stared at the mob.

"We're dead meat," I whispered. "9-ers" are circling like wolfs." A shout exploded from the apparent leader, a brunette with blue-shaded eyes. She busted a bottle across the roof, denting the frame inches from my face. A cloudburst of cheap alcohol rained down the windshield.

"Get out of town and stay away from Lovell boys," she screamed as jeers from the group squealed at our closed windows.

I turned on the windshield wipers and prayed that the alcohol would evaporate, leaving no smell. Dad would have enough questions about the dent. "Guess we'll get out of here," I said. "That bunch of creeps can keep their boyfriends. Let's get out of 9-erville, but I have to check out the windshield first."

Stopping a few blocks away under one of the only street lights I opened the door. It made a grinding noise, but I didn't pay much attention. Leaving it open, I ran my finger around the rim where the bottle had landed. Oh, boy, there was quite a dent, one that my dad surely would notice. How would I explain this one?

Slipping back inside, the door wouldn't completely close. "How in the world did that bottle of booze do this to the car door?" I asked Jean.

"You're really in trouble. And I can smell that stuff from here."

"Okay, okay. Let's drive over to the filling station and see if they can fix the door."

We pulled up by a pump and some kid came out to fill up the car. "Yes! He can wash the windshield. But he wasn't much older than we. "Let's hope his dad is a mechanic and he's knows about cars."

I got out before he got a chance to ask, Fill 'er up?

"We've got a problem we hope you can fix," I said. Jean sat in her seat.

"Let me take a look."

After a few unsuccessful attempts, he told me he'd be right back. Lugging a crow bar the size of a jack hammer, he stuck it under the hinge and gave it a tug. The whole door groaned as it settled back, but not on its hinges. The thing wouldn't shut at all.

"Oops, I'm so sorry," he said. I'm thinking, you're sorry all right and so are your skaggy little girl friends down on main.

I held the door shut all the way home.

"Dad can probably fix it," I told Jean.

"I never did like 9-ers," she replied.

The next morning I told Dad the car door was acting funny and we had gone to the station for help. He went outside, as I ran to my bedroom. I think I might have fallen down on my knees and plead for divine intervention.

"Whoever tried to fix that door was a loser. And somehow while he was cranking on it, he dented the window frame. Next time just drive it straight home," Dad said.

Lovell girls with their over-teased beehives didn't scare me, even if we topped their hit list. I knew their precious boyfriends were out cruising for chicks. All of them were fickle, including my former boyfriend.

This weekend the tables had turned and their boys were cruising in our territory.

Jean suddenly laughed. "I think they're following us. Should we stop?"

"Those guzzling, smoking, loser 9-ers from last weekend didn't look like the kind that chose great guys. Let's ditch them," I said, romping on the accelerator.

A pro at eluding riff-raff, I sped down the blocks past the city band shell, the tennis courts and the park, county-9-ers right on my tail.

"Watch this," I said.

Jean held onto the door handle as I tapped the brake, not slowing properly to maneuver the ninety-degree turn. Unknown to me, the rack was not welded onto the bed, but sat loosely in the corner slots. The whole rack lifted off the truck bed, crashing back into place as I straightened out.

"That thing came clear out of the holes," I said. Exhilarated by the game, challenged by the bouncing rack, I formulated a plan.

"I'll lose them in that dead-end alley." Confident I could slip in unnoticed, I still didn't appreciate the bulk of a ¾ ton truck finessing hairpin corners in a game of chase.

Shifting back to second, I let the clutch out, hefted it back into position with my toe, and picked up speed on the next block. I had forgotten the new stop sign by the grocery store. Slowing only slightly, I sucked in my breath, mumbling about my luck. My deceleration gave time for a couple of 9-ers to hop out of their car and jump on the rack.

Dead-end alley was out. New plan.

"There's two hanging on the gate!" Jean said, her head cranked around to report this new predicament.

"What should I do? Talk to me, Baldy!"

"If you keep ripping around those corners the rack's going to go."

"What else do you suggest?" I asked, feeling like I was in a James Bond movie without rehearsals.

"That one in the blue coat is gorgeous," Jean said, calm as Cat Woman applying lipstick during a bust. "You got us into this Jugs, now get us out."

Speed was my only weapon, no matter the risk. I took the next corner as hard as I dared.

"You lost one," Jean said.

I looked in the side mirror, a crack down the middle briefly splitting the rolling form of a 9-er in the ditch.

Twisting around, I took my eyes completely off the road. "There goes the other one," I said as his buddy jumped, landing in a tangle of flinging arms and legs.

Jean wiped her hands together. "What do we do now?" she asked.

I slowed the truck, wondering if we should have met those Lovell boys. They were cute, but James Bond they definitely were not. "I'm not going back to reconnoiter. Their girlfriends can fuss over them back where they belong. Let's go drag main a few more times."

I still needed a boyfriend.

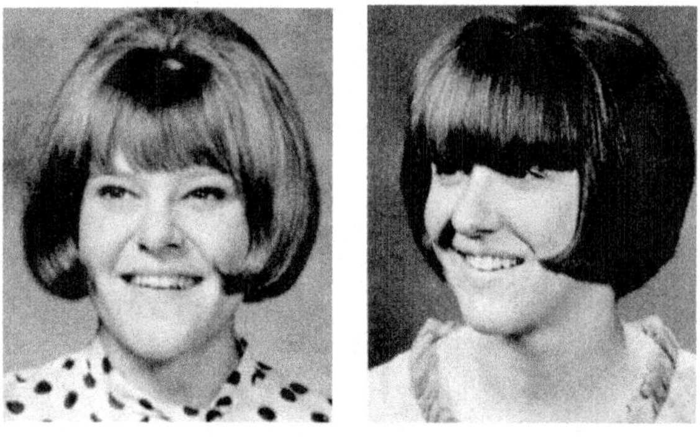

Me (left) and Jean, the year of our 9-er escapades.

Free Detail Job

Carl usually parked his old '72 Chevy pickup in the pasture behind our house. In desperate need of some paint and bodywork, this camper special with its lumpy seats was his project. I named the truck Rambo.

One Christmas I even bought him a custom made dash cover, *Rambo,* embroidered on the edge. Now that I think about it, I wonder if he liked that present as much as his red plaid suit.

As years passed, the varnished wooden bed was replaced, but Rambo resisted the body shop, rusting out around the running boards and spreading oxidation from the newest assault from our gelding, Cody. Forever mischievous and bored, he trotted over eye level to taste a turquoise fender. His sunken teeth tracks spaced evenly across the edge, lined perfectly, like a fat man targeting one row of corn on the cob. We'd been awakened at night with Cody's tactics. Bored, he would stand by the truck antennae, grip it between his teeth, bend it back and let it fly. Brrrrroinnnggg.

Another one of Cody's night capers was to sink his teeth onto the sprinklers protruding from portable irrigation pipes stacked in a pile behind the corral. Cody would lift the top pipe up so many feet and then drop it with a bang. Thwaaaaaang.

"There goes that noise again," I said one morning about 2:00 a.m. Carl stumbled out of bed. I heard him fumbling around the junk drawer in the kitchen. Then the back door opened and stayed that way for a good ten minutes.

"What was all that clatter?" I asked.

"*Your* boys ran the flashlight out of batteries again and *your* horse is at it again."

Both that horse and our truck were quirky.

I drove Rambo once in a while to take the kids camping; proving I was a real country gal who could tackle low gears and overgrown side mirrors. After all I cut my teeth on a stock truck. If I ever complained, I knew Carl's next sentence—"Love me, love my truck."

One day when I tired of the heaps of wood splinters, nails, and boards left from the re-siding residue around our house, I jumped into the truck to take charge of the cleanup on my own.

I had previously swung the gate wide and reconnoitered the area. It would be a tight fit for Rambo, but the side mirrors would fit.

Work-gloved and ball-capped, I turned the ignition and balanced both hips over the rumpled seat. Stretching toward the gas pedal and crunching into reverse, I let the clutch out and crawled toward the gate in the back yard. I could drive a stock truck around hair-pin curves in race mode. This would be easy.

Backing between the posts I swung around toward the biggest pile of debris.

If they could see me now.

I hefted boards, evading protruding nails by the keg—fragments of our house's wooden facade. Orange paint chips blew off the boards, and stuck on my face. The dude we had hired to tear off the wooden panels and replace them with vinyl siding should have been out here, not me. He was still on my list. Carl knew he was out of work and so he had hired him. Finishing half, money up front, he vanished for a month or more. Finally when we got ahold of him, he demanded the rest of the money before completion. Now onto his scheme, Carl declined the offer and the guy walked off the job.

I grumbled as the sweat poured, my arms and back began to throb, and I pictured the out-of-work bum, sipping lemonade on a porch of some other poor soul's remodeling project.

A couple of boards hung over the end of the truck bed, old buckets dotted the top of the load. But I had got 'er done.

I was ready to pull Rambo away—leaving a clean perimeter. The truck was now off kilter with the target, but with reverse—forward—reverse—forward, I was near achieving a straight aim at the open gate.

"Get me out of here," I pleaded to no one.

Removing my cap, I pulled it back over my wet hair and straightened my back, checking both mirrors. Slowly I backed toward the opening, my eyes darting from mirror to mirror.

When I felt one fender touch the gatepost, I bumped it a bit, hoping it had scraped the same place as Cody's teeth imprints. Carl would never know. Pulling forward more, the squeezing felt tighter and I put it in reverse to straighten the cumbersome machine. With too much correction, I felt Rambo bump into the opposite gatepost. I was tired of this jockeying. I gave it gas, felt the pole give and finally I was free.

Sighing, I shut off the ignition, put the gears into reverse to curtail any rolling, and slid out to the ground. As I ran my hand down the length of the truck, confirming our great team effort, my fingers fell into a horizontal dip. The whole side had a deep scratch, newly wounded from the gatepost. Holding my breath I went around to the other side, aided by grasping the top of the bed. I ran my hand down the side and felt the etching of the other post in a deep scratch down the length.

Oh boy, I thought, I'm in deep doo-dah now.

When Carl got home from work he didn't even notice the yard, let alone the truck.

I knew I had to fess up and so I chose the *show and tell* method.

"Come outside, I want to show you something," I said.

Looking around he noticed the junk removal. "Did you clean that by yourself?" he asked.

"Yep. I drove Rambo back there and loaded all the junk. Could you take it to the junk yard this weekend?"

"Let's go see how full it is, there are some barrels and wire by the shed I need to haul out too."

Grimacing, I walked toward him as I reminded him—"You know how much I love your truck."

"What did you do?"

"Well, you know how you've always wanted to have new bodywork and paint? I've already given the truck a custom look—matching racing stripes."

Garden Dance

I found her out in her garden, just outside the apple orchard. Wheel barrowing down the grooved path, she stopped to wipe her brow, a backhanded swoop pushing a stray lock of gray hair from her face. Pirouetting with a prop, she turned and backed into the open gate.

My friend invited me into her sanctuary, surrounded by a wire fence; neatly stretched and lashed with twine; sturdy enough to keep out velvet-nosed deer seeking tender shoots.

Streaming sunshine pelted the plot, illuminating hues of color—gold sun, free nectar for the garden. Water-filled plastic milk jugs stood guard by new plants, catching the day's sun to emanate warmth—hot water bottle-like protectors on chilly nights. Empty jugs ran up the fence posts, looped in symmetrical knots.

Spots of green peeked through the woody grape vines, growing tangles over the corner arbor. A patch of onions stood high in the perfect rectangle dug just below ground level. She led me to horizontally laid carrot tops, their lime-colored fuzz highlighting dark potato plants, flowering behind. Off to the side, raspberry bushes thorned around the spot where soon she would pick plump, ripe berries.

Her husband saved wood scraps, grayed with water and age and built a frame for her cucumber plants. The glass covering stopped frosty nips. She would serve firm, seedless cucumbers long before her neighbors. Bean sprouts inched up stick tripods; leaving plenty of room for mounds of pumpkins and squash as they vined forward, orange orbs hidden in umbrella leaves.

She had ordered exotic seeds and roots from colored catalog pages; studying varieties while snow whipped the window behind her shoulder. I marveled that crisp celery stalks grew adjacent to purple eggplant, all nightly wrapped in yards of clear covering, even into July.

I lingered and tiptoed through the little paths, soaking up sun and woody smells. I snapped back to busyness with a glance at my watch, excused myself, and told my friend I would find my way back. Walking forward, looking backward, I saw her silhouette leaning on the shovel handle, glazed in brightness, water jugs jingling against the fence.

Glamorous Bosoms

Must beauty these days be equated with bosoms? The thought gives me a rise—in sympathy. One day in the eighth grade I woke up to weighty orbs sitting on my chest. What was I supposed to do with these unwanted protrusions? While the rest of my friends sought padded bras, I was forced to the support section, way before my time.

Young men in the high school wolf whistled, then huddled with their friends and snickered about my knockers. By sophomore year "Jugs" was my nickname—slouching my game. If I rounded my shoulders and pointed both shoulder blades forward, I camouflaged a bit of the mass. Or so I thought. For years straps have dented permanent troughs across my aching shoulders.

Boobs go on parade now. Television programs and commercials plop their best chests in front of the screen. Slits to the naval and necklines reveal the fruits of expensive surgeries—grapefruits. Do their shoulders ache?

Victorian women flaunted their cleavage, tiny waists accenting what was above. Scarlet O'Hara showed cleavage, her corset plumping whatever nature had doled out. Can you imagine these women today, first in line for breast augmentations?

But, on the other hand, the native women I peeked at in National Geographic looked quite content with their lot in breasts. Pancake-shaped bosoms hung to the belly button, free as the birds. Buttons sat in pairs on some, barely visible to the naked eye.

Now I don't want to be accused of interrupting some ladies' free agency. They can pump up, plump up, pull up, point out, and roll away if they want. In fact, sometimes the knife sounds appealing. Maybe I can share with someone less endowed. I'll search the internet.

Pyro on the Place

Picking up line two at the office, Jeff's mother gave me the newest. "The boys forgot the food cooler at your house," she said. "I can't go back up. Jonathan wanted me to call you and see if you would go get it and drive up the mountain."

I'm thinking—I'm going to kill him, but politely assure her that we would get the cooler to them. Let's see. Ten miles to home, ten miles back, ten miles up to Spirit Mountain, ten miles back.

He'd been planning this overnighter with his scout buddies for weeks, but traditionally, scattered details left trails of loose ends. Mothering across the mountain, I feared he'd be hungry, his thirteen-year-old body demanding continual sustenance.

Breaking the news to Carl, I got the raised eyebrow arch—known to question the intent of our youngest son's motives.

"It's all their food, honey, we've got to go up there."

"Tell you what. You go ahead and grab something to eat and head to that meeting you have scheduled. I'll go home and get the cooler." Thirty minutes later I picked up the phone—mid-bite—anxious for the news on the abandoned cooler. Laughter interrupted Carl's rendition and I almost choked up a French fry.

"YOUR son is at it again," he sighed across the phone line. "There is no food in those coolers, only stacks of fireworks, covered with several pairs of swimming goggles—and I don't think they have swimming in mind. There's enough ammo to start and finish a war—and not a hot dog in sight."

Carl had put the kibosh on the pyromaniac's plans, but he felt pity for their empty stomachs. Unloading layers of fireworks topped with perfect rows of swimming goggles, he happened upon a few hotdogs, a half-empty bottle of catsup and a bag of Cheetos. Hiding the fireworks in a (hopefully) safe place until the Fourth of July, pondering what else the boys might need, he wondered if they had any matches. "Duh," was the word describing that thought.

As he approached the turn to Spirit Mountain, a huge sign shouted from the side of the road—NO FIREWORKS ALLOWED.

He told me about finding the boys sitting on their sleeping bags, docile, as if they were malnourished. "Well, guys," he said. "Looks like I caught you in the act. You boneheads, you can't have fireworks up here, OR shoot fireworks up here. This is BLM land."

They had a fire started in the pit, of course. He pointed at it and ordered them to the cooler. "Get those dogs cooked, eat some chow, and behave yourselves."

He drove back into town thinking, mission accomplished. We reminisced about other Jonathan antics, laughed a lot, and slept fairly peacefully that night.

One of the moms brought the boys home the next morning. She said they were tired, dirtier than usual, but acted like they had had a great time.

Jonathan dragged along to the shower and afterwards I picked up a trail of his dirty clothes. What is this, I thought as I held his shirt up. Several burn holes, powder marks and smoke filled the stinky thing. Same thing with his jeans. I knew they didn't have fireworks at camp. Maybe they had lit off a bunch before they left.

Years, I mean years later, Jonathan fessed up. The boys had snuck another whole box of fireworks into the "designated driver's" car heading for Spirit Mountain. What they really wanted was more ammo AND the swim goggles in the second forgotten cooler. None of this quiet sparkler and fountain stuff, they wanted war games—shooting Roman candle balls at each other. At least they knew how to protect their eyes. Carl had denied them the only hint of safety implementation, but all eyeballs where still intact.

Failing

Grandpa's Parkinson's disease had finally worn his eighty-six-year-old body down and by the Christmas holidays he was permanently placed in the nursing home for constant care. The aides got him up twice a day so he could silently sit in the overstuffed chair by his bed. When he did try to converse, it was with mumbling close-lipped unintelligible words. His trembling hands were bony and transparent veins flowed to neglected fingernails trapping pieces of last night's dinner. His great white hair, once slicked back in royal ridges, was shaved, revealing white flakes of dried skin, as dry as his protruding old bones.

He hadn't had his irrigating boots on for years. A few years before, he did however raise his own protest when the price of haircuts went up and George McGovern lost the election. He let it grow out—down to his shoulders, and held it in place with his old cowboy hat. Raggley as some old hippie he made a statement, I guess.

A few of his grandchildren decided to try one last traditional Christmas dinner with him at Mother's house, and hatched a scheme to spring him from the home. We didn't really get permission, but figured he could handle an hour if we could get him out of there. Stiffer than a corpse, his extremities were unyielding, extremely fragile, a combination requiring patient engineering to maneuver him into the backseat of a car. We were worried about the cold, but put a blanket around his shoulders and kept the heater cranked high.

With three of us helping him out of the wheelchair, something akin to a fireman's carry was invented to load him, gently pushing the top of his head down so he wouldn't bump the roof, like some criminal being whisked away in a squad car. We laughed like escapees on the lam as his mouth cracked into a mischievous grin.

Turkey whiffs drifted through the kitchen. Family talk, buttered rolls, and candied yams remained the same. He ate slowly, most of his mushed dinner spooned, his water glass held to his mouth by other hands. On previous years, after dinner, he always unlatched the violin case and fiddled old favorites like the "Missouri Waltz." Christie was home for the holidays and had her violin handy. She played a bit of "The Fox." We all joined in time for the verse about the grease:

He ran 'til he came to a great big pen,
Were the ducks and the geese were put therein,
"A couple of you will grease my chin,
Before I leave this town-o, town-o, town-o."

Grandpa raised his shaking arms in a hearty attempt to clap his hands. They both moved toward each other a good three inches, silently symbolizing the rhythm he felt. His cheap white tennis shoe rose off the ground and thudded on the carpet, tapping only one time.

How far, but close those farm memories brushed my mind. Aunt Beverly and her divinity, Grandma boiling water for iced tea, Grandpa getting out the little Ford tractor with the hay fork.

He couldn't even heft his violin.

Loading him back in the car was harder this time. He was wearied as what little stored reserve had been used up in all the fun. He couldn't help move his body at all and as Jay bent his old head into the roof of the car, this time it settled and stayed in a bowed position. The once tall, muscular farmer was now a bent, wizened old man, too tired to move. Settled back in his bed, he seemed more content with the white world of his hospital sheets. Our caper completed, his grin barely visible, he remained a willing captive of the nursing home patrol until his death.

Horal (Jake) Brian Sheets. He tested his hippie phase late in life.

Grandpa enjoying his "freedom" for an afternoon. Both he and I are pleased we pulled off the caper.

Hay on Fire

Jonathan—the kid that started his chemistry tests early. Two-years-old and he was dumping shampoo and cream rinse down the tub. Mixing formulas of toothpaste, hair gel and salt.

As he got older he did high-end experimentation—like dumping bottle rocket powder and other firework entrails into piles. He was about twelve one July when he took his experiments to his friend's house. The Cody wind was blowing a gale, making it impossible to light his powder pile dumped from a haul of fireworks. Being the brains of this latest caper, he told Jeff he knew how to keep the match lit. Cupping his hands, lowering his face over the ammo, he lit the match.

"Look Mom, no eyebrows," (or skin on his cheeks, forehead, ear lobes, etc.) Another trip to the E.R. The staff there was going to have his name permanently engraved on one of the beds. He was infamous.

That same Fourth of July, a lady from one of the trailer courts in town had called Carl with a news story. Being editor of the local newspaper did lend to some interesting tales, and he thought her story was worth writing. She had called the fire department because the kitchen in her mobile home was filling with smoke. The fire department was at a party. The Eagles Club had set aside an evening of gratitude for the local firemen. Most of the entirely volunteer department were there and most of them had joyfully "imbibed."

When the fire alarm went off, they all rushed down the stairs and banged into the locked door, "like birds hitting a windshield," a new rookie chortled. The Eagles Club is private, and the door automatically locks. Someone knew the secret combination, (a.k.a., the door lock) and off they went. The fire chief made the rookie ride with him, assuming the kid was too drunk to drive.

A few guys went to get a fire truck, but a fair contingent drove straight to the smoking trailer. The stove was on fire. They shut off the gas and decided they should pull out the stove, probably to see if the wall was scorched. That's when one of the firemen noticed his necktie was stuck in the oven door. Not only stuck, but in flames. He ran to the sink.

Looking around, the Chief determined the proximate cause of the smoldering stove was the lady's housekeeping. He gave her a fair tongue-lashing as only a man of some authority who has been interrupted mid-revel can do.

It didn't take Sherlock Holmes to track down the story. Carl set an appointment with the fire chief, who was more than willing to defend the event – off the record. He said he would help get Carl up-to-speed, but the whole affair was just a run-of-the mill event. And besides, he argued, his volunteers, drunk, were still better than any department in the state.

They used donations to stock a refrigerator with alcohol, and volunteers regularly met to polish the equipment and drink. It was a social event – a cultural thing. Without that, no one would volunteer.

Carl wrote the story straight, page 1. The city rebelled in defense of their fire department. Businesses pulled their ads. Friends refused to talk to Carl. The entire department marched into City Hall and resigned. The mayor refused their resignations, praising their work and adding a rebuke for the local press. Carl just let the story run its course without much further comment. There were other tales that one of Carl's friends offered – like the day a main street businessman and volunteer fireman nearly hit a child while driving a fire truck—drunk.

Most of the community seemed to conclude the entire kerfuffle was the result of Carl's being a pompous Mormon jerk. One day during that heated time I was checking out in line at one of the two grocery stores in town. A clipboard hung there, filled with lines and names. I honed in on a name—one of our Mormon friends. Looking up at the top I saw a petition titled "Support your Local Firemen" with names spilling onto the second and third sheets. Political posturing?

And here's where Jonathan comes in again, with a bang.

I was unloading the groceries. After leaning under the sink to put away cleansers, I happened to glance out the back door window. Jonathan was sprinting down the hill toward the house, yelling,

"Fire."

He blazed past me to his bedroom and I could hear his fervent prayers. "Heavenly Father, I'll never do it again. "I didn't mean to do it! I didn't mean to do it! I'm sorry. They're going to kill me."

I went into action. He went into hiding.

Being on the farm, we irrigated with a pump and unless it was turned on, we had water weak enough to dribble about two feet. I had to plug it in and hook up the hose. Our horses were whinnying, running circles inside the corral. Billowing smoke soon took over a pile of lumber meant for building a barn. I got as close to the flames as I could and blasted a steady stream. Hacking my asthma-irritated lungs out, I was afraid I was going to have to call the fire department. Help me. Those guys weren't our best friends at the moment.

I battled on, and finally, seeing no fire, I thought maybe it was going out, but then, to me, the billowing white smoke meant it was going to burst into even fiercer flames.

I called the fire department.

I heard the sirens before I saw them coming through the pasture. The fire had pretty-much torched the partly constructed barn. It had attacked the hay stack, leaving the horses with a few days of burnt offerings.

But, it was out.

I shouted "thank you" as they pulled away. One of the guys on the running board boomed in a loud voice, "Well, do you think we should all go have a Dr. Pepper?"

Ewwwww, I thought.

I ran back into the house. "Jonathan!" I yelled.

"I stacked a bunch of loose hay over some firecrackers and lit them to see how high the hay would blow," he explained.

I called Carl at the office.

He wasn't there.

He told me his story later. He had been downtown and heard the fire whistle, but knew his crew was monitoring the scanner and would respond if it was important. He walked into his office through the back door and went to work. Sitting in front of his typewriter, writing his column, he glanced up. The whole window was filled with staff members' faces pressing against the glass, the most incredulous looks on their faces.

Head of advertising opened the door and poked his head inside. "Haven't you heard?"

Without a who, why, what, or how come, Carl uttered one word.

"Jonathan."

"Your haystack is on fire," the informer added, with a look more of a question than a statement.

Carl wrote a thank you to the fire department in his column next paper day. The whole thing died down as fires do. A few years later however, in a small town in Wyoming a volunteer fireman pleaded guilty to aggravated vehicular homicide after he rolled a tanker on the way to a grass fire. The accident killed a 16 year-old female fire department volunteer. His blood alcohol was twice the legal limit. He was sentenced to 14 – 18 years in prison, plus a bit over $9,000 restitution – perhaps to cover funeral expenses.

The state fire marshal in Cheyenne responded with new rules. There were no petitions.

Bombs Below

Our oldest son, Dustin, did not have a reputation like his little brother's, but I learned one day that he was just as adept as Jonathan at crazy stunts and capers.

Lazing around on a day off work, I was upstairs on my bed painting my fingernails. Somewhere on the second hand, I suddenly felt the house shake. A horrendous explosive sound whooshed up under my mattress, and I was off.

Running in panic, I was plunged into smoke heading up the stairs as I was heading down. Out of breath, I ran through the laundry room and opened the garage door. Engulfed in smoke, it took me a few seconds to recognize Dustin's friend, Clark, from down the road. Clark was a quiet kid, his blonde hair always parted perfectly, his clothes pressed. He wasn't perfect then.

He was splayed against the closed garage door, looking like he was in a lineup, ready to be frisked.

Clark was standing, was Dustin down? A few more seconds and a somewhat weak, "WOW," floated from the middle of the room. Dustin stood, some implement in his hand, his face covered in powder.

Were they close to death? Illogical thought, but I was in the Twilight Zone, shocked. "I think I'll stick to computers from now on," Clark said.

As I hit the garage opener, Dustin began his story.

"We tried to make a bomb," he said, dazed—okay stunned.

"Are you okay? You're lucky you didn't blow your head off. What in the world did you guys do?

"I can't hear very well," Dustin said.

"My ears are ringing," Clark said.

"I can understand that. Mine are too, boys."

"We went the cheap way," Dustin continued. "You don't use Lysol much, so we shot a hole in the can with my BB gun. The Lysol drained right out."

This is worse than I thought. Lysol would not dribble out peacefully. More like spew out dangerous fumes. "And then?"

"Well, Clark was watching the neighbor's house while he was gone and he found some really cool gun powder in his garage."

Oh, boy. The neighbor had been irritated the week before because our irrigation water ran two feet onto his property. What if he knew those boys were pilfering gun powder?

"And then? You lit it."

"No, I found a piece of metal in Dad's reloading equipment on the shelf over there. I had to close the hole. We were going to put a fuse in and take it out in the pasture so you wouldn't even know."

I wondered what other war games they had been playing back there behind the sagebrush.

"So it didn't explode spontaneously, did it?"

"No. I think this was the dumb part. I used Dad's solder gun to solder the patch. I barely started. Smoke and fire started blowing out and I told Clark to run. He couldn't get the doors open."

"Why didn't you bolt?"

"My legs wouldn't work. My brain was thinking, I'm a dead man, but if I wasn't, I'd have to tell Dad."

Shaking my head, I surveyed the garage. The can was blown into jagged metal. "Where's the cap?"

"Look up there," Clark said. He had come to his senses some and had surveyed the damage.

Yep, the cap and tube from inside the can were melted to the ceiling. Tiny pieces of shrapnel had embedded themselves into nail cans, tools, and the garage wall. Black residue lived there for weeks.

"I'm going back to my room," I said. "My nerves *and* nails need repair."

"I'm going back home," Clark said.

"I'm going to rethink this bomb thing," Dustin said.

Years later Dustin told me he did succeed in setting off a bomb in the pasture behind our house. He also admitted that he was the one that taught Jonathan to play war with Roman candles. "Clark and I used to go up in those hills behind the pasture. I would hide below in this pit and Clark would shoot at my head. Lucky I still have my eyeballs."

"Spare me any more details. Your surgery career could have been forever gone—blind, maimed, dead?"

"Yep, I worked on a few of those body parts in the ER just this week."

Hen Party

Someone with a staff as long as Moses' beard began pulling sisters off the stage. "It stinks," a brother in the audience yelled.

"Boo!"

"Hiss!" harmonized a quartet from the High Priest Group. Sister West stood and pelted the stage with cherry tomatoes left from the salad plates.

Jerking awake, I tried calming myself by repeating the instruction Sister Jones had given me—"You can do anything you want. You're in charge."

The annual Relief Society birthday hadn't changed in a hundred years—dinner, lace-edged posters of each Relief Society president through the years, a skit dotted with sun-bonneted sisters stitching a quilt…snore.

The tradition needed some pizzazz.

I called my friend Jan the next morning. "I'm in charge of the birthday dinner."

"That's terrific, how can I help?"

"We're going western. We'll get Brother Jones to call a square dance, serve fried chicken and have a skit—no quilts allowed."

"You're so fun. I have a great idea," Jan said. "I've got this funky chicken music I used at aerobics last week. We can get Cathy and Erin and we'll dance in a kick line."

"A chicken kick line. That's unique."

"Push the envelope. This will be a hoot."

Or a cluck, I thought.

Never one to procrastinate, I called a food committee, a sister to be in charge of the square dance, and assigned Jan the chicken costumes.

I enlisted my fellow Relief Society sisters to make invitations. "I need the back pockets from 35 pairs of jeans," I told Sister Kimball. "We'll print the invitations and glue them on the backs of the pockets."

"You're in luck," she said. "I save old jeans to make quilt blocks."

In the previous two weeks I had imagined all degrees of table decorations; from flower-filled cowboy hats, to ribboned branding irons, to borrowing Sister Meeker's chicken collection. And then one day while I was ruminating on the appropriate menu, a vision of a horse roundup circled my brain and I joined the cowboys around the cook fire to share their grub—beans.

Before I could dunk my biscuit, I knew what to do. Pork 'n Bean cans! The colorful red labels would bring the old west right to the table. The cans would be opened only partway, leaving the lid attached and bent to the side. Wheat stalks interspersed with sagebrush sprigs would fill the cans, lending color, while emitting pungent country odors.

Stacks of hay bales would have been perfect decorations, but the fire code prohibited such décor and heaven forbid if you lit candles (or campfires) in the cultural hall. It would be just my luck that partially opened tin cans would be banned, but I remembered the adage "it's easier to get forgiveness than permission." I sent a sign-up sheet around Relief Society, asking for ten sisters to donate a large can of Pork 'n Beans—unopened.

Saturday was a special day—the day to get ready for the birthday dinner. I scoured our tack shed for saddles, blankets, old horse shoes, anything cowboy to dress up the stage.

Arriving at the church in the early afternoon, I dragged box after box through the kitchen and into the cultural hall. Just as I draped the last saddle over the saddle horse, ten boy scouts bounded into the room, two of them dribbling basketballs.

"So, you guys are supposed to set up tables?" I asked as Brother Walker, their den leader, whistled through his fingers. Metal folding chairs clanked under the long tables. As I turned around to check a noise on the stage, one of the scouts waved his hand in the air, bronco style, while bucking back and forth on the saddle. "You're too young to rodeo," I joked, holding my breath that he wouldn't be pitched head first into my horseshoe display.

Two of my friends popped in to help set the tables and pour the water. The smell of boiling potatoes and buttered corn on the cob drifted from the kitchen and mingled with the sagebrush. Pork 'N Beans bubbled on the stove.

"Oh, look at the cute decorations," one of the sisters said when people started drifting inside. "Who would have ever thought of using tin cans for the tables?"

"And sage brush," snickered another. "It's as common as weeds around here."

Wait until the chicken dance, I thought. It's not all that common.

The young women of the ward began serving the meal. I feared the mashed potatoes were mushy, but the chicken and beans looked okay. More worried about the unplucked chickens dressing in the bathroom, I headed down the hall to find the rest of the kick line.

As I dressed in my chicken outfit, my worries surfaced.

"We don't have any choreography," I said to Jan.

"They'll be laughing so hard, no one will even notice."

We're on in fifteen minutes," I told the flock.

"Break a leg," Erin said, jumping up and down with one leg extended, her knee bent, and her foot circling in air.

I went to check the microphone on stage.

The guests gobbled chicken with piles of mashed potatoes and gravy and homemade biscuits served from cloth-lined baskets. The helpers in the kitchen broke out brownie delights.

When guests began twisting their chairs around to view the stage, I knew the crowd was ready for the usual poster-laden program. I was almost excited to hee-haw around, until Sister Brown climbed to the stage, moments before we were to go on. "Two of the ladies had to go home. They're allergic to sagebrush," she told me.

What are they doing living in Wyoming, I thought.

Jan had done a fabulous job with our costumes—pillows filled our yellow tee shirts, construction paper beaks jutted from our baseball caps. Our feet were shod with stuffed, yellow work gloves tied to our shoes. We had spent hours filling plastic Easter eggs with chocolates and taping them shut. Throwing them to the audience was to be the finale.

My nerves shivered in a ripple to my stomach.

Strutting to the microphone, I looked out on the darkened audience. They weren't laughing.

Maybe I could still dig out the president posters from the Relief Society closet.

I strutted over to turn on the music. Chicken sounds clucked from the tape player as the four of us began to scratch the floor and flap our wings. Raising only sporadic laughter Jan urged, "Do a kick line," in a desperate whisper.

This is stupid I thought.

"Throw the eggs!" I ordered.

None of us realized what velocity a plastic egg could attain. The four of us, hyped up from the kick line, picked up handfuls of eggs and feverishly threw. With athletic prowess two pairs of missionaries stood and caught most of the eggs, deflecting them from people in the audience. They had come for a free meal; playing catch was an added bonus.

We were nearing the end of our stash when someone in the kick line threw an egg, winging sister Tuttle in the eyebrow.

Anyone but her. "We've hit sister Tuttle," I groaned. "We're dead ducks."

Sister Tuttle never had a bad hair day. Prim, staunch, she followed the rules. She played the organ every Sunday without fail, slipping off her heels before donning ballet slippers to work the petals. Perfectly postured, she never missed a note.

I rushed to her side. "Regina, are you alright?" I pleaded.

"That was an unruly display," she said. "Didn't you think before you started hucking those loaded eggs?"

"I'll get some ice," I said, escaping her tongue. I just knew she was going to sue.

Two forlorn ice cube trays sat in the freezer in the kitchen—empty. Now what? There was certainly no steak inside, only a dab of salad and two cubes of butter. Where was the green Jell-O when I needed it?

By the time I got back, things had cooled down. Sister Tuttle sported a wet paper towel over her eye and the missionaries were complimenting her on her bravery.

"I guess I'll be okay, Harry will help me to the car."

I'll never be asked to head another party, I thought. Regina would pass the word around the entire stake. "Sister Bechtold should have to visit the bishop." She'd say. "I almost lost an eye."

"Jan, get brother Waldron up here to call his square dance," I said. The distraction might make people forget the egg barrage.

I started praying. Again.

More than half the crowd left after the dinner, leaving only some die-hard country dancers. The primary president had changed into her bilious square dance skirt. I'd never seen wider rickrack. The rhinestone eyes bulging out of the buffalo-head closure on her husband's string tie caught the light and almost blinded four people.

Couples dos-i-doed and promenaded around the squares until the closing prayer. My husband stayed in the kitchen the entire time. He didn't know me after that chicken performance.

The next day at church I met Sister Taggart in the foyer. "You did a good job last night. It certainly was unique."

As I rounded the corner to the chapel, I heard one of the sisters say, "And she didn't even mention the past Relief Society presidents."

I slunk toward the door to hide inside but the bishop was there shaking hands. He laughed, extending his hand. A huge bandage wrapped around all of his knuckles.

"What happened?" I asked, momentarily dropping the chicken memory.

"I cut it on one of those Pork 'N Beans cans cleaning up last night. It only took nine stitches; it will be fine in no time."

Oh man, it never ends. Tears pushed on the back of my eyeballs, threatening to drain. I couldn't cry in front of all these women. Finding my husband, I slid into the pew, plopping my scriptures and jacket next to me in pretense of saving at least two seats.

The prelude music began. Sister Tuttle, sitting straight as a wagon tongue had traded her white ballet slippers for purple. They accessorized the bulging purple bruise over her left eye she wore like a new Easter hat.

She never missed a beat.

Reflecting on the previous evening—chicken feathers, sneezing, eggs landing like hand grenades, and square dance skirts sized like inflated tutus—I decided right there to do a more cultural, spiritual theme if I was ever in charge again. Maybe something from the Hawaiian Polynesian Cultural Center.

I wondered if Jan had a connection with anyone that owned four grass skirts.

Mr. Bike

One of the town characters was a young boy who biked everywhere. Joe was disabled-- harmless, but would noiselessly appear suddenly around corners, startling anyone lost in thought. Long hairs protruded aimlessly out of his young face, some pointing upwards toward his coke bottle, black-rimmed glasses. His disheveled red hair, untamed by plastic teeth, balanced on top of his sloped head as coconut layers on some red devil's food cake. He never spoke, but at times mumbled in recognition to someone on the street.

His stiff hands attached to the handlebars, wrapped around like bird's claws frozen on a wooden perch, his hunched back surrounding the space he possessed. We nicknamed him Mr. Bike and would time our lunch hour by his arrival in front of the high school. Gremlin-like movements accompanied his aura as he dismounted, his thumbs poking immediately into his jean pockets until gravity dropped them to his sides and he would compulsively put them back. Standing robot-like, rarely looking from side to side, his whole body had to rotate to be turned, like he was welded at the neck joint below those scraggly boy-beard hairs.

Thirty years later, I returned for my high school reunion. Nostalgic, savoring the old times, I headed for the bakery to the crème-filled Long Johns of my youth. Parking several blocks away, I decided to walk the length of Main Street, reminiscing about where I had purchased those pink-striped culottes, looking for the drug store where we bought nickel candy bars, and listening for old echoes of blaring horns from gas guzzlers dragging main.

Deep in reverie, I was remembering the theatre where I saw the controversial movie, *The Graduate,* "Here's to you, Mrs. Robinson" lyrics running through my head.

As I rounded the corner I caught a whiff of popcorn. Feeling someone's presence, I quickly stepped out of the way, avoiding a collision. My heart racing, I looked Joe directly into his coke-bottled eyes. Mr. Bike, now a wrinkled, even stiffer old man with arthritic thumbs, poked into his jean pockets, silently shuffled down the sidewalk.

I wondered where he had parked his bike.

Mama Married a Mormon

I didn't really like coffee. Even after dumping streams of sugar into the dark, acrid liquid and lacing it with cream, my ten-year-old tummy could handle only a few sips. But the thrill of getting away with a minor offense appealed to me.

After a few cups of contraband over several weeks, I gave up and told Grandma I didn't like it.

However, I couldn't get enough of steeped tea. I loved to watch Grandma as she tore off the waxed sides of a milk carton bulging from a frozen block of ice inside. The block crackled, groaning like a sinking submarine as it descended to the bottom of a bubbling kettle, while the sizzling water lapped the tea bags. A cold glass of iced tea just didn't seem as sinful as a cup of coffee.

My grandparents hated Mormons and never wanted my mother to marry my dad, even though he was a "Jack Mormon," a member who didn't quite live the religion. Sometime in my teens, Dad told me about the jabs he took from his future father-in-law when Mother announced their engagement. Grandpa had snickered, "You going to marry Mormon?"

Mother shook her head. "I'm going to marry Vern. Mormon is a prophet in their scriptures," Mother replied.

"Those Mormons stand naked in front of each other when they marry," Grandpa told her. "You better watch out for that kind."

"They don't stand naked in front of anyone."

My grandfather continued ridiculing what little he had heard about the faith. "They have polygamy. Do you want another woman in the house?"

"That's not practiced anymore and hasn't been for decades. Those that still practice are NO longer Mormons." Mother had been studying pamphlets and asking a lot of questions of her friends that were members. "I know lots of Mormons and they're good people."

Grandma popped up, "They want to buy up all the food so the rest of us won't have any."

Dad's irritated voice ratcheted to swearing as he told me more about the confrontation. He said Mother just ignored them and went forward with her plans. I was convinced he was still ridiculed, though Grandma and Grandpa never slammed him in front of me.

I wondered why my grandparents were so gullible.

Granddad was born in Missouri. He grew up in the middle of Mormon-haters—descendants of those that expelled the group from the state. He only had a third-grade education, but pondering reasons for his bias, he should have known better. Even though I was only a teen when Dad told me, I didn't believe that "standing naked" lie.

Grandma was raised on a mountain ranch, miles from the nearest Wyoming town. She must have heard about Mormons when she went to business school, or maybe she finally agreed with one of Granddad's views.

My grandparents did not attend my parent's wedding.

Within a few years Mother did join the Mormon Church, secure in her faith that this was the life she wanted, even if Dad rarely attended. Mother took us kids to church every Sunday and Primary every Tuesday. My grandparents thought Mother was obsessed and possibly possessed.

Granddad rarely laid down his insult stick. When I got hand-me-downs from my aunt, Granddad would say, "Are you going to give them to Mooor-mon?" dragging the first syllable in nasal tones." That didn't even make any sense.

Despite the fact that I broke the church's health rules sipping Lipton tea in Grandma's country kitchen, her talk about hoarding food with no thought for others left me fuming. Some ancient defense mechanism cranked on my feelings. "That isn't true," I said. "There's plenty of food for everyone."

"Not if all the Mormons take it," she said, opening a can of grapefruit sections.

I watched as the breakfast ceremony continued: sunny-side-up eggs in a saucer flanking perfect pancakes and strips of bacon crisped to the color of warmed molasses. I couldn't understand why Grandma thought there wasn't enough food.

"Didn't Granddad want to build a bomb shelter out in the yard?" I asked.

Grandma spooned the grapefruit into a Mel Mac bowl, the last rite before calling Granddad to breakfast.

"Horal had some crazy notion but he never did it."

"Wouldn't he have stored food in there?" I ran my finger under the rim of the syrup pitcher, catching a couple of drops before licking them off my finger.

Grandma repeated her daily announcement, like a ceremonial creed. "Horal, your breakfast is ready. You washed?"

Granddad arrived on schedule, sat down, and buttered his pancakes.

The preparatory ritual was ended and so was the discussion.

I was glad.

I'm going to Flunk

I had a bigger problem than defending my religion looming in the school building.

Her name was Miss Nelson.

Through the years, her reputation had reached even a focused student like me. I caught myself studying her as she monitored the halls. The tucked-in sweaters over her ample bosoms looked stretched to capacity. Her football-helmet hair topped a stubby neck. The yellow residue between her fingers inched into her nails, marking them in nicotine stains.

Renowned as the toughest teacher in the sixth grade, I had crossed my fingers behind my back every time I saw her, hoping the gesture would keep me safe, like garlic warding off vampires. But as I opened my school registration packets that fall, I knew my finger crossing had betrayed me.

"I'll never get good grades from her," I said that night at dinner.

"You're a smart girl," Dad assured me. He stabbed the last pork chop from the serving platter and placed it on my plate, knowing they were one of my favorites.

Mother added, "Just study hard and you'll make it." She cut green beans tidbits for Christie, my one-year-old sister sitting on her lap. "You've always done well in school."

Although I might display my naughty side at home, I was always good at school. I liked finishing the assignments and awaiting the teacher's red-penciled above-average grades. The rules seemed to steady my behavior, the rewards satisfying my need for understanding and verification.

My report card reflected A's; my behavior confirmed by superior ratings. I couldn't stomach the thought of getting a "B," let alone a "C," or below.

Distraught, I could see Miss Nelson's tobaccoed tongue darting at me like a frog snatching a fly. Eye to eye she would rail, "Why can't you understand this? Are you dumb?"

My sister Cheri was five by then, but did not attend kindergarten either. My curly-headed bouncy sister probably couldn't have sat through kindergarten anyway. She wiggled so much during the meal; she bumped her milk glass, spilling it into her plate. Green beans floated like mossy logs. Mother got up to clean up the mess.

Tony chewed on the marrow of his pork chop bone. He always did that with his meat. Already frustrated about my impending failure, I didn't need Neanderthal man sitting across the table grinding on a bone.

"Dad, make him stop gnawing. It's disgusting," I said.

Dad smiled, picked his own bone up and sucked on the remains. "That's good calcium."

"He's not a dog," I whined.

I glared at Tony, daring him to argue, but he continued dredging that bone through his teeth.

I stood and shoved my chair back so hard it toppled to the floor. "He's dumb and I'm going to be dumb too if I have to go to HER class."

I stomped off to my room, prostrating myself on the same chenille bedspread that served as my study spot every evening. I had heard about the homework Miss Nelson inflicted, her unsolvable math problems, and her insistence on perfection. I imagined my superior report card branded with the word INFERIOR diagonally burned across the boxes.

I thrust my mind into the future. My life would be ruined. I was a poorly dressed, never-went-to-kindergarten dummy and I had proven it. I would never graduate; go to college—a failure, living on the street holding a tin cup like one of Dickens' beggar waifs.

Failing was bad. I woke up in a panic every day, exhibiting anxiety in its purist form, unrecognized by my parents or me.

The first day of class, I found my desk and sat rigid as Miss Nelson's reputation. From my desk in the middle of the room, I watched her every move. Primly postured behind her desk, she assigned sections in each textbook. As we alternated reading aloud, I observed that she continually opened and closed her desk drawer. She would then place her hand over her mouth in a not too sneaky mannerism, move her shut lips in and out, and suck on something. The rumor around the playground was she stored rolls of lifesavers in that skinny drawer to quell her nicotine cravings. Personally, I hoped it was Wintergreens, in case she ever affronted me eye to eye.

In the class picture that year, my parted hair lies flat on my skull, kinking up at the ends from being unevenly wrapped around pink foam curlers. My gathered cotton skirt accents my childish thick waist and is a longer length than the rest of the lineup. Some of the girls are wearing nylons; my anklets contrasting like mukluks worn to a ball.

At recess I heard students in my class talk about the homework load Miss Nelson inflicted, her advanced math problems, her insistence on perfection. I imagined my superior grades dropping to inferior. Every night I would finish my homework, surprised that I really did understand most of it, but still bracing myself for the next morning.

But before sleeping I would lie in bed, going through the day in my mind, worrying about each subject in descending order, from the first class to the last. Tossing and turning, my covers resembled a wrung out bath towel, as uncomfortable and messed up as my perception of sixth grade.

I became an insomniac.

Sixth grade. The infamous Miss Nelson and class. I'm on the bottom row, third from the right. Note, I'm the only one in the row wearing anklets.

The Ghost of Miss Nelson

My chenille bedspread was one of my best friends. Between reading textbook chapters, or in the middle of an impossible assignment, I would tip my pencil upside-down and drive the eraser through the valleys between the flowered bumps, pretending I was lying on a magic carpet. The coverlet would fly at my command, fringes waving in the breeze, to places that could make over a second-hand sixth-grader.

Pearl lips, brushed with sheer white lipstick, would accentuate a brand-new hairstyle—my burnt hair healed, never again to frizz under a Toni home-perm solution. Adorned in the latest outfits, I would stroll to my desk amid reverent whispers. As the popular girls looked me up and down, they would glance at each other in puzzled awe.

I flew through dreams of acceptance—a respite from reality.

My anklet socks discarded, I would be among the trendsetters, snapping nylons into my rubber garters. I was so pretty, even Miss Nelson would look up, staring so hard that she would accidentally shut her finger in her lifesaver drawer.

But reality always crowded back. As my daydream would end, I found that the eraser was leaving red streaks and minuscule beads of rubber, sharply contrasting the white chenille.

Stacking my books on the dresser, I pulled my flannel nightgown over my head and ordered my brain to overlook my fear of another school day in the company of Miss Nelson. My fear of the kids was nothing in comparison to my fear of her.

I longed to hide in the sweet nothingness of sleep, forgetting about my grades, my teacher, and my social status. But this normal safeguard eluded me.

As I eased under the covers, tightness enveloped me like a dress two sizes too small. I had to wiggle my feet to loosen the top sheet. My mind insisted that I wasn't through worrying. Wide-awake, I turned onto my stomach and bounced my foot around to find a cooler spot. Yanking the sheet completely free, I threw the covers over my hip and stuffed them between my knees.

I needed air.

I tried counting sheep, the kind that bound over the fence in perfect formation—with perfect grins. The last sheep in line blinked and suddenly Miss Nelson's protruding eyes appeared, glued to the end of a pair of springs, broinging back and forth, inches from my face.

Shivers overtook me. I ran to my mother's room.

"Mother, are you awake?" I asked.

She rolled over and flicked on the nightlight. "What's the matter? Are you sick?"

"I'm scared and I can't go to sleep."

Roused by now, Dad added his solution. "Drink a glass of warm milk."

Mother pulled her covers tighter around her neck. "Read for a while and you'll fall right asleep."

Drinking a glass of warm milk reminded me of drinking baking soda water for an upset stomach. That wouldn't do. I really didn't want to barf in my bed.

Reading might work however. Thirty minutes into "Wuthering Heights," I still hadn't fallen asleep and Heathcliff was taking on tones of Miss Nelson in my head.

I hollered, "Mother, I still can't sleep."

"Think of something nice and you'll drift off," she replied.

I quickly figured out that was nonsense. I could think as nice as I wanted and all I saw was my teacher's puckered mouth, her yellowed fingers pointing through the air, zeroing in on my stupidity.

Night after night I tossed on that bed, convinced that I was going to flunk. I probably was dumb. Who else would eat legless grasshoppers and nurse a kitten? Maybe I deserved this fate, for all the times I threw fits when Mother told me no, for standing with a nude neighbor boy on the ditch bank.

Some mornings it was after five a.m. before I finally dozed. The alarm clock's glow-in-the-dark hands circled the face so slowly, I could have lived in the next time zone.

I survived this muddled condition for six weeks. The day report cards came out, my heart beat so fast it could have whipped cream. I sat at my desk, staring at the cover for a good ten minutes. If I didn't have my grades, what did I have? Wiggling my toes inside my shoes and biting my hangnails, did nothing to calm my pitted stomach.

Finally I ripped open the envelope. Laying it on my desk, I closed my eyes and I said a little prayer. Slowly opening them, I ran my finger down the column.

My grades remained straight "A's."

I never got close enough to Miss Nelson to smell her rancid breath. Like the girl in the poem, I was very, very good in school that year.

One night soon after the report card, as I lay in bed staring at the alarm clock, I drifted peacefully off to sleep.

I think I was thinking about something nice.

They Smacked the Gavel without a Sound

Before the "demise," I was secretary in the first little copy shop we bought. There were three of us—Carl, me, and a pressman that had worked for him when he edited two semi-weekly Wyoming newspapers. Within a year we had purchased a larger building and hired more help.

A short time later we bought out another printing company and remodeled a bigger building closer to Main Street. We were on the move. I held my breath, and the edge of my desk. Now in customer service, I put my whole self in work mode. Dedicated to a fault, I would push through any obstacle to get the customer's jobs on schedule.

One evening, I had a deadline for our largest client and time was short. They needed a proof for a brochure the next morning and I wasn't going to let them down. I had missed the regular Fed Ex pickup, but I would drive it to the airport and deliver it myself. Everyone else had left the shop except the gal in the stripping department working on the final mock up. I cheered her on as I filled out the forms and then grabbed the goods.

The airport was about a mile and a half away. I envisioned some good airport employee saving the day and getting that package aboard. (You must know that the airport was very, very small. Planes with rubber-band propellers—chain curtains between the pilots and passengers.)

My resolve waned as I drove up and saw the plane just beyond the gate—engine on, pilot in place. But, I wasn't licked yet. Heading for the gate in the chain length fencing, I silently commanded, "open sesame." The gate was locked. Looking around I spotted a keypad about eye level on the adjacent brick wall.

Saying a little prayer, I punched in 6 random numbers and stood a moment in silence as the gate slid open. I think I saw angels.

The pilot looked down from the cockpit. He was cool as a Popsicle. I held my overnight package aloft and like the runner in "Chariots of Fire," I lunged in slow motion, the movie theme song pounding in my head. Steps from the plane, the pilot cracked the side window (or was it the wing window). "Please take this package," I said. "I have a deadline" After lifting my delivery as high as I could, he stuck his hand out the window and took it without a word.

I walked away like it was a normal way to shortcut procedure. Carl couldn't believe it of course. "Only in Cody, Wyoming," he said.

My client called the next morning with corrections on her brochure, never knowing the lengths I had gone through to keep her on schedule.

Carl is quiet, a totally nice guy, but strung a bit taut. He'd keep pulling the staff out of trouble, putting more stress on himself. He rescued the back-shop foreman from time crunches several times. One of our best customers in Montana had a standing order for church bulletins every Sunday. If the job wasn't ready by five o'clock on Friday night, Carl would personally deliver them to the loading dock. Many times he hauled cases of other brochures, forms, books, etc. We had started a printing office in Billings also and so had a ninety mile "paper route."

Staying late one night catching up on bids due soon, I took a break to look for Carl. Sometimes at that time of night I'd find him in his office, snoozing on the bare floor. This time I was stumped. Maybe he was in the warehouse, but I was too tired to wander around paper shelves.

Determined to wrap up one more detail, I sat down at my desk.

Crash Crash Thump Shatter Thud!!!!

I made myself look up toward the ceiling where the commotion was coming from. Directly above the copier, the ceiling was falling and what to my wondering eyes should appear—Carl's boots, his knees, his legs dangling there. Checking on insulation problems in the attic, he had not stayed on the 2x4's. He wasn't thinking or wasn't balanced, or both of the aforementioned. Sheetrock wasn't made to hold a guy like him. His legs stayed there for a very long time. I kept asking him if he was okay. No answer. Slowly, his lower half raised up through the roof. Poof, he was gone, leaving only a heap of powdered chunks on the copier.

Carl was always promoting, checking the payables, working late hours, dedicated to his business.

One of Carl's friends had a son that served a mission for our church in the south for two years. "Not one person ever fed him or his companion in their home," his friend told him. Carl was chagrined, and decided right then that the missionaries in our area would have a meal with us once a week. The old building we were in had a long history and no eating area.

Carl installed a kitchen sink and counter and he was in business. He cooked lunch every Tuesday for ten years for any missionaries serving in the area. Those Tuesday mornings were sometimes agonizing for the crew, lunch smells sliding down the stairs into the pressroom. One of those mornings someone in bindery came to find me to show me a surprise. Pointing to the ceiling under which the "kitchen counter" stood, soup was seeping down the ceiling seam and pooling in a large dark spot. Carl's crock pot overfloweth.

The only contingency to Tuesday lunch was a rule that each new missionary had to sign the wall behind the tables. The names always brought up discussions and questions. Signing Brother Bechtold's wall became quite an honor in our mission zone.

"When we fill up the wall, we'll quit feeding these guys," Carl told me.

And then came the gavel.

After almost twenty years, thirty employees in two different shops, and not one missed payment to our local bank, they lost faith in us and gave us two weeks to get out. Carl had gone to ask for some help to meet discounts on some of our payables. Some new guy from the east pulled our records and decided we weren't going to make it.

Over lunch one day, this guy told Carl, "You're bleeding and we're going to stop it." What he really stopped was Carl's appetite and peace of mind.

One of the first things we did was buy a gallon of paint. The wall adjacent to the counter in the eating area was soon a spotless white, every missionary's name obliterated. "We don't want these names left for just anyone to see. This is a special place," Carl said. There wasn't room for another signature anyway.

The wall was full.

Nests and Needles

"Are there bugs under there?" my four-year-old grandson, Kade, asked.

"What if there's a dead rat all squished with its eyeballs popping out?" asked his twin, Kallen.

I took a quick breath and erased the bug-rat image. Setting the picnic basket down on a rock, a scruffy blanket I had drug from the back of the car and slung over my shoulder, slid to the dirt. "There are only a few harmless ants, some spider webs, and a bed of dried needles inside," I told the boys as I shook the blanket free of dried grass. The pine tree's boughs scraped the dirt, its circumference spilling into the driveway.

Fifteen years before we had dug the pine from my mother's garden. It rode home in a bucket, the top of the tree grazing the roof of our old station wagon's back end. Small enough to need only one string of lights that first Christmas, we wrapped them around and around the boughs as easily as if the pine were a toy. As Christmases came year after year, we gave up the decorating as the girth of the pine tree spread like Santa's velvet waistband.

Not mentioning the fact that this was my first time under the pine boughs, I was the first one inside. I hoped my expectations matched my imagination of the fantasy world weaving around the trunk of the tree.

"Let me go under first and straighten the blanket. You two can come in when I give the command," I said to the twins. Lifting a scratchy bough, I scooted the blanket forward with my free hand.

Pine smells entered my nostrils and filled my being. Large enough for four adults to lie down, the moments passed as I took in the mystery and adjusted to the lower light. I smoothed the blanket, patting down the lumps of needles underneath, my rear end still protruding from the cavern.

"I want to see the eyeballs," came a voice from behind. A push rocked me off center and my hand landed on the pine needles scattered across the floor.

"Okay, crawl under," I ordered in my grandma-sergeant tone. There's plenty of room in here."

Both boys crawled inside, hunching on all fours as they took in the hollow under the tree.

"It's poky in here," Kade tentatively spoke.

"But where's the rat?" asked Kallen, pawing through needles around the edges of the circle.

I scooted the food basket under the branch in the far corner, smoothed a dried needle lump under my leg and laid on my back.

"This is a perfect home for a deer; soft bed, a roof, and cover to hide for a long, long time. I'll be the mama doe. There are a lot of twin fawns in the forest."

"Birds love trees too," I said, glancing around. "Bet there's a nest in here somewhere. There *is* one," I said, making a telescope out of my fists and squinting through the sunlight shafting down the holes through the foliage. "Look right up through the middle and where the sun hits that branch, see the bird's nest?"

"I've seen bird nests before; I want to poke a dead rat." Kallen was the feisty adventurer—the boy found chasing the ducks in the back yard, pumping high enough to snap the swing chains, or squeezing cat food between his fingers to see how it felt.

His brother, wanting a better look at the nest, cuddled on my shoulder and peered at the spot. "Grandma, do you think there are babies in there?"

"I think it might be deserted," I told him. Maybe a fairy family took up residence when they flew south. Papa fairy probably flies by the bedroom window every night you're here to check on you. "

"Is he the tooth fairy's dad?" he asked.

"I bet these are regular flitting fairies," I said. I tickled his tummy and walked my fingers under his neck. "Flit, flit, flutter," I teased and my little Kade giggled the laughter of snips and snails and puppy dog tails.

"Lay down by us." I beckoned to his brother. "Duck before that little girl fairy flutters down and kisses you on the tip of your nose."

"No girls allowed in here. Only you, grandma, this is our club house."

"Can we keep it our secret?" Kade asked.

"We'll never tell anyone," the grandson with just a hint of cat food odor answered. "If the bad guys get close, we'll laser them until they're dead."

I could almost hear the needles as they fell on our faces. The wind roared around the tips of the branches, ignoring the trio inside. A spider ambled around the outline of his web.

After the bank foreclosure, we lost our country home and the pine tree went with the contract. The money went back to the bank although there was barely three years left on the mortgage. It was two years before I was strong enough to drive close enough to check the pine that had once encroached upon the driveway.

As I rounded the corner and slowly headed up the drive, I stared at the gaping space between earth and the bottom of our tree. The new owners had sawed off many of the lower limbs to allow more room for cars to back around the driveway.

My eyes adjusted to the hole as the wind ripped through the hollow. The fairies were gone, uprooted by the teeth of a hungry chain saw. They must have flitted around the window for several days before they found another club house, another set of wondering hearts, or maybe a couple of little boys, soon to lose their baby teeth.

"What are these little boys made of? Snips and snails and puppy dog tails." (Left - right) Kallen and Kade.

On Bums and Such

Bodies are so strange. My college journalism teacher's torso—perfectly normal above the waist hoisted hips so big they waltzed for ten minutes before settling back on her legs. "Class, I know you won't believe this, but I've been informed that I'm expecting twins. My Lamaze class will have to hire a fork lift."

We all laughed, amazed at the candid manner she accepted the shelves protruding from her waist. I should have recited my mother-in-law's old joke; did you know polyester pants come in three sizes? Small. Medium. And I DON'T believe it. But, I just stared in awe, wondering how the podium hid all that flesh.

In the old days women paraded around in bustles as proud as a peacock with double tumors. The bustle accentuated the tiny-waist look, I suppose. However, stepping sideways through a door jamb doesn't seem that alluring to me.

Dad had the opposite problem. Folks accused him of having his bum shot off in the war—his work pants always hanging a couple of inches below acceptable. "A family trait," he'd say and walk away.

He passed it along.

In my day I could buy a pair of skinny jeans, straight up and down to fit like a sausage casing. Now-a-days the low cut, hip hugging, belly showing fashions actually come in junior sizes for very large girls. I'm junior in height, senior in fat. The pants fit in the dressing room, but walking across the parking lot, stepping out of the car and crossing the lawn seems to signal detachment.

The neighbors must forgive me—my arms too loaded to get a good hike on the waistband.

I'm the one that needs a barricade.

I've tried every size, every style. I've been in dressing rooms from here to there and sent off numerous catalog orders. My pants still fall. I've tried belts, suspenders, and threatened to go back to jump suits or house dresses.

A few summers ago, I ramped up my resolve to get healthier and work out. With a body style closer to whatever the designer of low riders had in mind, maybe I could finally find the perfect-fitting jeans.

I had walked off some of the extra pounds sitting around my waist. Of course with any good thing, comes opposition. My bum had flattened even more. One day while unloading sacks of groceries, my granddaughter warned me that my pants were sliding down.

"Celie, I'm losing weight," I said, with a note of pride in my voice. I hitched up my belt loops. "I can't decide to buy new pants now or wait until I lose more."

"Grandma, buy them now and do us all a favor," she said with that sly little tone of adult humor she employed quite regularly.

Oh, my, gosh. If anyone knew what went through my mind sometimes. Bums are probably off limits, even in moments of private contemplation.

I'm still hoping for a dramatic style change on the runways this year. Maybe pants with a waistband, jeans with ties—something for all womanhood, not young girls with hourglass proportions.

Someone must realize bodies are strange.

Stupid Tax

Dustin started his acting career in junior high when a theatre company from Montana came to town. A role in "The Wizard of Oz," showed how much talent he had. He ramped up his comedian routines at home, adding impersonations.

He'd get Jonathan laughing, even though Dustin was on Jonathan's black list. Dustin continually harassed his little brother. Like the time he took the top bunk-bed mattress off, hid it and picked on his brother until Jonathan chased him around the house, eventually into the bedroom. While Dustin sailed across, knowing to place his weight on the frame, Jonathan went diving down to the lower bunk. When Jonathan came to his senses, Dustin was long gone.

Jonathan told me that he was in the garage working on one of his swords and Dustin came down to harass him again. Jonathan chased Dustin with the electric drill. (But not very far.)

"I would have killed him," Jonathan said, "if the drill wouldn't have run out of chord."

Jonathan and his friend, the drill.

And so Dustin would have us all laughing until we couldn't catch our breaths. His Indian dialect, Spanish accent and movie star impersonations were dead on.

One night right before dinner, the phone rang.

In an Italian diction, someone asked, "Is this aMrs. Bechtold?"

"Yes."

"This is aPepe's Pizza and we havea a pizza ready to deliver."

"I didn't order any pizza and I don't know any Pepe."

"But it hasa peperoni, and amushrooms, anda extra cheese."

"I hate peperoni. You must have the wrong number."

I started to hang up and Dustin returned to English right quick.

"Mom, its Dustin. Want me to bring home a pizza?"

Okay, I laughed.

A lot.

Which reminds me of another guy trying to sell stuff. A middle-aged man came to the shop one day, his red striped tie and blue suit perfectly pressed. A bit of hair wax stuck loose hair strands down on top of his balding head. I usually shooed salesmen right out the door because Carl always reminded me that he was paying for his employees' time, not for some salesmen's. He caught me off guard, I guess, because the next thing I knew, he had boxes of light bulbs lined all along the front counter.

"Here's a light bulb every business should have," he said holding the closest one up like the Olympic Torch. "It will last longer than anything in stores and will give you brighter light."

"We use fluorescent lighting here."

"No problem ma'am, I've got those out in the back of my car."

Ding, Ding. A memory surfaced of Carl and I answering an ad for a sewing machine the second year of our marriage. I still can't believe we bought a sewing machine straight from the trunk of some shyster's car. I won't even tell you what brand it was. (Cause I have never heard of it and probably no one else has either.)

"I don't think so," I said, ready to call up one of the burly bindery workers from the back shop if he gave me a hint of trouble.

"No, I swear. Our fluorescents can't be beat." He picked up another box, six white bulbs nestled in paper wrapping, looking like lovely hens sitting on their nests. "We use these at home. My wife always wants to travel with me to witness to the truth of these bulbs. She's never seen anything like them. We have four kids and a couple of grandkids. These bulbs are bright enough to see what they're up to, and don't need changed for years."

I was tempted to demand a look inside his car trunk. I bet there were dozens of cheap fluorescent tubes in there, and a couple of sewing machines.

"Okay," I said finally. I had been saving a *Book of Mormon* to give to someone who might enjoy reading. I opened my desk drawer and held up a copy. "I'd like to give you a gift. This book is a history of people on the American continent, just as the bible is a history of the people where Christ ministered. It's called the *Book of Mormon* and it's a true book. One that may inspire you and cause you to ask questions."

"I've heard of the book."

"If you promise to read it, I'll buy two boxes of your light bulbs. They're very expensive, but I'll try them out and you can try the book out."

"You've got a deal. I'll read your book, and you can tell folks about your success with these." He handed me two boxes and I wrote out a check.

I figured he needed to sell a lot of those things to feed four kids and two grandkids. Besides, if I could interest anyone in knowing the Savior better…

Carl changed out most of the light bulbs at home, even though he wanted to know why we couldn't wait until the old ones burned out. "Where did you find these, anyway?" he asked.

"Oh, I succumbed, and let a salesman in the shop. He took me by surprise and I did buy. I want to see if they really burn brighter and, he promised we wouldn't have to change them for years."

Within weeks, light bulbs were burning out all over the house.

"Well, that guy with the wax really pulled a slick one," I said.

"I told you not to let any salesmen in the door," Carl said.

"Oh, like that dude you let plop his briefcase down on the counter? Remember he immediately, without asking, whipped a flask of combustible liquid out, poured it all over the briefcase and lit a match?"

"Yep, he was something. At least the fire hydrant he was selling put it out quickly," Carl said. "I think I remember you looking up, standing up, and telling him to 'GET OUT.'"

"Okay, salesmen (or women) are not coming inside the building ever again," I said. "We'll print the biggest *NO Soliciting* sign and tape it across the front of the building."

I didn't have one of the light guy's business cards and so resigned myself to buying boxes of my old brand of bulbs. I still hoped the dude with the kids had read my book and would come back with a few questions, but leave his so-called, eternal-burning light bulbs at home.

A few months later, I answered the phone, "Yellowstone Printing. How may I help you?"

"May I speak to Mrs. Bechtold?

"This is she."

"I'm so glad I caught you in. I see that a few months ago, you purchased two boxes of our fantastic light bulbs from Randy and I was wondering if you could give me referrals."

My foot started tapping. "No salesman will be allowed in this business again, and as for...... your light bulbs. What a rip off. You guys are liars and cheaters."

"But wait, maybe you got a hold of some duds. Our bulbs are guaranteed."

"Well, I'll guarantee I'll never buy any more of your cheap, undependable, and overpriced light bulbs or tell one of my friends to try and GOOD......"

"Wait Mom, its Dustin. I get it. I get it. So you really DON'T want any more of those special light bulbs, but aren't you curious to know if he read the *Book of Mormon*?"

"No I don't want any more of your stinking light bulbs ! ! ! " Me at work at our office in Cody, WY.

Buyer's Remorse

You would think I would be totally onto salesman's strategies, but no. Let me describe the tactics of the best salesman I ever had the short pleasure to deal with. I do mean the pleasure was short.

Tending my two young grandsons, Tristan and Jett, has been another blessing, howbeit a challenge. In my sixty fourth year, I'd get a bit tired by the end of the week. I had a Monday off and decided to treat myself to some mall shopping. Used to popping in and out for any errand, I lingered, trying on blouses and a couple of sweaters. (I had already purchased a new pair of jeans, classic fit—guaranteed satisfaction.) You guessed it—I'm wearing a belt to hitch 'em up.)

Window shopping by a couple of stores, purse over my arm, my new shirts lovingly wrapped and lying in a shopping bag, I remembered I had no reason to hurry.

A nice looking young guy stepped into my path, wielding a nail file cube. "May I show you our newest product?" he asked as he held out his hand and mine met his. It was like some involuntary twitch that one couldn't control. I stood, and he filed my thumbnail. "You see all those cracks in your nail? Do your nails usually look like this?" I'm nodding yes and yes. "Ridges in your nails are the problem, watch this." He filed for a few more seconds, showed me the shine and immediately proceeded flipping the nail block over and buffing while he got to know me.

"How many daughters do you have?" I answered. "And daughters-in-law?" I answered. He showed me my thumbnail. It had never looked so satiny. Whipping out a bottle of cuticle oil, he dropped a perfect dab on my nail bed. He assured me it would soak in and my nail would stay shiny for two weeks. I whipped out the credit card as I walked closer to his booth and the credit card machine.

"Today it's only $60.00 for the whole kit, which includes our popular hand lotion."

I gulped, briefly thinking about when I had only five measly dollars spending money for a whole month. The thought went away real quick. "Okay." It was extravagant, I didn't need it, but I wanted that kit. My nails deserved it.

I looked around the booth as he made the transaction. Oh, my word. The sign advertising the complete beauty and skin line as ONLY two thousand dollars popped out, unashamed. I thought it should have a drape over it, or the salesman should whisper such a number. I gulped, wondering if he was a money launderer right here in Utah County. Why wasn't I not running for my life? At least heading for the complete-set-of-scriptures-cd booth down the corridor—to something halfway familiar. Then I could veer off to the buttered pretzel stand around the corner, and away from this beauty trap.

"Oh, I see you've noticed our pricing," he stated.

"No one in their right mind will pay two thousand dollars for skin products. I think I'll have to remain plain."

He pulled out the stool. "Just take a minute and let me show you our secret." I think I saw him swaying slightly back and forth like a snake charmer. You have all afternoon, you have all afternoon….I deserve some pampering.

I sat on the stool.

"Utah is a dry state." (Get it?), he said. Let me show you the secret of lasting beautiful skin. Moisturizing, moisturizing. In Israel we have discovered the revitalizing nature of the Dead Sea sand," he said. I'm picturing the Dead Sea Scrolls, scraps of dried papyrus brittle as old bones. "Our products are infused with diamonds." I'm thinking diamonds specs will cause a rug burn. He held the hand mirror to my face. "Which side do you want to be wrinkle free?"

Duh, make it both so I don't walk out of here spinning in circles. I pointed to a place where wrinkles lapped each other. Why was I wasting his time, anyway? This was a make-believe-moment without a chance of owning this luxury. Just let him finish and let me go home.

He gently applied the masque and rubbed the spot. He added the vitamin C concoction that was to activate the masque. He wiped the spot, then applied the revitalizing skin cream. Lifting the polishing cloth, he held the mirror up REALLY close and revealed the spot. It WAS less wrinkled.

"There's not as many, but they're still there," I said.

"This is the first application. You must use it daily."

"Well, thanks for the demonstration." I pushed myself a bit up from the stool.

"You can't leave without this wonderful product. You deserve youthful skin. You work hard and need to pamper yourself."

I was in the zone somewhere in Israel, picturing beautiful, youthful women kneeling on the Dead Sea shore, massaging sand into their face pores. The scene changed to my return from the sea, my friends whispering words like, "I wonder if she had a facelift? Has she found something new on the internet? She looks twenty years younger."

"I can't afford this, even if I look like a supermodel. It's not going to happen," I said.

He reached out and cherry picked different boxes and bottles. "Now, say if I give you the cleanser, revitalizing skin serum, mask, toner, anti-age defying, chin lifting serums for seven hundred and fifty dollars?"

"No way. Besides I'd have to call my husband."

"Your husband would want you to have this. When my wife comes home with an eight hundred dollar purse, I don't ask her how much she paid. She is beautiful and deserves beautiful things. You deserve beautiful things."

"I don't have my cell phone," I said. "I'll think about it."

"We talked about your daughter and daughter-in-laws. You have three, correct?"

I thought about how beautiful all three are. "Yes, I do."

"Well, I'll tell you what. I'll throw in three nail kits for their Christmas presents, no extra charge from the price I quoted for all these products." He fanned his hand over the loot and reached across for a bar of sand soap. "AND, I'll throw in this soap for your husband. It's only available through us—and…."

"I know, I know, it's straight from the Dead Sea."

I turned to the kid he was obviously training to break women down and said, "See how to do it, kid?"

He didn't answer. Didn't admit a thing.

Okay, I do work hard. I do deserve this. I need this. My skin is parched and wrinkly and old.

I heard the snake charmer's flute—beckoning, luring, hypnotizing. I could actually feel my wrinkles diminishing. Far away, I also heard the fact that I've already paid sixty dollars for one nail kit. My ears shut on that thought.

Carl would understand. Especially after I gave him exotic sand soap. "Okay," I'll give you seven hundred."

He whipped out his calculator for the third time. "I'll absorb the fifty dollars, I want you to have this that much. And, I'll put my card inside so you can call and then bring me white chocolates to thank me for introducing this gift into your life."

I walked away, two more shopping bags added to my shirt bag. Floating, I thought of the change coming in my face and in my life. I'd be more confident, stylish, out-going, and just plain beautiful. I slipped into the car and picked up my cell phone from the passenger seat.

"Honey, I bought something for myself today. Now, hear me out."

"How much did this *sale* cost me?"

"You know I've been dwelling on all the wrinkles I'm getting and I've been worried about getting old and you told me not to even think about a face lift. I did something I never do. I spent more money than I ever had on the spur of the moment. It's not like me at all, but I bought a beauty and skin routine from one of those booths at the mall."

Dead silence.

"Cindy, (He always calls me by my nickname, except when he's serious, mad, or skeptical) how much did you spend?"

"I deserve this. I work hard. I need some extravagance once in a while," I said.

"How much."

"Well, it originally was two thousand dollars but I got it for only seven hundred dollars."

"How do you feel?" he asked.

"What do you mean? I feel fine. I feel like this was made for me."

"I'm on the freeway we'll talk at home," he said.

I did feel fine, we could pay this off. How many times had HE bought something I didn't think he needed?

By the time I made it home, I wanted nothing more than to take the stuff back and throw it at the nice salesman. Chocolates? I wanted to give him a grandmotherly blessing—expose his snake flute for what it was. I felt terrible. Like a bad little girl who had a lot of wrinkles, right in the middle of her forehead. Why had I signed that credit card?

Then I knew why Carl had asked how I felt. That guy was practiced. I was primed, soothed, cajoled, and led into a fantasy land.

Carl met me at the door. "I feel awful. I made a huge mistake. I'm sorry. I'm so sorry."

"I've done a lot worse than that," he said.

When our son-in-law, Bill, makes a money mistake he calls it "stupid tax." This was "stupid tax," I said.

Carl concluded, "We've all goofed and wasted money. Don't worry about it. As long as you have it, enjoy it.

You really do deserve it."

Orchestrating a Salad

Carl builds a salad as preparing for an audience of sage concert buffs. Fully orchestrated in sections; cherry tomatoes tumble in percussion, diced carrots fiddle through layers of crisp lettuce, chopped bits of green onion burst in flavorful arias. Triangle green peppers slice through the melody and land beside cucumbers, round and strong as cymbals clanged in perfectly timed moments of silence. Spicy vinaigrette blows over the members, opening palettes tapped by trumpeting smells and tastes. Sharp, tangy tones tuba deep senses-- melding flavors, colors, and pitch.

He conducts the rendition as if dressed in black tuxedo—his apron strings cascading down the tails. With gusto, he lifts the wooden utensils to toss the selection. Peeking through the kitchen door, I see the tails, the strings—the momentum as elbows flying, he directs the flipping wooden wands.

Crescendoing toward the finale, he adds some sunflower seeds and garnishes with squiggly cheese pieces—as rigorously he beats time—instruments mix-mashing towards completion. With one downward beat the movement is over, the height of fulfillment resolves as the bowl topples--clangs and clatters down the counter and onto the floor, flinging veggies everywhere.

The conductor is stone still, as the music abruptly stops.

Bears Beware

"How far are we going in?" I asked Carl as we discussed our upcoming pack trip.

"Two Ocean Pass," he said.

"How far?" I asked again. Like, how many hours?"

"Not that far. His camp is in the Bridger-Teton National forest. Scott takes in hunters all the time. Probably about 7 hours.

"What? Carl, are you nuts? I haven't ridden a horse in years, for even seven minutes."

"It will be fine, Cindy. You can do it."

"We'll be clear to the Canadian border."

"I'll take care of you. We're not going foreign. Still in Wyoming," he said.

Dustin was nineteen in 1992 and had been called to go on an LDS Church mission to Argentina. We wouldn't see him for two years and Carl wanted some time together before he left. The pack trip he had arranged was a week long. I worried about the cost, but Carl assured me that his outfitting friend, Scott, had agreed to trade his brochure printing bill for extra horses and he would also guide us to camp.

Okay, a little trail ride would be fun. I enjoyed camping—I could throw in some bacon—fry it up in a pan.

I called Monika and told her the news. "Can Bill get off work? Will you let Kelby go? Your dad thinks he'll have fun." I'm panicked inside, thinking about a three-year-old playing with a bear cub, or bleeding profusely, the nearest doctor three mountains away.

She loved the idea. Everyone did. Even though horses really weren't Dustin's thing, he wanted to be with the family. Jonathan would be a high school senior that fall, surely he wouldn't cause any major catastrophes, although he would be riding Foxy—the one that bucked him off on the wagon train rendezvous the summer before.

The good old pickup I loved, Rambo, pulled our cheap, rusted-out, orange horse trailer. Inside were our two horses, Cody (the antennae flipper) and Foxy (the old gray mare).

We circled the vehicles up in front of Scott's outfitter cabin. He roped the gear on pack horses—our sixteen-inch iron camping skillet, utensils, metal plates, food coolers, clothes, tents, sleeping bags, sun screen, flashlights, Carl's old guitar, fishing gear, and two surprise items that a friend assured me would keep bears plum away.

A bit warm at the first of the trail, it cooled as we ascended. I was soon humming "Moon Shadows on the Trail," right along with *The Three Amigos*.

"I'm sure we'll see a plethora of bears," Dustin imitated, loud enough to get my nerves rattled.

I had one of the gentle, (larger) horses. Docile enough. I knew Scott had a gun or two so bears were no threat on the trail. Yep. But bears didn't know that. We each had a canteen, a cowboy hat, and, too early on the trail, I had a very sore bum.

Scott called a time out and I slid down from the saddle. I can do this, I thought. Bum's sore, legs a bit stiff, but look at the flowers, the trees, the sky. I sat in a meadow, picking wild sunflowers with Kelby on my lap.

A couple more hours and I definitely wasn't sitting high in the saddle. In fact, I had slumped further back to ease my blisters. I was shouting, "are we there yet?" I prayed for rain, anything to get us off those horses.

Everyone else was stiff when we got to camp. I was crippled. Scott came to unsaddle my horse and spotted two sore spots on his back where I had shifted my weight. The poor horse was more saddle sore than I.

Everyone knows setting up camp is first on the agenda. While the boys were pitching tents, Carl picketed our two horses on Scott's lines. They started chomping grass. Five minutes later, Cody (aptly nicknamed Houdini) was loose, wandering through camp. Scott, thinking Carl needed a real cowboy's skill, nonchalantly said, "I'll picket your horse."

Carl smiled.

A few minutes later Scott walked back, Cody directly behind him. "You've got someone following you," Carl said.

Scott turned to look. "Hump, you were right. That horse *is* good with his teeth."

Carl had ridden Cody on a mountain cattle roundup the summer before. He was the official photographer for the trip. One of the calves busted loose and headed up the mountain through the trees. He couldn't get it on horseback so he tied Cody up to a little tree. When he returned later to mount up, Cody was gone.

Carl walked along the trail for a half an hour or more until one of the girls on the roundup stopped her horse and chatted for a minute. "Have you seen my horse?" he asked. "The bay?"

"You mean the one dragging the tree down the trail?"

Carl didn't laugh.

With Cody back on line and the camp ready, Jonathan (One Match) gathered wood. It stayed within the fire pit.

"Monika, let's get supper going," I said. "I'm dying for fried potatoes and onions." She helped. We cooked and washed dishes, heating water on a grate.

That evening the real test came. I dug in a canvas duffel bag and pulled out my two secret items. "Attention family," I announced. "These two lights are going to keep away bears. Someone at the sporting goods store told me about them. They're battery-operated compact miracles that flash a blue light. One at each end of the camp will deter any bear looking for trouble."

"Mother," Dustin said. "How are we going to sleep?" Everyone else grumbled.

"You're tired, you'll sleep. And so will I. Bears are probably attracted to hair dye and I just had mine done."

Carl shook his head.

He set the lights in two trees on opposite ends of camp.

I slept soundly, even the first night out. The light blue flash blaring through the canvas every thirty seconds soothed me. The next morning it was Carl grumbling. "I thought for sure we'd have an airplane in our laps this morning, the way those lights were flashing."

I slept every night. Hey, they worked. Not one bear came scratching at our flaps.

There's nothing like a few days in the Rocky Mountains to take away everyday stress. Fish are plentiful. Thousands of stars shine and smoke drifts into skies so blue they seep into your soul. Monika and I cooked, washed dishes. Cooked, washed dishes, and then whined. Three days out, our men caught some fish and cooked them themselves.

The ride back was all I had prayed for on the way in. It rained the whole seven hours. We donned our cheap yellow ponchos and kept going. Our three-year-old, Kelby, loved the rain. He knew all the horses by name and was dust and soot up to his cowboy hat.

His dad, Bill's, reputation followed him along the trail. He had taken sick during every vacation he'd ever taken. Something about stress let-up. I trailed behind his horse, his slumped-over form resembling a wounded cowboy slung over a saddle in *Gunsmoke.*

The shower at Scott's cabin almost made up for sore bottoms, wet jeans, and horse hair.

Blisters healed, memories stuck. I'm broke in now and ready to give a piece of wilderness advice.

When camping in the woods, don't forget the battery-powered runway lights and watch out for airplanes.

Kelby and me picking wild flowers in a meadow at Two Ocean Pass.

You Need a Job

"You find any work today?" Dad asked, setting his lunch pail on the counter. His oil-stained fingers flipped the latches open and the remains of a scrambled egg-whites-only sandwich stared out of creased waxed paper.

"Nothing yet," I replied. "Just like you always tell me, 'keep beating the streets.'" My words came easily, I really had been looking. (Always after noon when I stumbled out of the sack.)

Mother slipped into the kitchen, retrieved the scraps and stuck them in the dog dish.

"Those egg sandwiches don't feed a man. Can't you put in the yolks?" he asked.

"You know you have to watch your cholesterol."

"I'd just as soon be plugged up with some good beef tallow. My starving to death won't pay the bills either."

As Mother carried the pail to the sink, he looked at me, age lines stacked on his forehead. "We're driving up the North Fork Highway tomorrow to find you a job. Those dude ranches are always looking for help."

Cowboys?

He wanted me to work with creeps in cowboy hats and pointy-toed boots? With no friends, no dances, no civilization—horse flies and hot dog roasts? Yee ha!

"I'll get a job, Dad. I'll look all day. I won't come home until I have one. Dude ranches aren't for me."

"Get packed, we're leaving early." His steel-toed boots flung little mud bits down the hall.

"He isn't serious is he?" I asked Mother. She poked the broom under the fridge attacking crumbs and dust. "You can't lay around here the rest of the summer. You're out all night and sleep all day."

My parents had sent me to California for the first half of the summer to get me away from my wild friends. I went to church again, babysat my cousins and tried to ignore the pain left by my boyfriend—Ken, the jerk.

I had calmed down, but as soon as the airplane circled over my old stomping grounds on my way home, I formulated plans to call my girlfriends and be at the weekend dance that Friday. I was itching for a party—dancing the Twist, the Freddy, like the Go-Go girl I was meant to be.

I refused to go into square dance mode—the dosado, allemande right, swinging with a hay seed to "Duck's in the Soup" with a bunch of tourists in one of those lodges.

The next day square dancing wasn't at the top of my worry list. Dad rapped on my door at an hour I hadn't seen for weeks. He picked up my suitcase and warned me to get hoppin'.

The whole family was going on this outing.

Thirty miles up the North Fork of the Shoshone River on the highway to Yellowstone Park, he pulled into the first drive with a readable sign. Two boards tilted on a rusty nail—Crescent C Ranch. A two-tire trail, gouged by vehicles and horses, sloped away from the grassy middle. If it rained, I'd be stuck in there until Labor Day.

"It's not open," I said as we rounded the corner to a vacant parking pasture.

Dad kept one hand on the wheel, the other rested on the open window. "There's two old boys sitting on the porch."

"Turn around. There's no tourists in this hole in the road." I sat up to catch a glimpse of the old boys on the porch.

A skinny dude wearing chaps and a hat the size of a milking bucket looked over at our car as Dad pointed at me. The other stood and stuck his foot on the seat of his wicker chair. Slowly he twiddled a long piece of wheat grass through his teeth and stared at me. He nodded his head.

Going once, going twice—SOLD to Crescent C for minimum wages—auctioned through my brain.

Two spotted heeler puppies appeared from behind one of the cabins, nipping at a cloud of bugs above the men. There was no hint of habitation by any female.

I was gulping sloggy tears.

"Don't make me stay, Mother. They're weird."

My sisters sat in silence in the back seat, their minds flipping into their own futures. Crying.

"They've got some bed making and odds and ends," Dad said, as he sank back into the driver's seat.

"I'll be good," I begged, my mantra since childhood pulsing in my conscience loud and clear, the good little, bad little girl poem magnified in capital letters. I COULD be very, very good. "I'll come home nights and work two jobs. Let me get one in town."

"She can't stay here with only men," Mother said.

Dad gave the two a salute and turned the car around. "We'll go further down."

The next ranch turnoff looked as equally foreboding as the last. A steel bridge arched over the river, white caps stinging gray boulders fell to eddies laden with water skippers. Any other time I would have soaked in the woodsy smells and thought about marshmallow roasting, but my adrenaline signaled fight or flight.

I raked the ridges for any sign of real life—young people, a store—something to hope for. Dad pulled up in front of the hitching rack at the next lodge, a pickup loaded with saddles the only vehicle around. As Dad walked up the stairs, a big-bellied woman nodded and flung a "howdy" at him. "Need a room? We're not full yet," she said.

"My girl here is looking for work."

The woman wiped her hand down the side of her Levis.

"You know, we're pretty far into the season, but somebody will be getting antsy and leave early. Check back in a week."

I resumed breathing in rhythm. "Looks like these ranches have their quota," I said.

Dad rubbed his chin. "Pahaska will need help."

"That's clear to the entrance of Yellowstone Park," I said.

"Pretty place with lots of kids," Mother added.

By the time we pulled into the parking space at Buffalo Bill's old hunting lodge, I knew I was going to finish the summer working at a lodge and I prayed it would be this one. One of my friends had spent a recent weekend hanging around this place and had met a couple of really cute boys, waiters in the dining room.

Dad went straight to the manager and within fifteen minutes I was shown a woman's wooden dormitory, my room, and the bathroom down the hall.

I walked back to the car for my good-byes, looking around for the cute boys my friend had mentioned. A dark-haired, black-eyed hunk stepped off the path as I walked by. "Are you a tourist?" he asked.

"No, just got hired as a fry cook."

"It's fun around here, but watch out for the cook. He spits chewing tobacco. None of the staff eats the food."

Smoking at the Drive-In

The night of my first job at the drive-in theatre concession stand, Mr. Paul hovered over me like a vampire driven to green blood—money in the till. I was confident that the brief rehearsal Dad and I had had would suffice for counting change back to the customer.

It was.

As the night progressed, Mr. Paul backed away, leaving me space to turn around without colliding with his nose. His till would balance.

As he relaxed, the rhythm of the drive-in theatre tangoed through the glass counters. I bent and dipped into the candy rows, retrieving whatever the customer ordered. Twirling around the popcorn machine, I dumped the salted kernels into the skittering oil, listening for pings against the steel kettle.

A quick two-step and I was in front of the grill, flipping burgers in time with the beat. Ketchup circled the buns where the patty would float on a fat onion slice.

The hustle of the customers deadened the movie sounds funneled through the speakers. I took a break outside by the projection room.

Captivated by the whir of the projector, I peeked through the open door at the black reels turning images across a shaft of light bursting from a hole in the cinder block building and onto the screen. Laden with dusted specks, I longed to slice my arm through the light, projecting my shadowed arm and fingers over the movie.

Instead, I went back inside to close down the snack bar.

Judy, the other girl scheduled that night, brought out the brick to clean the grill. The smell charcoaled off the heat and hung in the air as she removed the grease with white rags.

My job was to spray and rub the glass on the counters until all fingerprints were obliterated. Like a gypsy rubbing her crystal ball, my fortune revealed a plethora of candy—and, neatly stacked beside the sweets—several rows of cigarettes.

Judy had told me during her break that she was going for a smoke.

"What kind of cigarettes do you smoke?" I asked

"Usually, Salems—something menthol." She moved to the counter and pointed to her brand.

"Do you like to smoke?" I asked.

Judy turned back to the grill and nodded. "It's a habit now."

"What's it like?

"Don't even get started on them. I wish I could quit."

All the lessons at church about tobacco rapidly burned through my brain but left no mark. "I just want to try."

"You'll try it one way or the other. Buy a pack and we'll smoke one after work."

"You buy them for me so no one will know." I was brave, but only under cover.

We sat in her Dodge. All the cars had left the drive-in lot. Lopsided speakers hung from the hooks—some of the poles bent by reckless drivers. The air was crisp. The moon hung above the theatre screen, fire-yellow.

I followed her motions as she took a cigarette from the package. I took one from mine. She lit hers. "When I hold the lighter at the end, puff so it catches on fire."

I puffed.

"You probably will just want to puff on this one. You can get sick inhaling until you get used to it." Judy was inhaling and blowing smoke rings, powder-sugared doughnuts stacked inside one another.

"No, I want to do it the right way."

I inhaled.

I was twirling, but not toward the rhythm of the popcorn popping or the burgers flipping. Dizziness engulfed me, spinning my brain until my stomach heaved.

"I'm sick," I said feeling for the handle to roll down the window.

Laying my head out the opened window, I breathed clean air.

"I'm used to it now," I said as I took another drag on the stick. This time smoke hit my lungs and I coughed burnt cinders. My world went green. I started sweating and yellow flashes crossed under my eyeballs.

"I guess I'll throw this out. Maybe I'll try again tomorrow night."

And I did.

How absolutely stupid.

Pahaska and Jell-O

Sinking through the saggy springs on my newly assigned cot, I sat and checked out the knotholes in the wood-paneled room. Three new pairs of tooled cowboy boots stood in a perfect row under the bed a few feet away. A bucking bronco poster loomed above the pillow, the cowboy in tight jeans arching from the saddle, hand flinging through the sky.

Briskly, a girl stepped into the room, halfway out of uniform before really noticing me. She flung her clothes on the bed. "Oh, didn't know we had a new roommate, I'm Amy."

"I'm the new fry cook, Cindy," I said. "My dad just dropped me off to start work."

"This is the perfect summer job—the mountains—the cowboys," she replied with near reverence in her voice. Amy pulled on some jeans and a sweatshirt. "I'm going to the rodeo tonight in Cody with Trish. She's the girl that sleeps in that bed." Amy pointed at the cot shading the row of pointy-toed cowboy boots.

What had I gotten myself into? Both of these guys dug cowboys?

"I'm from Powell, thirty miles from the rodeo grounds and I only went on the 4th of July. I haven't been since I was a kid."

"How lucky can you get? I'd be there every night. Do you know any of the cowboys riding this year?" I didn't tell her I stayed as far away as possible from boot-cut jeans, pockets with whitened circles rubbed by chew cans, and hats with sweat rings. In my circle, these guys weren't "in," they were out.

"I'm not into that crowd much. I like a guy in a madras shirt and penny loafers."

Amy laughed. "Guess you don't want me to see if Clint has extra room in the car?"

"Nope, I think I'll look around and go to bed. My shift starts at 5:30 in the morning. I didn't even know there was such a time of day."

Amy pulled on her cowboy boots, a wad of dried manure stuck under one worn heel. She must have a pass to go behind the bucking shoots. As she stood, she tucked her cuffs inside her boot tops, a very uncool way to wear jeans, even if you were a wannabe cowgirl. She waved her cowboy hat, rodeo queen style, and bounded out the door. I hopped into bed.

Clint was one of the craziest guys I'd ever met. The next morning while I was under the full scrutiny of Christine, the breakfast cook, he winked at me as he stuck his order on the wheel. A waiter, he caught the adoration of all the employees by sticking his silverware sets in his back pockets, along with a bottle of ketchup. He consistently earned the most tips. I had to admit his cowboy boots fit his personality—freckles and all.

I might be able to stand this place, I thought, especially if Christine, my boss, would not question every order I placed on the grill. She was no *Aunt Bea* from Mayberry. She was a large woman, but there the similarities ended. Her bun was stuffed under a hairnet the color of wood. Her anklets shoved up the black hairs on her legs. She reminded me of a Scandinavian washer woman turned chef.

"Where's the two scrambled eggs?" She asked. "You've got six hash browns on those orders. Where's the sausage on number four?" She reminded me of Mr. Paul dancing around me at the drive-in theatre last summer, convinced I would mess up his till, but she was a much larger version. I didn't mess up Mr. Paul's till, or her side orders.

I gritted my teeth. "Right here," I pointed, "and here and over there." My orders were always sizzling in parallel lines down the grill. It miffed her. I knew I was a good worker.

"What do I do with this egg? It has blood in it?" I asked.

"Just dump the whole thing in the French toast bowl. We'll dunk the bread in it."

I about upchucked my bacon. There were dirty little secrets in grease-layered restaurant kitchens.

I had been warned about the biggest secret the day of my arrival. Drew, a grizzly old Navy cook, now cooked for the employee crews. He never shaved, never wore deodorant and always spit tobacco. His white apron tied twice around the middle was always smeared with splotches.

Drew lowered the beaters into the huge mixer used for pancake dough. "You kids look hungry. Got enough to make flapjacks for a submarine crew." I stared at him, hoping his tobaccy juice wouldn't fall into the batter.

"Do you guys eat in here?" I queried the group around me.

"We have to unless you want to pay tourist prices out in the dining room." Trish rolled her lip into her nose. I listened to her. Despite the row of boots and the cowboy poster, she was a lot of fun. She liked makeup, rock, and other normal non-cowgirl things. The kids liked her—let her be spokeswoman.

That evening about midnight, I met her in the hall returning from the bathroom. We didn't visit. I had a stomachache the size of a grizzly bear. My intestines felt like ropes wrung by another giant washwoman, even larger than Christine.

After six more trips to the bathroom that night, I didn't even try to cover the noise. By dawn, the illness abating, I lay on my cot, thankful to have only rumbling left to remind me of the searing pains of the night.

Amy was the first to wake up. "Something happened last night and I was sick as a dog," I told her in a weak little whine.

"Ick! Hope you're better." She crossed her pointer fingers at me like she was warding off vampires. Moans commenced from under the bronco poster. "I was in the bathroom all night with the trots," Trish rolled over and swept her long bangs away from her eyes. "That was the worst flu bug I've ever had."

"It must be a fast one—both of us at once." I stood up but crumpled back into bed, one leg swinging over the edge.

I wasn't hungry for breakfast. "Maybe I'll never eat again," I thought, as I overheard someone talking about diarrhea as they filled sugar bowls and cream pitchers.

"I was so sick last night I wanted my mom," Clint told Amy as he wrapped his silverware sets and put several in his hip pockets. He laughed, but held his stomach and rocked back and forth. "Wait a minute," Amy said. "What did you eat last night?"

"Drew's famous noodle casserole."

"I ate the chicken," she said.

I found Clint in taking a survey in the employee room. "Who ate the casserole last night?"

Several raised their hands. "How many of you were best friends with the toilet last night?" He laughed, but scanned the audience for a tally. Everyone raised his hand.

"Who ate the chicken?" The majority raised their hands. Who of this bunch got sick?

No movement.

"Drew has struck again. He gave us food poisoning."

In my mind I saw brown juice from Drew's chaw running through the boiling ribbons of noodles, little bits sticking to the Italian spices.

I would not eat his food again.

For the next few days I ventured into the worker's cafeteria at mealtime, checked Drew's current concoctions, remembered the night adventures with the casserole eaters and picked out a nice jiggly bowl of Jell-O.

My only variety the next few days was the color of the Jell-O. I was getting hungrier every day—so hungry I gave up and played tourist. I waited for the hostess to seat me at one of the varnished wooden tables and picked up a real menu and ordered in the dining room.

I inhaled the cheeseburger. After sucking on Jell-O for days, the side of fries were golden sticks of pleasure. But the reality of my situation came in the form of my ticket. Fry cooks only made $1.25 an hour and one meal came to $1.40. I shouldn't have ordered the cherry pie.

I settled on one meal in the dining room a week, snuck scraps from the breakfast grill and dived into my Jell-O at lunch.

"I'm starving to death in this joint," I said rather loudly one day at lunch.

"You don't trust ptomaine Drew's cooking?" Slim, one of the supervisors from the night crew moved over next to me, his plate filled with the "surprise of the day."

"How can you eat that stuff?" I asked, cutting my Jell-O with the edge of the spoon and piling it in little ridges across the smooth surface.

"I never get sick. Raised in the Louisiana woods. You know some of the old folks still let the dogs lick their plates clean right off the table." I looked at him real hard.

"You're lying, but you do know how to eat," I giggled. "Slim" is my Aunt Beverly's nickname too. She weighs over 300 pounds. When she gets on the scales it reads, "One at a time please."

Slim chuckled and took another bite. "You are a skinny little thing. Maybe I could have mercy and get us some extra chow."

"Christine has eyes all over her head. I can't even sneak a French fry without her pointing her claw at me."

"Tell you what. You meet me by the back door to the kitchen at one o'clock this morning and I'll let you in with my key."

Visions of piles of pulled turkey, roast beef, and cheese triggered saliva and I had to swallow several times before I could answer.

"What if we get caught?" I bit on my thumbnail, my eyes pleading with Slim to somehow pull it off and give me a guarantee we wouldn't be discovered and spend jail time in the meat cooler. Or possibly be strapped to the grill for ten hours while Christine dribbled scrambled eggs over our cuffed wrists.

"The cops would probably laugh. Especially if they ever ate Drew's cooking. Stealing sliced beef isn't a felon. Besides, we'll work in the dark. We're not going to get caught."

"Maybe one of my roommates will come." I pushed my chair from the table and whispered, "I'll be there at one. Be there or be square."

I asked Amy first. She instantly refused to go. "You're crazy. Stealing isn't the way to solve the problem."

Trish passed too. "I'll take a chance on the toilet again. My folks would kill me if I get kicked out of this place. Anyway, I have to be here 'til the end of the season to see C.J. win that gold belt buckle." She was Mormon too, but I never let on that I was.

Belt buckles and over simplification were not good reasons for starvation.

I wanted protein.

As I dropped a solid into the pool table, my heart dropped a notch with the thought of the upcoming heist. I didn't even try to sleep after the curfew bell rang, just sat on my bed in the dark.

Sneaking out was too easy. No chaperones on the doors, no locks on the dormitory and no guard dogs. I snuck around the walls and down the hill to the creaky screen door at the back of the kitchen. Slim was waiting.

I didn't want to get into the yellow light oozing from the porch light. Gnats and mosquitoes swarmed around the bare bulb and I had no desire to be spotlighted. "Let's hurry," I said as Slim pulled out a heavy key ring and poked a long key into the hole.

In seconds, we were inside the kitchen. "No lights remember." Slim touched my arm and I whispered, "I know this kitchen like I know what's in the French toast."

Sliding my arm along the counter, I felt for the clips on the meat cooler and slowly popped the latches back. Right in front, stacked in thin slices, the roast beef waited between sheets of slivered white paper. I reached for a pile and laid some in my hand. I made an order in my head. It called for cheese—cheddar. My hand advanced to the cheese slices. Make that a Dagwood. I added a bunch of turkey and unpeeled some greasy salami slices.

All of these went to Slim and I immediately started one for me. I couldn't wait for the bread as I stuffed meat in like a prisoner of war with real food. Closing the cooler, I led Slim over to the rolls and stuffed several in his pockets and mine. I wanted pickles, but ticking time troubled my conscience.

"Let's split. I eye this stuff all day on my shift. Can't believe we're eating the good stuff and Christine doesn't even know."

Slim and I rendezvoused at the back door three evenings in a row. More confident, we took bigger slabs of meat and wore extra layers with pockets to hide a couple pieces of pie and doughnuts.

As I glopped an egg into the French toast bowl one morning, I honed in on Christine's conversation with the morning supervisor.

"My inventory's off on the meat. I'm showing less than I should."

"You've got to watch these kids. They don't know an extra slice will cost the company."

"I watch every order. Something's going on." Christine looked at me, boring holes into my brain. "We're going to have to step up supervision."

I swallowed dry spit.

Slim and I reviewed the conversation at lunch. "Guess that ends our feasting," he said. "I get enough anyway."

"She can keep her roast beef and slimy turkey. I can live on Jell-O and an occasional slab of bread."

One of the kids would take pity on me once in a while and buy me lunch in the dining room. Everyone knew my views on Drew.

I was thin when I headed down the mountain to start college that fall and had no more appreciation for cowboys than when I saw boots lined under the neighboring cot, but I did know how to flip eggs without a spatula, pour pancakes without any brown circles, and appreciate Jell-O in any flavor.

Playing Deer

My nieces and I walked the path around the campground, stopping to pull apart a tall piece of snake grass and watch a chipmunk scurry up a scraggly pine tree. As they huddled around my pointing finger, I asked them to imagine an animal curled up in the hollow bed of needles under an umbrella overhang of tangled bush. Wondering who could make a home there, voices spoke of rock chucks, chipmunks, coyotes, deer, or even skunks.

My nieces screeched and held their noses.

"You aren't serious, Auntie Cindy."

"I'll protect you. Let them try something."

Remembering how good it felt as a child to lay on our red plaid car robe, smashing a "bed" in the middle of a thick, mature wheat field, I extended my imagination into the evening that night, just as the stars began popping. Still licking remnants of toasted marshmallow from the corners of our lips, we gathered a couple of old blankets and a flashlight for each child and headed out to play "deer."

Holding hands we headed for the secret spot I had noticed on our walk that day. Some of the girls were timidly pointing rays of light straight-ahead, afraid of straying from the path. I heard Kallen ask Kade if remembered the bird nest in Grandma's pine tree. The twin boys leapfrogged ahead and as I called them back to the group, they moaned at our slowness.

I called a halt directly in front of the large clump of foliage twisting around a trio of pines. Directing the kids to shine the light into the sticks and leaves, a hollowed den appeared, covered with rusty colored pine needles. Amid "ooh" and "awesome" we laid down the blankets and one by one crawled through the twigs to crouch inside. Hanging the flashlights up above, an eerie glow warmed our room.

Now, if you were a deer, you'd lie down all curled up like the letter C. I pretended to be the mother deer as the fawns spooned around me, cradled in the quiet space of forest rest. We talked of nature and fairies and woodland nymphs. The smells of pine and waning campfire smoke permeated our play and the moment locked in my heart.

One of the girls wondered if a bear could fit in our den. The others rattled nervously and asked how far we were from camp. I told them bears usually stayed out of these areas because of all the people, but my heartbeat quickened. I decided it might be time to go play a game of Yahtzee and we emerged, like scouts exiting a pup tent. I think I picked up the pace as we headed back to our camper, stars bright, warm night, pure delight.

Wyoming Water and Fire

There was only charcoal left from our lunch bonfire and a few sticky marshmallows dripping off nearby willows. Little footprints headed off in scattered directions and clothes dappled sagebrush branches, drying for the next round of water contact. It was the fourth of July, 1977, and we were at Yellowtail, county 9—water skiing. I'd learned to slalom ski and that time only lost consciousness and my bikini top once as I slammed into the bank in a heap.

Always afraid my kids were going to drown, I nagged them not to go out into the water higher than their shins. Janice, one of my nieces, still remembers me nagging Jonathan to get back to shore before he drowned. It never worked. Most of the time they floated on beached logs and drug moss by the handfuls out of the reeds.

But after many water fights, throwing rocks for Willard, the black lab, and building rafts, the kids were ready for the next phase—the Olsen fireworks. The lake, now placid, the dipping sun spread shimmering light pockets warming certain spots in the water. Like a perfectly made bed, the covers had been lifted, shaken a few times, smoothed, and tucked into the sand. Adults felt the tug to ski off into the sunset one more time, but children can be persuasive.

Willard was in no mood to leave either. He had swam out every time he was called to snag the tow rope and pull the boat to shore. Still sorting rocks to find the right size, he begged to play fetch.

Some folks say that the family dog looks like their owners. I say Willard acted like his.

He soon hopped into the truck, feeling the grit of drying sand like everybody else.

At home, Mother hauled the ice cream machine outside to the sidewalk. My sunburned skin whined a bit, but I headed to the grill. Dad had built it out of brick with adjustable racks that cranked up and down.

Kids swarmed over the silver swing set he had welded, complete with a teeter-totter and custom built horse. The gallant steed's metal head supported his wooden body, its length carrying up to four kids pumping the silver handle back and forth. The other swings were chains with canvas seats, riveted in the perfect contour for little pockets to sit and fly.

That year Dad had seemed to revel even more in the action. Usually he would escape for a breather from the noise and sneak off to the pool hall for a good round of pinochle with his buddies. But that day he stayed and if we headed toward the door to run a quick errand, he'd stop us and say, "Stick around. Let's round up those kids and I'll show them how to burn some snakes." Able to remove a baked pie from the oven with no potholder, Dad knew about fire.

Children wrote their names in the sky with sparklers and when a breeze woofed by and extinguished all the matches, Dad pulled his welding torch from the bed of his truck, struck a blaze and held it to the tips of the fattest sparkler ends—the ones that couldn't be lit with a wimpy match anyway.

Willard had been lapping the children, building himself into a frenzy, evidenced by his wagging tail knocking children off balance and sending them shrieking to the adults to "Make him stop!" As the fountains erupted Willard circled. His curiosity and craziness got the best of him as he raced in, knocking one of the cones over with his nose. We looked to Dad to ban Willard from the firing range, but knew he'd say it would take a blistered nose to end his games.

Jay planted a Roman candle seconds before seven balls would shoot out in succession. Willard grabbed it, just after the second shot. He chomped it sideways in his mouth, running in front of the crowd, explosives blasting like a machine gun.

People ducked their heads in perfect syncopation, like a chorus line dipping one after another. Then Willard rounded the corner, a weapon resembling a square bullet box clamped in his mouth. Most ran for cover, others ran to turn on the hose, as there was a fire in the haystack. The older kids wanted more. The younger kids wanted their moms. Crazy antics with Willard— the dog blessed with a cement skull.

Smoke built as the finale began. Spider veins crawled through the clouds. Balls of color reverberated, warheads burst—pre-mapped by powder patterns loaded in tubes. Tell-tale wrappings littered the ground.

It was Dad's last fourth. Next year the fracas would move up the road to Jay's house.

There never would be another year like 1977.

The Gun

At sixteen, I was absorbed in my own world of mascara, brush rollers, and pink bell-bottoms. Busy doing my schoolwork, I grumbled when Dad commandeered us all to pick the rest of the garden produce. Frost had been forecasted and he needed all available hands to bring in the remaining crop.

Every fall the same ritual was performed, our maestro, the bite in the air—hurrying our efforts—reminding us nature's chorus was changing key. Once outside, the cold made my nose run, dripping into the muddy ground where days before rain had soaked the resting produce.

My fingers stung as I plucked wet tomatoes from the vines, tangled along the ground. Soon stooping had caused a lengthy twinge in my back, but resorting to tugging the cucumber vines up to stomach level, I could relieve the strain. Pulling the prickly ends loose from soggy stems, they tracked dirt down my clothes.

I had traditionally helped with my personal garden duty that spring. Dad and I always planted cucumbers. He shoveled hills while I dropped in tiny white seeds. I now gathered these cucumbers come full circle.

The garden unburdened, we all returned to warmth, rubbing stiff fingers, sloughing wet apparel in the utility room. After a hot bath, I could finish my homework. It was quiet—all the kids in bed. I glanced at my watch, gauging how much work I had to do before I could curl into bed myself. Paddling to the kitchen for a drink of water I thought I heard the words, "That sounded like a gun." Curious, I headed toward the living room. Before I could ask any questions, Dad was by my side instructing, "Cindy, get in your room, there's someone outside firing a gun." Scuffing his heavy work boots across the tile, he hurried to the closet for his rifle.

Knowing my father could overreact; I had to see for myself what triggered his fear. Nudging my way past him, I peered out the back door into the driveway. My boyfriend sat in the passenger's side of a car I had never seen before, facing a kid I didn't know.

"It's Kenny. I've got to go see him," I said, as I reached for the handle.

My dad, visibly shaken, reached out to stop me. Mother had joined us in the hall. "Vern, put your rifle up. We should call the police."

"I'll run them off with this," he said, lifting the rifle in the air.

"It's just the car back firing," I argued.

"Don't you leave this house. Those boys have been drinking."

"How do you know? Kenny's come all the way from Cody. I have to talk to him."

Spinning around, I shot down the hall, through the living room and out the front door. Running down the sidewalk, I reached the driveway just as the car peeled out into the highway.

I could hear my dad's footsteps close behind and shouted as I ran after the vehicle, "He's not going to hurt me. I just want to talk to him."

"Come back."

"No," I volleyed over my shoulder, still running, Dad in close pursuit.

I knew that I could outrun him, but guilt sponged over me. Dad had not been well. However, my need to be in Kenny's presence outweighed Dad's problems. I kept running. I had to see him and I was determined to prove there was no gun in that car. He was my first love, the boy who kissed with movie star gusto. I was in love.

Kicking up gravel, I soon touched the highway, brushing the mailboxes as I rounded the corner toward town. Out-distancing my dad, I could see him falling back. He turned back to retrace his steps—walking now, but I kept going, determined to catch those guys.

I recognized the car I'd seen out the back window as it screeched to a halt at the end of the secondary intersecting the highway. Approaching Kenny's open window, I spotted his tipped beer. His curly hair brushed his eyebrow. He winked at me as he motioned me nearer.

"Hi, how in the heck are ya?" His standard greeting assuring me of his love.

"What are you guys doing?" I asked, between gasps. "Why didn't you stop and come in?" I could smell alcohol fumes on his breath. Dad had been right.

Kenny lowered the can and pointed to his comrade, saying his cousin had just gotten into town and they were just putting down a couple beers.

"So why didn't you come in?"

"Thought maybe you were asleep."

"You guys have really upset my Dad. Do you have a gun in there?

"Nah, we don't even own a gun. It's Wheeler's car making the noise. Just come for a ride with us."

"No, I can't, I know my dad is still looking for me."

Kenny turned to his cousin, instructing him, "Let's go to the Downtowner, we're out of beer anyway."

"Call me Friday," I pleaded. The car peeled out again just as Dad and Mother pulled up in our old Buick. "Get in the car," Dad said, breathing heavily.

"Don't you know you could have been hurt?" Dad began, turning the car around.

"I can take care of myself. Just take me home. I didn't go with him, did I?"

"Your dad only wants to protect you," Mother added, her voice firm. He shouldn't have been running down the highway in the dark. Neither one of you should have."

"Where are we going?" I asked as he passed our turn off and drove further into the country.

"I've got to calm down. I can't run like I used to. Had to get the car out to catch you."

"You didn't need to run after me at all."

"That boy is a drinker. You need to stay clear of him." As he raised one hand from the wheel, he shook his fist at the front window. "I wanted to punch him."

Mother once again tried to calm him. "Now, Vern, you can't do that. She's safe now."

As he slowly brought down the fist, he opened it to slide his hand across his chest.

"Dixie, my chest hurts," he told my mother.

"Is it bad?" she leaned over to touch his shoulder, repeating again, "Neither one of you should have been running down the highway."

Scared, I imagined doctors resuscitating Dad in the cold hallway of the emergency unit.

"Stop the car and we'll get you to the hospital. I didn't mean for you to get sick," I told him as I leaned forward and put my hand on his shoulder.

"I need water," he said, pulling over. As the car crunched dried hay stubs on the edge of the barrow pit, Dad stopped and put the car in gear. After opening the door, he stumbled through the grass and dropped. His crouching form sought relief as he edged closer to the irrigation ditch. Cupping his hands, he drank mouthfuls of seedy water to smother the pain.

He was only 45 years old. I had won the footrace, but prayed my dad was still in the battle. Guilt undulated along my skeleton, halted only by my continuing worry. His retching coughs spasmed as he hung his head in the weeds.

Mother emitted a small "Oooh."

As his stomach quieted, he dipped for another gulp of water, and then stood, slipping back inside the car. His shirt was wet from dripping water and he gripped his chest like he was forcing out an embedded arrow.

Through the dim light from the overhead bulb, his white skin mottled, and as Mother touched his forehead, she raised her voice commanding him to "change places and let me drive you to the hospital."

"No, I'm going home. I'll be ok, I just need to lay down."

I sat in silence, remorse my only ally.

Quiet as the eye of a tornado, we returned to the house. Dad rushed to the refrigerator, grabbed a jar of sweet pickles and crunched each one, then downed all the syrup. The brine's acid seemed to always settle the erupting bile. Pushing a mound of ripened tomatoes away, he leaned on the counter, his empty pickle jar touching his arm; only cloves and spices left clinging inside the jar.

I sat at the kitchen table, arms folded, doodling a few stray grains of salt across the plastic cloth with one finger.

"I'm sorry Dave," I said, using the nickname I saved for when I really wanted something.

"I wish we were back in the garden picking cucumbers."

Deep down I knew those two had a gun.

Pumpkin Pie and Gooseberries

We lived eight miles from Cody on a hill above the alkali flats. The neighbors to the north were parents of an only child. Gilbert was large for his age, freckle-faced, and older than his years.

I liked the kid. His green, somewhat crossed eyes, endeared him to me as well as to his cat, Leonard. Leonard had the exact same green, somewhat crossed eyes. He was as big as any housecat I'd ever seen. As white as dry ice and as evasive as a cricket chirping in the next room.

One summer day I got a craving for turkey—Thanksgiving style. I was willing to put the time into making a feast. I even made pumpkin pies and cut up little veggies to serve with French-onion dip. The smell was powerful—remembrances of Thanksgiving dinner, turkey liver—Aunt Beverly thumping around the house.

I sat the food on the counter and went to tidy up for the feast. Maybe ten minutes passed. As I headed to the back door to holler for all the family, I stopped, unable to take in the scene.

The smell must have been scintillating to another guest—an uninvited one. Sitting ON the pumpkin pie, Leonard was feasting on our dinner—shredding turkey meat between his teeth. He was a fast eater—half the thing was gone. For a split second he stared at me, those green, somewhat crossed eyes flaring. He jumped, landed on his feet and sped through the open front door. Yep, the door was open. The door was open?

Gilbert and Dustin were dueling with wooden swords down in the driveway. They proclaimed total innocence as I inquired into the matter.

Ten minutes later, Jonathan ran into the living room to ask if dinner was ready. I pointed to the counter.

"Someone left the front door open," I said. "And that dad-burned Leonard ran out chomping on the turkey."

He ran to his bedroom as fast as Leonard had run out the door.

I heard his voice rise once again in fervent prayer.

The next spring another family moved to the east of us. The father was a retired Hell's Angel; the mother, a mental health counselor. Do opposites really attract? I loved to go down to their house to see all his biker souvenirs and weird medieval collection.

They had two kids, one son named Michael, and one daughter, named Lucy—very close in age. The kids were shy and a bit sneaky. The two would come up the lane to check out our ducks, Hanky and Panky, and play with our dog, Peaches. Sometimes I wouldn't see them for weeks, then I'd see their eyeballs peeking around every corner.

One day, I came home to find at least six police cars, two fire engines and a herd of men standing around the water pump hole in front of their house. Someone (some kid someone, I bet) had removed the cover and Lucy had fallen into the 6 foot pipe casing. One leg was bent under and she was jammed tight. Her head was at least two feet below the surface. I wondered if she was playing spy and got in deeper than her imagination. It wasn't long before the men had he out.

Mike and Lucy also liked to come up and pick green gooseberries off our bushes by the retaining wall. I knew they loved them, seemingly as much as our kids loved to sneak gooseberries off their grandma's bushes. I never told the two to scram.

I'm pretty sure they had gooseberries on their minds one Sunday afternoon. Carl headed to church for early meetings and I drove our

Subaru wagon in with the kids. A warm spring day, I had thought about skipping, but what kind of an example would that have been.

After the services, Carl had another meeting and I wanted out of there, so we didn't hang around. I drove down the main lane, pulled into our group of homes, turned a quick left. On automatic pilot, the smoke didn't really register until I was almost to the scene. Fire engulfed the whole gooseberry bush and was burning toward the huge pine tree in the turn-around. Once again, I ran to the turn on the pump in the back to get more water pressure. Jonathan ran off to get the neighbor, and between the neighbor's hose and ours, we doused the fire.

After the smoke and flames were nothing but steam, I peeked into the crime scene. Yep, a couple of separate handfuls of scorched gooseberries lay in piles on the ground. A few remnants of stick matches scattered at the scene were evidence enough, but Mike and Lucy never confessed. I interrogated them face to face. "Nope, we weren't even around your house."

Soon after, Carl drove up the road and stopped to check it out.

"Where's Jonathan?" he asked.

"He's innocent this time," I muttered. "There's a consensus among us that most likely, although they haven't been proven guilty, the neighbor kids have been at it again."

"It's some kind of a sign," he said. "Do you realize you just got home from church and now have witnessed your very own burning bush?"

Amen—and amen.

Snow Plows

Bronchitis.

But I was determined to go to Vale, Colorado to ski. The president of the newspaper chain Carl worked for had set up a three day holiday at one of his friend's condos. Sounded exciting, classy—fireplace logs burning into the night. (cough cough)

We had tried out the slopes at our local ski resort that year, primitive but functional. One would sit on a wooden circle attached to a rope while being towed up the hill. Novices, Carl and I had more fun watching our kids ski down, then take lessons or practice on our own. Six-year-old Dustin, showing no fear, *snowplowed* straight down the hill over and over.

Well, even if I didn't ski on this trip, I could say I had been to Vale. I bought a blue ski outfit and packed. I threw in a new blue-knitted cap covered in white snowflakes, warm thermals, and my inhaler. (cough cough) Carl wasn't going to commit to the sport of skiing just yet, so he broke down and bought a pair of jeans.

Carl drove, I coughed—until we climbed higher in elevation. I alternated between coughing and complaining. I'd been on plenty of snowy Wyoming roads in the dead of winter. Ones where Carl had to stick his head out the window to spot reflector poles. I'd traveled with him over mountain passes hauling our home-made trailer, *Big Bird,* full of band equipment. I politely held my screams until we had finished fishtailing through ice patches. The trailer was sky blue, a carefully outlined white dove painted on each side, an olive branch sticking from both beaks. I believe it was Carl's statement to the sixties—symbol of peace.

I wasn't mellow or polite at all this time. Snow was falling, flakes bigger than industrial-sized cotton balls. We made our own tracks in foot-deep snow—visibility—zip. Where were the snowplows? I didn't even want a fireplace. My lungs were burning enough, ribs aching more every time I coughed. (and coughed) Too bad I forgot to pack my prescription cough syrup. With a couple tablespoons of that, I'd feel happy to cough.

"Cindy, we're fine. We've been through a lot worse roads," Carl said.

"Just pull over. We'll sleep in the car," I replied.

"I told you I didn't think you should go on this trip, but you insisted. We're almost there. I haven't wrecked you yet."

When I wasn't opening my jaws to cough, my teeth were clenched so tightly I had a headache. We came in about one in the morning—our usual travel arrival time.

All night I tossed on the bed, sure I was still on the road, my eyelashes batting snowflakes, my teeth grinding ice.

My bronchitis was some better the next morning.

"You look like you're feeling better," Carl said. "Everyone else left for breakfast, but I wanted to let you sleep."

"I dreamed the whole night that we were swerving through killer snow," I said.

I sensed he didn't want me to go into details as I have a habit of pinning him down in the mornings to listen to my long, boring renditions of dreamland.

"Let's try the wanna-be hill a few times. The rest of them are showing off on black diamond runs all day."

Hauling my new skis over my shoulder, I felt like I fit in. The snowflakes running down my ski mask were so tiny they were more like rain. We practiced on the bunny hill the whole morning. Of course, we were initiated by falling several times, but it was fun.

After lunch, I admitted that I wanted to try the big girl slopes.

"Are you sure you want to go up there? You know, you do have to ski down."

"Yes, dear. I understand the logistics," I said.

"You're on. Let's hit the slopes. We're ready for the green trails."

At the top, the folks in the chair in front scooted and skied off. In seconds, we were next, the drop off much steeper than I had pictured. I knew how to turn, glide, snowplow to slow down. I hoped I knew how to dismount without running off a cliff.

"It's scarier up here than I thought," I told Carl.

"Just relax. I know you can do it. Want to try a black run?"

I glared at him.

The next thing I knew I was traversing across a fairly easy hill. Back and forth, I had the rhythm and the balance. Carl was doing better than I, of course. He was kind of cute whipping around those turns.

"Let's go again," he said. "Are you up for it?"

I had been coughing harder and my legs were getting tired, but I didn't want to waste the chance.

"I can do one more run. How about the same one we just went down?" I asked.

He was already ahead of me moving toward the lift.

This time when the chair reached the top, I felt panic setting in. What's up with this? I thought. We'll sail down and then have a totally tubular dinner with the crew.

"Come over this way," Carl called. "There's an intermediate trail that looks great."

I skied over and looked down. I crossed my poles. "No way."

"Ah, come on. I know you can do this."

He took off.

I looked over the hill and… coughed. Suddenly, I didn't like skiing and I didn't want to go down some dumb mountain. What had I been thinking? Carl was around the corner waiting for me. I had been straining every muscle to slip down that mountain, without actually skiing. Panicked, I would traverse and instead of turning and going down, I turned up the mountain and stopped, clinging uphill as long as my muscles would let me.

"Honey, you've been doing great. Just let go and ski," Carl said when I finally reached him.

"I let go and I'll have two broken legs and be in traction until the Fourth of July. I'm not going down that mountain."

"You have to go down. You can't stay here all night. I'll ski a ways farther down and wait for you to catch up."

I now had a death grip on my poles, digging them in so hard I might have hit pay dirt. I just could not force myself to traverse that mountain. Pointing my skis straight down was suicide.

I took my skis off, put them over my shoulder and walked. No shame, no dishonor, I was going to live to see my children again.

Carl waited for me at the bottom.

"Well, you solved that problem, Loucie. Let's go get ready for dinner."

Retelling stories of the day, one of the other editors at our table launched into a laugh. "Hey, at lunch I was looking out at the bunny slope and saw all these blue stripes up and down the hill. I finally figured it out. Somebody must have hit the snow (literally) wearing new blue jeans.

I looked at Carl. He looked at me. I looked at Mr. Observant. "That's hilarious," I said.

Carl quipped, "Someone was skiing a blue streak."

The skis are even on the ground. Just look at that form.

Shopping Carts are Evil

You've heard those women who sneer, "I've raised my kids and I'm not raising my grandkids. I've done my duty; they can raise their own kids." And then I reply, "You bunch of wimps." They know I take care of my grand boys five days a week—six-year-old Tristan, and two-year-old, Jett, a rascal extraordinaire.

Stuff happens and Jonathan and Amber needed my help. I adore the boys, glad that I get "overs," employing more patience and skill than I did the first go-around. But I must admit one week I nearly defected to the wimps.

The first thing Jett always says when I get him out of the car seat (all thirty five pounds of him) is "run away."

"No you're not going to run, you're going to be a good boy and stay with Grandma." He's obsessed with tractors and I bribe him with two new ones if he behaves. I'm in luck. The sidewalk is just a step over the curb and right in front of the Dollar Store door I spot it, a small shopping cart with a kid seat. The force is with me. In fact, there are two carts, twisted side by side, braced against the wind. No problem. I hoist him into position over the holes, but he isn't going to cooperate. He sticks both legs in one hole and I begin to tug. Struggling, I almost have him lifted to freedom when the cart catches his shoe and starts rolling straight for a van parked smack in the front of the cart.

I try to swing the cart away, but with Jett's awkward position, and me totally off balance trying to keep him from launching onto the sidewalk, I fail. The cart bumps the front of the van. That's when I notice a lady sitting in the driver's seat watching the whole slapstick routine. Oh no. Apology due. I silently run through my spiel and grit my teeth.

I try to swing the cart away and place it parallel with the sidewalk. Bad choice. The shopping cart's partner rolls straight to the same spot on the woman's van. Oh no, matching scratches.

She finally gets out. I'm having a hard time here," I utter.

"I see that," she says.

"I'm so sorry," I mutter. "I hope there aren't any dents."

"These carts are pretty light. I think we're fine.

You might be fine, I think. Why didn't you step out of that car and help me in the first place? With that nine-seated van, you must have hauled gaggles of kids to the dollar store. May the bird of Paradise Fly up Your Nose I think, and where's an elephant when you need it? Jett's screaming by this time, and the wind handicap has won, but I'm still trying to jockey two unwieldy carts to the front door.

"Just let me do it," the woman finally says. "You go ahead."

Her little irritated tone could have been averted, if she would have only helped. Maybe she wanted to see an old lady wrestling with her grandson because her own mother told her she would never babysit her grandkids.

Everyone that knows me could tell you I was not going to give up finding Jett a tractor (or two). Determined, I worked my way down the center of the toy isle so Jett couldn't reach either side and stopped in front of the tractors. No problems, he chose the green one and started peeling off the wrapping. I rounded the corner to the cleaning product aisle. Coming straight at me, another shopping cart, and who do you think they be? (Hint, it wasn't the butcher, the baker OR the candle stick maker.) It was van woman.

Embarrassed, I muttered something like "Don't get close to me. I don't have a license for this thing." She smirked and rolled away as I picked up Jett's tractor from the floor. He'd tried to open it but had only ripped off the top. The bar code was still there. No sweat. One little tear is nothing compared to car dents. I pushed the offending cart over to check out, paid, and lifted Jett out.

Please don't let me run into the van woman one more time. (Literally) Once outside, I sneaked a peak for would-be dents. Conscience clear, I whisked Jett into his car seat. I admit I was breathing hard, my back ached, but I wasn't about to declare wimp-hood.

I waited quite a while to risk another runaway cart episode, but I needed groceries and Tristan and Jett could come along. What could be so hard? Steer the cart down the middle, remain calm at all times. Enjoy the outing.

Jett put both legs in the cart in different holes! Off to a magnificent start. Like Sesame Street grocery lists, I repeated in my mind. Bread—milk—baby food. Bread—milk—baby food. No tractor toys this time.

Tristan pointed at something he wanted on the very first shelf we passed and I lost my focus. Why couldn't this have been the cereal aisle? Pickles weren't even on the list.

Crash.

Splinter.

Splash.

Immediately vinegar assaulted my nose, but it took a few seconds to register that my sweet little grandson had managed to reach a jar of dill pickles and drop it on the floor. I started sweating.

No way to cover this one up. My conscience wouldn't allow me to run.

"Tristan, watch Jett for a minute while I run down to the check stands and find someone to clean this up."

I triple checked that my cart was in the middle and warned Tristan not to move it.

Ta-dah-da-da-dah-da. Once again "Chariots of Fire" song lyrics accompanied my sluggish legs. And then I saw him—a guy with a red apron and store badge.

"Sorry, my grandson dropped a bottle of pickles right down this aisle. It's got to be dangerous."

"Don't worry mam; I'll get it cleaned up right away."

Run for our lives. No one will know if we split the scene, but once again, I had a mission and I wasn't going to be a quitter. I was not repeating this event the next day. I can do this, I thought.

"Tristan, you're being so good, want to push Jett to the baby food aisle?"

Bet you think he rammed his little brother into another disaster, but he actually was a better driver than I.

"Jett, do you want some yogurt treats and mac 'n cheese?"

"Roni, roni, roni," he chanted, adding a couple of rounds of "tractor, tractor, tractor."

Well now, things were going well, no more grabbing and throwing. I threw in a couple of toddler meals and looked around for something else he would eat. He was between baby and people food and spit out any kind of pureed, mushy, or bland bites.

"I know, Tristan," I said. "Jett liked those little Vienna sausages I tried the other day. I got out the catsup and that did the trick."

"Okay, then can we get some fruit snacks and leave?" he asked.

"Yes, I've had enough for"—I said as I reached for two Vienna sausage jars. Just as I got out "one day"—Jett reached for the jars and because I didn't have a good grip on the two, they crashed to the floor.

"Grandma, you're in trouble," Tristan said.

"Oh, oh," Jett said.

I didn't say a word.

No way was I going to track down the guy in the red apron again. He was probably still inhaling pickle juice.

"Tristan, run find a guy to clean up this mess, but make sure it's a different guy from the first one. Make sure now. I'll meet you at the checkout counter."

He ran.

I ran, pushing Jett on the ride of his life.

Once again my conscience told me to pay for all that floor food. I got in line with a checker I didn't know and rattled off the sin list.

"Okay," she said. No other words escaped her lips.

No words escaped mine either. I didn't even repeat my phone number for the rewards card.

"Grandma, do you think they'll let us back in that store?" Tristan asked.

"Not until Jett is at least five," I muttered as I strapped Jett back into his car seat.

Cat Nap

It had been a long day at work—number one client whining, late lunch, messages jabbed on my spindle in reams. I couldn't let the crew see me sweat, so I applied the old saying about the duck swimming peacefully on top, feet paddling beneath. I let my anxiety out through my feet, tapping under my desk like a jack hammer.

I picked up the phone with my professional voice, "*Yellowstone Printing*, how may I help you."

"Mom, I filled up the tub to give my cat a bath and I got really tired and laid down."

"That's great son," I said. "You have scouts tonight. Rest a while."

Wait a minute, my son does not report his naps. "Jonathan, what's going on? Where's the cat?"

"I went to sleep and there's just a small hole in the laundry room ceiling."

Don't panic, I told myself as I envisioned him lying on our bed upstairs, bathwater gushing over the tub only a few feet from him. A little water is easy to clean up, but--did he say hole?

My toes were tapping like a machine gun on the front line. *Oh boy, I'll..........*

"I cleaned up most of the water. Oh, mom, I used all the towels to mop it up. I put them in the dryer, but it won't go on."

Wait a minute. The dryer is downstairs, directly under that bathtub. A trickle would not be on the laundry room floor, a flood would. My feet were now frozen in place. Let the world see my icy sweat. "Listen to me carefully. Back out of the laundry room. I'll come home. Anddddd stay out of there."

He's alive, he's alive, and that's all that matters. I've done multiple damage control with this child before.

I hadn't even thought about the cat. Had it drowned and been quickly buried in the yard? No, he was probably curled up right cozy on the bed in our room. How long had Jonathan and Rover been asleep?

Racing up the driveway, I entered the laundry room, through the garage. It was worse than I could have ever imagined. Water was still dripping from a hole in the ceiling the size of a kettle drum, landing on the dryer. It was nearly two inches deep on the floor. The situation was exacerbated because the builder had sloped the drain uphill. I knew we should have reported him to the carpenters union, the police, or *someone.* I waded through and pulled open the dryer. A load of wet towels filled the cavern. Jonathan could have been electrocuted.

I needed to hug him, and then thump him on the noggin.

Towels were draped over the top, down the side, on the floor and out the door onto the basement carpet. A damp smell drifted around the room.

Looking around more, four or five inches of water had crawled up the sheet rock and across the mopboards, clear to the bathroom.

Dollar signs poked my eyeballs.

The dryer unplugged, I started to clean. The towels were so heavy it would take a crane to get them into the washer. I ran upstairs to call Carl.

"We've got a little problem in the laundry room."

"What did he do now?" he asked.

I explained as gently as I could, but I think he visualized the destruction. "How much is this one going to cost me?"

Jonathan was on his bed looking mighty humble. Rover was on his belly, snoozing away.

"Do you think Dad will let me keep my cat?" He asked.

Jonathan had not even tried to dry the carpet by the upstairs bathtub, the scene of the crime. I found where the water had settled and broken through to the laundry room. Sheet rock on all four sides of the linen closet bulged from the mopboards.

I wished my stressful day had continued at work, not here standing in water and rotting sheetrock.

"I'll just cut out the floorboards and we can have a laundry chute right above the washer," Carl said, as he studied the linen closet damage. "I've thought of doing that already. Save you lots of time hauling dirty clothes down the stairs. You can shoot them right on top of the dryer." Didn't he realize most of the time I set the laundry basket at the top of the stairs and gave it a shove anyway?

He sawed out the area only to find a 2x4 blocking any chance of dropping clothes. Weeks later he hired an out-of-work carpenter

Jonathan has always loved animals.

to come patch the ceiling and put new sheet rock up around the mopboards. Was this guy a cousin to the no-show house sider? The job was botched. Perfatape bulged around the hole in the ceiling. He hadn't spackled the sheet rock or painted it so we had a lovely souvenir of the whole escapade. Carrrrrrrlll.

I think I passed my "bad little girl" genes on to our youngest son.

Shriners' Cakes

The Park County Fair was still an important part of my life, despite the fact that there were fewer and fewer two-headed pickled cow jars, fat ladies, or snake-eating weirdo side shows.

Monika had been in 4-H since she was old enough to join, I made sure of it. She advanced through sewing flowered aprons, to wool suits. From chocolate cookies, to fancy cakes. It was fair time again. The call came for cakes for the cake walk and she jumped in.

"Let's get out the decorator tips," I suggested.

"Okay, I learned how to make a crumb coat, I can probably handle those."

"You pick the theme," I said.

Several topics later, she had it. Most of the cake walkers would be little kids. There was a carnival on the fairgrounds, why not make it a clown cake?

"Sounds great."

Of course we made the cake from scratch. "Oh no," Monika said. "We only have one egg."

"Not to worry, there's fresh eggs right up the walk," I told her.

When we bought the house, Carl immediately had to have baby chicks. He announced the name of our three-acre ranch the day the chicks arrived in the cheeping cardboard boxes. The name was............*Oleo Acres*, one of the cheaper spreads.

He never did get the sign made.

We kept two ducks named Hanky and Panky, a few dozen chickens, and a couple of turkeys named Wishbone and Drumstick. Our lop-eared rabbit, Thumper, was the cutest critter on the place.

We had a lot of tourist shops in Cody and many carried the latest mythical animals—stuffed jack rabbits sporting tiny pairs of deer or antelope horns—jackalopes. All the tourists thought they were a specific breed.

One day the boys went to the hutch and found Thumper dead. Unbeknownst to me, Carl had the taxidermist stuff him, add a pair of deer horns and touted him as a jackaLOP. I wouldn't have known about this travesty, but the taxidermist called me to say "Carl's rabbit is ready to pick up."

"What rabbit?"

He didn't?!!

"You'll have to ask Carl about it," the animal stuffer said.

Carl showed me Thumper one time only. He thought he could trick some tourist into buying him for big bucks. I thought Thumper was much cuter alive.

Well, Thumper was stuffed, but we had nice laying hens up in the coop.

"Monika, run outside and gather a couple eggs. You'll have the yellowest cake there." I was always a bit hesitant to use fresh eggs, but Carl insisted they were safe since the chickens roamed the alfalfa field eating pure bugs—no additives.

The cake came out of the oven deep-yellow perfect. Monika laid a smooth crumb coat and went in for the frosting. Piping a nice lace bead around the top, we declared it a blue ribbon winner. Maybe even grand champion.

Until we got to the clowns.

Squeezing a ribbon of plump frosting for a body, we held our breaths and waited. The blob remained sitting on the edge. "I have a

Not clowning around, she won!

great idea," Monika said. "I'll pipe some legs dangling down the side. Classy. Now for the head and pointy hat."

"Squeeze a dob of blue on the point to look like a pompom," I said, as the clown body began to sink. "It will firm up."

"It's definitely not the 4-H way," Monika said as she squeezed a nice little pink face and changed tubes for the hat. Before the tip was even a possibility, the frosting flattened.

"Oh, my, gosh." I started laughing uncontrollably. "It looks like one of those Shriner dudes riding in their electric turtles in the Fourth of July parade. Can't you just see their flat-top hats with the tassels flapping in the breeze?" I literally had to sit on the floor to keep from laughing myself dizzy.

Monika smiled. Demure little girl with a mother on the floor.

We scraped off the clown, got another tip and added more powdered sugar. This time when she squeezed, the little bodies held. We even found some tiny umbrellas to set off the clowns.

She won a blue ribbon. The cake was definitely baked the 4-H way.

She Squealed

A first year schoolteacher, on the lowest pay scale in the state, Carl struggled in Shoshoni, Wyoming, population, five hundred. In addition to teaching English, he drove the school bus, was the junior class sponsor, watched over the AV equipment and was the yearbook coordinator. Even though these extra time-takers added a few dollars, his monthly salary barely covered the essentials, forcing me to stretch his check in every direction.

Five dollars in my wallet was a luxury, like silk lace on flour sack undies. Monika and I were headed to the "big" town thirty miles away for some groceries. I had five dollars, spending money for the whole month. I didn't really want to blow it, but my stomach decided I would. Monika, just a toddler, followed me into Kentucky Fried Chicken. Catching a whiff of grease as I held open the door, I explained our dining-out adventure as we entered, the occasion taking on proportions of Roman banquet tables, heavy with gigantic drumsticks and barrels of succulent potatoes.

Monika, delighted with a small drumstick, giggled as I lifted the Jell-O lid, wiggling the cherry color, promising it was all hers. Original coating seasoned over my wing dinner, guarded the tender meat of my memory.

Not wanting to hear the teasing and, "I didn't get any chicken," I didn't mention the stop to Carl.

The next monthly grocery run, Carl was with us. Holding my breath as we rolled by the restaurant, I silently chortled over our escapade. Standing on the console in our Plymouth Duster, balancing between us, Monika suddenly pointed her finger at a familiar red and black sign and excitedly spouted, "Tucky Chicky. Tucky Chicky," until her dad paid attention.

I cringed.

"A-ha, how does she know about Kentucky Fried Chicken?" he asked.

My cover blown, I admitted to our extravagance and after the anticipated whining, "I didn't get any," he laughed, hugged his curly blonde baby and bragged about how well his daughter could talk, how smart she was to pick out the Colonel, and how cute to tattle tell on her mother.

***

When Monika turned five, Carl couldn't help adding stories about five-year-old Monika's antics in his bi-weekly newspaper column:

> My Kindergartener, Monika, was quizzing me last night. "What did God make people out of?"
>
> "Dirt," I responded, feeling sure that she had learned something new in Sunday school.
>
> "No, Daddy, you're wrong. Formulas."

Same year, different column, Carl included another five-year-old fear that she passed along to her brother.

> Monika came home the other day reporting that, "If we don't quit walking across that lot, the PRINCIPAL is going to GET US!" No doubt a terrifying thought for one kindergartner who has never seen the principal. Later in the evening, as two-year-old son, Dusty, was having trouble falling asleep, he asked, "Will the 'prince-pal' get me?"
>
> "No son."
>
> "He be nice?"—"Yes son."
>
> "Can I ride the prince-pal?"—"No son."

Strange how those childhood fears get started.

And our little girl made it into another column, as Carl wrote;

Women movie stars have long been a mystery to us all. They are forever getting up in the morning with perfectly groomed hair. Monika has it figured out though. She went to bed with her cotton bonnet on. Why? "Because those girls in 'Little House on the Prairie' wore theirs to bed, and when they got up they didn't have any tangles."

He tattled again to his reading public:

Cindy had just taken her hair rollers out Sunday, and Monika was admiring one of the cone-shaped ringlets produced thereby.

"Your hair sure is neat, Mommy. It looks just like a tornado!"

And, the last one I kept a clipping of—

Children have the perfect solution to almost everything. Cindy was feeling bad about her softball team's loss last week, and Monika asked why she was so sad. After receiving a proper explanation, she suggested, "Gee, Mom, why don't you just join the other team—they won!"

Oil Barrels and Enquiring Minds

Carl and I were in love. But, introducing him to my family made me nervous. We decided to go on a Saturday afternoon when all the kids would be out of school. Hoping out of his old Ford, we rounded the corner by the lilac bush, just in time to see two of my younger sisters wrestling over an oil barrel. Cheri won, after pushing Christie hard enough to knock her into the stinky ooze. As Christie fought her way to air, she shot out of the fallen barrel and slid on the slick grass, belly-first through prisms of blue and brown.

Mother came from the garbage barrels, her pants plastered with chicken feathers, remnants of a still warm hen she had been plucking. She headed toward the mayhem to separate opponents and directed us into the house. I held my breath, hoping my brother, Jay Tony wasn't gnawing on another bone. He was the only one who got steak around our house, always after a wrestling meet. He'd scarf them down, on the edge of starvation. His breakfast had consisted of half of a fried egg. No lunch or dinner at all. At practice he'd bury himself under the rubber wrestling mats to sweat off more ounces to make weight.

Not to worry. He wasn't even home—off with one of his buddies pheasant hunting.

I held Carl's hand and headed for—whatever. Cathy, the youngest, had been going through her standing-on-her-head phase for weeks. Obsessed with timing, she wasn't about to break her record to meet her sister's boyfriend. After asking several times, Mother got her to land and hop to her feet, her skirt and braids falling into place. She then set her vocal chords into cow mode and mooed in the most authentic imitation imaginable. Maybe she would grow up to be a cow girl.

Christie had long since run into the house. Usually she was so quiet. One could easily find her curled up in a ball in an overstuffed chair reading a book.

Just my luck, Cheri had succeeded in luring her outside just at the WRONG time.

Things bore a tentative calm and Carl seemed resilient, even amused. I heard Dad's work boots on the linoleum before I saw him. Heard his lunch box hit the snack bar and then his call, "Dixie." He walked into the living room, work boots and all, and as Carl stood to shake his outstretched hand, Dad said, "I'm hungry. Are you? Let's get us a glass of bread and milk and onions."

Carl politely declined.

"Good for your liver they say," Dad cajoled.

Dad got sick of repetitive meals, especially when Mother got in a groove and stayed for weeks at a time on one menu. She fessed up that Dad had left her a "love" note in his lunchbox a few weeks before.

Please discontinue chicken noodle soup until further notice.

Love Vern

He'd get a craving sometimes after work and stop at the grocery store. We LOVED those evenings. He would bring home paper sacks full of great food: potato chips, pickled peppers, tins of sardines and kippers, olives, cookies, and my favorite—pickled pig's feet. I don't think Carl knew about our secret delicacies rebellion.

Love me, love my family.

Dad finished his milk. I hoped Carl hadn't gotten too close because I'd been blasted with his bread, milk, and onion breath many a time.

I was in the bedroom trying to talk some lady-like behavior into my sisters. Cathy was searching between the mattresses where she hid her candy stash. Cheri was petting the cat, and Christie was innocently curled up in another chair.

Taking a deep breath I headed back to find Carl. I heard Dad interrogating him. "You go to college where Cindy goes? Get an education. Don't get stuck out in the oil patch, eating chicken noodle soup every day. What are you going into?"

Carl told him about his English major, but they got into a good discussion about Carl's photography passion.

"I've seen some of the photos you take," Dad said. "Good pictures of Cindy."

"Your daughter is a great subject. I spend lots of time in the school's dark room."

I didn't mention that I spent a lot of time tracking him down to that same darkroom.

"What kind of a car do you drive?" Dad asked.

"An old Ford Galaxy," Carl replied, both of us wondering where this was going.

"Would you go to the gas station and pick me up a *National Enquirer*? My enquiring mind wants to know." He handed Carl some coins.

Dad's funny, I thought. Maybe Carl would remember that and not all the other antics my sisters had pulled. Besides, I wanted out of there before Mother started burning pin feathers on that just-plucked chicken. She used the gas burners on the kitchen stove and the stink always drove me out of the house. On plucking-eating chicken days I feasted on potatoes only.

Back in the car, I waited for the family review. Carl sat laughing. "Your dad is great," he said, "but do your sisters always act like that?"

Years after our wedding day, Mother told me that after the third round of "Cindy photos" Carl had taken out to Dad, he had said to her, "That's the one she'll marry."

Fathers know best.

Carl and I during the time of the "introduction.

Coincidence?

Grumbling parents complain about their kids moving back home. We pulled the reverse and moved into OUR daughter's home after the untimely demise of our business. We lived in an apartment in Monika Bill's, basement. I tended their four kids while Monika finished her degree at BYU and then entered law school. Carl hunted for a job for three years and learned what most people think of anyone… at, or over fifty.

One day he went for an interview with a small startup company. It was a demanding set of qualifications, targeted at someone who had experience in multiple roles. The guy was in flip flops and cutoffs. Carl in a suit. The dude looked Carl up and down and said, "Actually, we were looking for someone a bit 'newer.'"

At a well-established software company looking for a PR and marketing writer, the manager surmised, "I don't think you would be challenged by this job. You could do the job 110% today. We're looking for someone who can do 20% and would be challenged by the other 80."

Another interview in downtown Salt Lake City started out more encouraging. They invited Carl to bring in his resume. "Yes. He'd like to see you now," the receptionist said. The recruiter, head shaved except for the goatee, in the style of the day, was pondering Carl's resume. But then he looked up, paused, and passed it back across the desk. "I don't see anything here that is relevant for this job."

Carl later told me the details. "Not being relevant. That was the heart breaker. All of the experience, the accolades and awards of years, but none of it relevant." He had then walked across the street to the exquisite architecture of the Joseph Smith Building. He sat on one of the concrete planters a few feet from a homeless fellow holding a cardboard sign, "Will work for food."

Me too, thought husband, we're just going about it different ways. A few tears dripped down his nose onto the concrete. Relevant?

The homeless guy scooted around to sit on the other side of the planter.

But yes, he finally landed a job by knowing someone in a corporation. But nine years later he still wonders if he's relevant.

In my life, his relevancy has been proven myriads of times.

Like the weekend both Monika and Bill went out of town and Carl and I were in charge of fourteen-year-old Kelby, ten-year-old twins, Kallen and Kade, and six-year-old, Celie.

No worries. We'd been raising kids for over thirty years and knew the ropes. But we were about to experience a knot in a rope we had already untangled at least once.

The first evening everything was status quo. The kids were fed, the twins had only climbed up the walls in the hall a couple of times and hadn't landed on Celie.

Kelby had been hanging out with friends but was home early. Bedtime with no problems. I peeked in on the twins and was instantly reminded of the story about two little three-year-old brothers. Monika was standing at the door listening to their goodnight prayers one evening. It was Kade's turn to pray. Kade was extremely grateful that night, thanking Heavenly Father for each member of the family, naming each specifically. He was thankful for his monkey bike, his food, trees, clothes, and on and on and on. He was even thankful for the top bunk and the bottom bunk and....then.

Kallen blurted out, "Just say amen, Kade. Just say amen."

I felt a bit of regret because I hadn't kneeled down with them to say goodnight prayers. I hoped Carl had covered everything in his prayers. He was already snoozing downstairs. The kids accounted for, locks were checked.

Ah, to sleep. Perhaps to dream.

Somewhere around one o'clock a.m. I jumped out of bed with a scream. The fire alarms on both floors was going off. "Quick, Carl I'll go upstairs. Look around down here. I have to check the kids."

Running race speed, I flew upstairs, expecting a billowing smoke encounter any moment. After all I was acquainted with fires. I wondered if the twins were on their knees praying. No fire, no smoke, only that wailing, good- for- nothing alarm. My ears felt like someone was poking tweezers clear through my eardrums.

The twins slept through the noise. I couldn't believe it. Celie was up wandering around. I told her Grandpa would have the fire alarm shut down any minute and she should get back in bed.

Running toward the back of the house, I opened Kelby's door, wondering why he wasn't trying to find us. The alarm suddenly shut off and just as I opened Kelby's door, Carl walked in behind me. Something wasn't right. Kelby's knitted hat was lying on the pillow, but not on his head. I pulled the covers back over the lump and other pillows lined up like a giant hot dog.

Panic, was my first reaction. "Where is he," I frantically asked Carl.

"I don't know, Cindy, but he'll be back."

"Oh my word, not again," I said. "He's his mother's child."

When Monika was sixteen she experimented with rebellion. (She's her mother's child.) In the wee hours one night, our cat jumped in Carl's face and startled him awake. "What's this cat doing in the house?" he asked.

"Just stick her outside," I said.

He pushed her out the back door, but just as he dozed off again, the cat was back—in his face. "Alright, something's wrong."

Carl went to check the doors and I joined him to check the basement. We caught on right away. The basement window was wide open. Rover had crawled right in. Monika had crawled right out. Every time she pulled something though, Carl always found her.

This was her payback, but we were the ones in charge.

"What are we going to tell his mama? What are we going to tell his pa?" I hummed a fifties tune. "They're going to kill us."

I had gone outside several times thinking maybe he was with friends—out sleeping in the open, communing with nature. My heart rate was through the roof.

About two o'clock I was looking outside again and here he came walking in the back way. He was dead meat.

We had hauled an extra chair to his room and were sitting quietly as he walked in. Cool as a Coke, he sat down on his bed.

"Where in the world have you been? I've been worried sick," I asked.

"I just needed some time to think," he said.

About what at two in the morning? I asked.

"Oh, you know, what I'm going to do after high school, where I want to be."

Carl hadn't said a word.

"You expect us to believe........" Carl stopped me.

"Calm down and we'll talk about this when his parents are here."

Oh, my word. The kid had me frantic for hours and I can't talk?

"That fire alarm didn't go off for no reason. It was a warning for us to check on Kelby," I said.

"He's safe. Let's go to bed," Carl said.

Cats and fire alarms. A fella can't get away with anything.

Kelby sticks by his story to this day. He's twenty-six.

Kelby is the first grandson. The one that was three when he asked me, "Mamom. Do you ever run?"

He had me running that night.

Bombs Below

Our oldest son, Dustin, did not have a reputation like his little brother's, but I learned that he was just as adept as Jonathan at crazy stunts and capers. Lazing around on a day off work, I was upstairs on my bed painting my fingernails. Somewhere on the second hand, I suddenly felt the house shake. A horrendous explosive sound whooshed up under my mattress, and I was off.

Running in panic, I was plunged into smoke heading up the stairs as I was heading down. Out of breath, I ran through the laundry room and opened the garage door. Engulfed in smoke, it took me a few seconds to recognize Dustin's friend, Clark, from down the road. He was a quiet kid, his blonde hair always parted perfectly, his clothes pressed.

He was splayed against the closed garage door, looking like he was in a lineup, ready to be frisked.

Clark was standing, was Dustin down? A few more seconds and a somewhat weak, "WOW," floated from the middle of the room. Dustin stood, some implement in his hand, his face covered in powder.

Were they close to death? Illogical thought, but I was in shock.

"I think I'll stick to computers from now on," Clark said.

As I hit the garage opener, Dustin began his story.

"We tried to make a bomb," he said, dazed—okay stunned.

"Are you okay? You're lucky you didn't blow your head off. What in the world did you guys do?

"I can't hear very well," Dustin said.

"My ears are ringing," Clark said.

"I can understand that. Mine are too, boys."

"We went the cheap way," Dustin continued. "You don't use Lysol much, so we shot a hole in the can with my BB gun. The Lysol drained right out."

This is worse than I thought. Lysol would not dribble out peacefully. "And then?"

"Well, Clark was watching the neighbor's house while he was gone and he found some really cool gun powder in his garage."

Oh, boy. The neighbor had been irritated the week before because we let irrigation water run two feet onto his property. What if he knew those boys were pilfering gun powder?

"And then? You lit it."

"No, I found a piece of metal in Dad's reloading equipment on the shelf over there. I had to close the hole. We were going to put a fuse in and take it out in the pasture so you wouldn't even know."

I wondered what other war games they had been playing back there behind the sagebrush.

"So it didn't explode spontaneously, did it?"

"No. I think this was the dumb part. I used Dad's solder gun to solder the patch. I barely started. Smoke and fire started blowing out and I told Clark to run. He couldn't get the doors open."

"Why didn't *you* bolt?"

"My legs wouldn't work. My brain was thinking, I'm a dead man, but if I wasn't, I'd have to tell Dad."

Shaking my head, I surveyed the garage. The can was blown into jagged metal. "Where's the cap?"

"Look up there," Clark said. He had come to his senses some and had surveyed the damage.

Yep, the cap and tube from inside the can were melted to the ceiling. Tiny pieces of shrapnel had embedded themselves into nail cans, tools, and the garage wall. Black residue resided there for weeks.

"I'm going back to my room," I said. "My nerves *and* nails need repair."

"I'm going back home," Clark said.

"I'm going to rethink this bomb thing," Dustin said.

Years later Dustin told me he did succeed in setting off a bomb in the pasture behind our house. He also admitted that he was the one that taught Jonathan to play war with Roman Candles. "Clark and I used to go up in those hills behind the pasture. I would hide below in this pit and Clark would shoot at my head. Lucky I still have my eyeballs."

"Spare me any more details. Your surgery career could have been forever gone—blind, maimed, dead?"

"Yep, I worked on a few of those body parts in the ER just this week."

***

We should have known Dustin would be creative. From an early age, he was showcased in Carl's newspaper columns:

> Two years old is a difficult time of life. Dusty is two and seemed to really enjoy "Snow White and the Seven DRAWERS." Problem is, the only part he seems to remember is the witch. He's hiding under his covers again.
>
> Two years old is a time of getting the details almost down pat, and missing the point. We finally got him to quit saying "shut up," at least. But last night his father was putting him through his paces. "Put that lid back on your pop! Sit still and quit kicking your sister! Don't jump on your mother when she's trying to drive!"
>
> His response?
>
> "Simon says don't talk, Dad!"

Dustin was in the newspaper again when he was almost three. Carl wrote:

> Son Dusty will be three late in June of this year and the series of birthdays in our family this spring has been causing him some problems. Everyone is getting presents except him. Wife Cindy keeps telling him that his birthday is "a long ways off." Finally running out of patience last week, he requested, "Mom, would you drive me to my birthday?"

And this column was dedicated to tattoos—

> My son Dusty has problems with the word tattoo. He got one of those lick-em, stick-em water color tattoo things from the Cracker Jack box and ran around showing off his "tic-tac-toos."

Rendezvous at the E. R.

And then there was the time.....

Monika, had come home to visit and brought the grandkids. One night we had a cozy dinner and adjourned to the living room to visit. We were talking about how the summer before, her brothers Dustin and Jonathan had spent every free moment at the gym.

"Well, can you keep it up until you're seventy?" I asked. "Your great grandpa still ice-skated on the canal on the homestead AND could stand on his head."

Jonathan said, "The ice-skating sounds doable, but who wants to stand on their head anyway."

"I could never do a somersault," I said, "But I could stand on my head. Watch this." I double-checked that I wasn't wearing a skirt and then knelt in front of a blank wall, just in case I'd lost my touch.

One of them said, "Don't do it, Mom. You'll hurt yourself—or the floor."

Lippy kids.

Carl said, "There she goes."

I repeated a few Zen hums in my mind and focused. It took a few kickbacks, but I did it. My body sat on my head like an elephant balancing on a circus drum. The pressure was unbearable. I had put on some weight, but come on. I quickly lowered myself to the floor and felt my head spin back into correct position.

Nobody else tried it.

The next morning I opened my eyes and slammed them shut again. I thought of Carl's dumb joke—*some days I wake up Grumpy, but most days I let her sleep*. Not very funny and neither was this.

I was sick!

I crawled out of bed (literally) and on my hands and knees headed for the bathroom. I was so dizzy I could hardly move. The heaving began and didn't abate. I somehow crawled back in bed and called Carl at work.

"I'm really, really sick. I can't even stand up without heaving and spinning uncontrollably."

"Do you want me to come home? It's probably just the flu."

"This AIN'T no flu."

"I'll be there as quickly as I can."

Monika was my witness. "She's really sick, Dad. I think you should get her to the doctor."

After coming into the bedroom to check, he looked at my face and the bucket by the bed and called the doctor. I could hear him asking. "Should I call an ambulance?"

I said "Yes," as loud as I could whisper.

"I'll bring her right in."

"I need an ambulance," I said. "I can't walk across the room. I'm so sick, honey. I can't do this."

"The nurse said you probably don't need an ambulance, I'll take you in the car."

"Oh, no, I'll puke all the way!"

Carl helped me up and wrapped his arm around my waist to steady me. Every time I stood up from then on, I threw up. Collapsing in the hall, he picked me up and carried me outside, down two flights of stairs, and got me into the car.

"I'm not walking into that doctor's office. Take me to the hospital."

"He's got to check you in. You can do it."

All I wanted to do was croak. “Every time I stand, I’m going to heave,” I warned.

I got out of the car in front of my doc’s office and true to my word, left my mark on the sidewalk.

“I think we better admit you,” Doc said. “You’re dehydrated and we’ve got to take some tests.”

I could barely make out if he was the right doc, let alone care. I stood up to get into the car. I stood up as I got out of the car. I was getting weaker. I finally got to the room and plopped down.

Into the room came the nurse, pushing a scales. “We need to weigh you Mrs. Bechtold.” Her sing-song cheerfulness almost made me puke. Oh, I was already doing that.

“Nooooooooooooooooooo.”

“You don’t understand,” Carl said, “Every time she stands she throws up.”

“Well, it’s the rules. I’ll just get the little pan.”

“I’ll help you stand up. One more time and you can lay down and rest,” Carl said.

Yep, you can guess the next line about doing it again.

I laid in that bed for almost a week. Fell in love with anti-nausea pills. One day a phlebotomist came in and recognized Carl sitting by my bed.

“Oh, is that your mother?” he asked.

I turned and looked at him with my yellowed skin and blurted out, “Mary Kay, you have failed me.”

I had all kinds of tests.

“I stood on my head the night before I came in, doctor. Do you think that could have done it?”

"That doesn't sound likely," he said, "We'll do some more testing."

That day my sister, Cathy, brought her three blue-eyed, curly blonde-haired girls to visit. They lined up by the bed. I recognized their voices, but instead of six blue eyes, I counted at least twelve. Everyone was yacking away, oblivious to how sick I really was. Monika's four-year-old was pretty quiet. I did hear him ask his mom, "Is Grandma going to die?"

At least he had an inkling of my situation. Monika's twins sat in their car seats cooing away. I wanted to be well, to hold them again before they left for Utah.

At the end of the week Doc came in and told me he was releasing me.

"What do I have?"

"We think it's a virus that attacked the balance organ in your left ear." I'm thinking viruses are blamed for most stuff doctors can't diagnose.

"I know you're still dizzy," he continued. I want you to stay in bed a few days and have Carl pick up a prescription of anti-nausea pills. What was he thinking? I still was spinning and looked *older* than Carl's mother.

I called home for Carl.

Jonathan answered the phone. He hesitated after I told him his dad could pick me up. "Mom, he's in the middle of something for work. He'll pick you up in a while."

Okay, that was strange, but I sat on the bed and waited, and waited. Finally a nurse walked in. "I'm getting worried. I called my husband to come get me over an hour ago."

"Oh, haven't you heard? He's down in the ER. He came in by ambulance, unable to walk."

"What in the world. Is he okay?"

"I'll call down there and ask about him. He's probably fine."

She came back in a few minutes with the great news. "They're releasing him soon. He apparently hurt his back. He called your sister to come get both of you."

I leaned my head on my forehead during the wheelchair ride to the ER. Carl was a bit loopy—muscle relaxers for back spasms. He slowly headed toward me while I asked what happened. "Your back hasn't acted up for a long time," I said.

"I haven't carried you since our wedding night."

"At least you got to ride in the ambulance," I said.

We both chuckled as Cathy grabbed our coats and stuff and headed us for her Suburban. Carl walked behind me pushing the wheelchair. I couldn't stand, he couldn't sit. Cathy helped me into the passenger side, shut the door and I leaned on the window to keep from spinning.

The nurse helped Carl the best she could. He belly-flopped into the back seat, his legs bent so the door could shut. Cathy got behind the wheel and shook her head.

Jonathan, a high school junior, had splint the scene. Home again, we hobbled back to our bedroom, both sighing as we hit the bed. To this day, I still call my bed my best friend.

Ten minutes later the phone rang. "I can't get it, if I roll over I'll lose it again."

"I can't roll over, I'll be in traction."

And the phone rang on and on.

It took months for me to recover. I couldn't walk down the hall without bumping off the walls. No driving for two months. Carl said it was the quietest he had ever seen me.

Years later I saw a medical show on television. They were talking about loose crystals in the ear that, when jarred loose can wreak havoc with balance.

In fact, in my sixties I went through a bout with dizziness, but only when I laid down or got out of bed. The otolaryngologist I went to knew exactly what it was—loose crystals in my ear. Positioning me on my side and placing my head at a specific angle, she tapped on my jaw just under the bottom of my ear lobe. As I sat back up the dizziness was gone. I tested out laying down and the same thing. I was cured. "The ear crystals can shift sometimes when you move your head too quickly," she explained.

"I bet it could happen if you stand on your head," I said.

CAUTION: Do NOT stand on your head after about the age of six.

Sour Notes

One Tuesday at the children's church class, primary, the teacher passed around the annual talent show sign-up sheet and I wrote down my name—in cursive. I wanted to show those kids I had a talent, despite my thick waist and hand-me-downs.

I had been practicing a new song in the intermediate Thompson book—one a little on the showy side with some tricky fingering. I spent the next three weeks perfecting it. Instead of practicing 30 minutes a day, I spent an hour. If I made a mistake or lost my place, I started over from the beginning. Over and over—I repeated that song until it was mastered.

The day of the talent show I tried to calm myself. My hands felt frigid, yet I was sweating.

"What if I make a mistake and have to start over?" I asked Mother. "You'll do fine," she said, stirring her casserole for the potluck dinner.

"What if I forget?"

I was looking for assurance, but Mother couldn't possibly know how it felt to play in front of a bunch of staring people.

"Just start over. No one will care."

That wasn't the answer I was looking for. I blew warm air into my closed fists.

She walked toward the oven, balancing the glass dish with one hand as she opened the oven door. "Take the music book if you want."

The oven door banged shut and I returned to the piano to practice some more.

I carried the piano book to the church that night, creased and flattened at the exact page, although I still pinched my fingers shut at my selection—just to make sure I could open it in a hurry.

Not touching a bite of food during dinner, I spent most of the time in the bathroom, feeling the urge to go, clinging onto my Thompson book, even in the stalls.

I paced the hall behind the stage, listening for each name to be announced. I secretly wished the girl before me would mess up—maybe croak on a high note or clear her throat real loud in the microphone—but she sang her piece without a mistake.

The applause lessened and I squeezed my legs together to stop both the trembling and the urge to go. I could do this. I had practiced.

I couldn't do this.

As I walked toward the piano, I felt like I had eaten my last meal. I sat down on the bench. The first chord was right, but from there I couldn't even tell in what octave I was playing. Starting over was not an option. I wanted out of there.

The discordant notes clashed and I surrendered somewhere on the last page. As I stood, the audience politely clapped. I walked behind the curtain and stood there for a long time, hiding. Two more people completed their acts before I slunk down to the chairs and sat at the end of the row.

Mother waited for me by the back door of the cultural hall when the show was over. In a weary, frustrated sigh, she put the whole thing into context.

"Cindy, you knew that song perfectly."

That Special Time

We all knew the boys and girls would be separated in seventh grade health class to watch THE film—the one where the lucky cartoon-smiling egg gets punctured by squiggly black things. In addition, the girls watched facts about the monthly "visitor" that each girl would get to know. The whole thing looked like a nuisance to me--yucky.

I didn't want any visitors.

One of the worldlier girls in the class said, "My aunt told me to take a douche bag on the honeymoon." This was only the seventh grade, I thought. Why would her aunt be talking about honeymooning? I wasn't sure I even liked boys.

Our teacher had just gotten married and smiled that just-between-us-girls smile as she replied, "Yes, most certainly. The act is lovely, but one needs to remain fresh, and you should also douche after your monthly period." I didn't know what a douche bag was, but I wasn't about to ask. I imagined it was a Greek ritual, having to do with bags of grapes.

"What's a douche bag?" One of the braver girls in the class asked. This girl knew a whole lot more about sex than me. She necked with boys downtown behind the movie theatre.

The teacher never even swallowed. "It's a hot water bottle with a tube. The bag is filled with water and dumped upside down, allowing the water to wash out the vaginal area."

Yikes! I'd had enemas before and there would NEVER be a bag loaded with water racing down a tube into my privates. That could blow your head off! I was never going to have sex and the monthlies hadn't appeared yet.

I was safe.

Mother had never even hinted about any 28-day visitor, let alone a douche bag. In fact, I was still waiting for her to notice I needed a bra. During shower time after PE, I checked out all the girls' bras. Some of them wore those training kind— all fluff for no stuff, but several of the girls filled one right out.

I intuitively knew that Mother was shy about this whole matter. Once when I had asked if her church friend was pregnant, she got this funny look and said, "Yes, Linda is expecting." I thought that would have been a good time to bring up the "talk," but she was embarrassed to even say the word, pregnant.

I didn't want to be the lone, bare-chested girl in the locker room. My undershirts just weren't doing the job. One afternoon after school, I worked up the courage to confront my mother.

I rehearsed my request to myself. Um, Mother, most of the girls in my class wear bras. No, that was no good—too straightforward. Or…I've seen some of the nicest bras in the underwear aisle at Samsel's Department Store. Nope, too vague, she'd change the subject on that one.

Mother was in the kitchen talking on the phone, rubbing her dishrag in a circular motion over the counter. I stood there, waiting for her to finish her conversation. The afternoon sun slid across the counter, lighting her hand as it circled the crumbs. The wash machine thrummed, spinning the clothes. I smelled baked potatoes. I thought there should have been music, to herald in the day I finally got the nerve to ask my mother for a bra.

I shifted from one foot to the other, my nerves shredded like a cat-clawed curtain. All the grown-up sentences I'd practiced vanished and as she hung the phone up. I stood for a few seconds, wondering how I was going to do this without embarrassing her, or both of us.

With one hand, I grabbed the bottom of my tee shirt, pulled it taut across my budding breasts and pointed at the button-sized bumps sitting on my chest.

"Look," I said, words totally inadequate for the importance of the occasion.

"We'll have to go look for some underwear," is all she said.

To this day, my mother has never said the word bra; it's still referred to as underwear.

Bra story. Part two.

(In case I didn't have you hooked)

The stars must have aligned to form the perfect setting. At a Fourth of July reunion in Wyoming, all three of my sisters and a couple of nieces were reminiscing. By then, I was at least sixty years old, Mother, eighty. Girl talk surfaced and someone dropped the nasty word *bra.* I jumped in, disclosing a secret I thought everyone knew.

"Mother has never ever said the word, *bra*."

"What?" my twenty-year-old niece asked. "Grandma, you have never said, *bra*?"

I wouldn't let it go. "No, she really, honestly has never uttered the word."

Mother sat, her modesty not allowing her to answer such a question.

Sadie asked, "Then, what do you call one, Grams?"

I answered for Grams. "Underwear."

One must know that Sadie is the youngest grandchild—her grandmother's pet. Full of fun and no inhibitions on the horizon, Sadie wouldn't let go of her newest revelation.

"Say bra, Grams."

Thus commenced silent staring at the woman in the rocker.

Silence bounced right back.

"Come on Grams, say it, say it. Bra. Bra. Bra."

Mother got a twisty little grin across her lips, "You mean, Victoria's Secret?" she asked.

I couldn't believe she said those words. Huh, I thought Victoria's Secret was safe from my mother.

Laughter dislodged and all of us were hysterical.

Secretly, I didn't think even Sadie could get her to say such a word. "You've got to say it now," Sadie said.

We all watched, willing the dreaded word to fall out.

"Oh, you girls," Mother said. And then it lurched out like a brief hiccup.

"BRA."

I should have heard music this time. All the years of guarding the three-letter noun.

"Say it again, Grams," Sadie yelled through the laughter.

"No, don't make her do it again," I said.

I kind of felt like a bad little girl.

Eyeliner in the Twilight Zone

Monika had come into the master bathroom to share the mirror, as other family members hogged the other one. I marveled at how quickly she had become a teenager. What a beauty. I dabbed on some blush and wonder cream—guaranteed to vanish wrinkles, zits, age spots and probably half your face.

Monika poised her eyeliner pencil, just as the drawer under the mirror slowly inched open.

"Did you see that drawer move?" I asked. She didn't respond—just kept drawing the line. I gingerly shut the drawer and straightened a flyaway hair. Seconds later we both saw the drawer slowly move toward us and felt it pushing on our thighs. Our eyes locked. Supernatural terror and images of Edgar Allen Poe's poems ran through my head. Monika's perfectly lipsticked mouth froze in a pink oval and her eyes filled with terror as it finally registered that drawers don't move on their own.

After our eyes locked, there was a three second silence—1,001..........1,002.........1,003........and then a duet of shrill screams, as we both ran out of the bathroom, into the hall. Shaking and shivering, our auto-nervous systems broke into laughter and we told an alarmed Dustin and Carl that there was a ghost in the bathroom.

We crept back around the corner and peered through the door. JONATHAN. Poking his head out from under the dark corner cabinet he slowly pushed the drawer open and closed, open and closed.

Lumber Wagon

I didn't trust our old Oldsmobile wagon. Once a classy car, it now wore chips and dents like an old fogie's face. I hadn't even wanted to buy it in the first place.

Carl did.

The check engine light was more on then off. He had broken down and filled it with a higher-grade gasoline the week before our trip and the check engine light finally went out. Would it last?

"We can't make it clear to northern Montana in that dump of a car. It's over 500 miles.

Carl tried to assuage my fear. "We need to support Dustin at his theatre camp. Remember it's his last year. You've never been to Missoula. Maybe you'll run into one of your old hippie boyfriends."

"I think Missoula's loaded with *granolas* these days. Quit changing the subject. What if we're stranded and have to hug a pine tree for three days?"

"I guess I'll play hero and hire a cab."

"Carrrrrl."

The wide-open spaces of Montana did take my breath away *and* my last ounce of patience. The old wagon had been showing the "check engine light" for the last two hundred miles. "Aren't you worried about the engine?" I asked my husband.

"I checked and it's still there," he said.

I wasn't laughing.

The car had done its duty, carrying 4-H kids on field trips, hauling cubs to scout meetings. Many times I'd load four bicycles, owners and their backpacks, water jugs, sunscreen and a flock of flies they'd let inside.

"This piece of junk is going to break down before we make it home," I said.

"Have some faith. This car is going to be around to take our grandkids to the coast."

I sucked in some words. "Hope they have taxies out here on the range. Maybe we'll hitch a ride on a couple of stray cows," I said. I stared out the window, a parade of mountains staring back. I turned back to talk to him, the scenery calming me some.

Glancing over my shoulder I watched a car approach and pass, slowing to match our speed. "There's a car pulling up beside us. I think they want to talk to you."

Carl rolled down the window.

"Your car's on fire!" the woman on the passenger side shouted. "You've been shooting flames for a couple of miles."

"Flames!" I screamed. "Stop. We have to get out of here."

"I suppose we ought to take a look."

"A look? Stop and let me out."

I ran around the back in time to see a puff of smoke flounce into the air. A black streak of burnt grass ran right to the bumper. "What are we going to do? I'm not getting back into that thing."

Hubby went across the road and stood while several cars ignored the thumb he poked hopefully into the air. More cars sped by.

"Nobody will give me a ride. We're driving back to the nearest town," he announced.

"You may be driving back but I'm not getting into that inferno."

"We don't have a choice, now get in."

I jumped up and down, stomping the grass down beside the burnt streak. "I'll die in that car." Visions of imploding panels caused me to step further away.

"It will be fine. It's only a ways back. I saw a sign."

"I don't need a sign to know there's a heaven, but I'm not going today, and, it might be fine for *you*, the fire was shooting out from under *my* side of the car."

I knew I'd be getting back into the car. I had no choice. I couldn't sit out there in the open beside the interstate weaving grass bracelets to kill time.

"If my life is no value to my husband," I mumbled, "I might as well go out in a blaze."

We found a one-man gas station thirty miles away. I sat on my hands the whole way. Mostly to keep them from strangling my other half.

Even on the range, a catalytic converter surfaced. They had the beater running later that day.

"I knew it could be fixed," he said. "This is a good car."

Back on the road, I stared at the scenery.

Missoula was what we expected—a hoard of college kids wearing glasses and sandals. Forgetting all about the car I enjoyed the romantic little stroll through the town. When we got to camp I embraced our son and asked him if he had gotten the package I had sent. Dustin hated zucchini with a double portion of yuck. I had picked some nice ones from the garden and sent the package as a little reminder of home.

"Yeah, I threw them against a pine tree."

Who did our son take after?

He was the best actor on the stage.

Dustin fell asleep the minute his head hit the upholstery. I yakked on and on about what an awesome actor he was and how I thought he needed a talent scout.

Carl, finished with the play, let his mind roll ahead. "I know how to fix that starter problem, too," he said. "I'm going to buy a spare battery and stick it in the cubby in the back. I can run a wire under the seats and connect it to the battery."

"You are NOT going to string wires under the seats," I stated.

Our son lifted his head a couple of inches off the seat and told his dad that he was pushing it too far.

Dustin, exhausted by all that play practice, slept the rest of the way home.

As we approached home I let out a sigh. The old wagon had made it. "The trip was great," I said. "Except for this lumber wagon on wheels."

Carl sped down the hill and made the yellow light.

"The brakes are gone," he mentioned as he shifted down and pumped the pedal. "I'm going to have to crawl home."

"You're going to crawl to the junk yard and leave this thing."

"Brakes we can fix," he said.

"If you repair this piece of junk one more time…"

He did.

While the wagon was in the repair shop, I secretly walked through my brother-in-law's car lot. I spotted it, bathed in ethereal light, its body beckoning me—a sporty blue Toyota. I pictured myself behind the wheel, sun roof open, hair flying in the breeze.

The wagon was back on its wheels. Later that week I asked my dear husband if he'd just look at a new car I had seen at the lot. "It's perfect," I said.

"I'll look but you know my plan is to keep the wagon running."

I held my breath every time I turned over the key on the wagon. I guess I'd drive it into my old age, wires strung under the seats, its fake wooden panels flaking down the highway as I lumbered along.

Hubby left for work the day of my birthday, not acknowledging a thing.

I wanted to forget about it anyway, forty is not a number to fling around. Besides, I had errands, bills to pay, boys to pick up—flocks of flies eager to hitch a ride. I walked down through the basement, my arms loaded.

The wagon was not in the garage. For a minute I thought it was stolen, but I mentally slapped myself and came back to reality. Who would steal that wire trap?

I walked outside. I had to adjust to the light bouncing off the polished blue of a brand new Toyota. A red ribbon the size of Missoula wrapped from bumper to bumper. I didn't know bows came in industrial size. THE Toyota, loaded: electric windows, sunroof, and six cylinder get-up-and-go fancy.

"Oh, no. It's so beautiful"

I knew way down in my palpitating heart that Carl would come through.

It Only Takes One

I didn't laugh about this one for a long time.

Every weekday when Kade was seventeen, I picked him up at the bus stop after he finished advanced classes at a local college. The bus stop was by the sidewalk next to the highway. Behind the sidewalk loomed a huge parking lot, once owned by a now abandoned grocery store.

I was tired that particular day. Actually not feeling well at all. *Okay, I'll get 'er done and come back for a nap,* I thought. I parked next to the sidewalk. Kade was already waiting. Not a good sign. At that time in his teenagership, he did not want to waste time. A bit on the serious side, he had an agenda and a schedule. I could already tell he was grumpy.

As he opened the door he started in on me. "Grandma, you can't be late. I've got a paper to finish tonight and it stresses me out when you're late."

Ungrateful kid anyway. After all I do for him.

"Kade dear, I don't feel well and so I'm asking you to be patient."

"Just get going. I'm really in a hurry."

My head ached. I was having cold sweats.

"Just give me a minute." I turned the key and put my awesome, now old, Toyota in reverse. Glancing over my shoulder, I saw the way was clear. Not in the mood for messing around now, I gave her gas and turned the wheel.

CRUNCH!

Kade didn't say a word.

I did.

I opened the door to check out what I hit. The only guy left at the bus stop immediately pulled out his cell phone. The look on his face said, "That old gal is going to leave the scene and I'm calling the cops." But he had no idea I'd had enough of being a horrid girl long ago and would never try a hit and run.

Jerk.

It was the fender and part of the door—crumpled like an industrial sized tinfoil wad. Of course it had to be an old boat of a car—dated somewhere between a Model T and a "79 Oldsmobile tank.

I called the police.

Kade got out of the car to look.

"But Grandma. You hit the only car in the entire lot!"

Okay, there goes his Christmas presents.

It took at least an hour for the police and the accident report. I called our insurance company and Kade moped.

The next day his sister, Celie, told me Kade was seething. He had been on a schedule which I had preempted. The only time that he came even close to being so mad was when Monika bought him a $4.00 chocolate-covered banana at the fair.

"Why did you spend that much money, Mom?" It's too expensive for a dumb banana, I won't eat it."

So Monika did.

Oh, for a $4.00 banana. I'll guarantee that driver pocketed the cost of about four hundred of those dumb bananas.

The Red Can-Can

I was eight the winter we spent in Arizona. That fall my doctor had prescribed a dry climate for my lungs. Mother told me I needed three months away from cold weather—to soak up some sunshine. I was so used to my asthma that I wondered if our country doctor had sent us away so he wouldn't have to make so many house calls.

Dad quit his job, rented our house and in three weeks we were on our way to Litchfield, Arizona. He had gotten a job welding for Boing Aircraft. We all adjusted to a tiny apartment that looked like every other apartment lined up for miles. We lived across the street from a stinky celery field and next to a kid named Elmer. That kid pestered me every day coming back from school.

We were there for three months. I don't think Dad called to get advice from my doctor, but I was coughing less and hadn't had a hospitalization once, so we packed all our stuff back into the station wagon, ironing board squeezed between boxes of dishes and clothes, bedding covering the sparse contents hauled to Arizona.

Dad said he'd take us to the ocean on the way home. I couldn't wait to collect seashells on the beach. I'd find the biggest one, curled like a tuba, pink-glazed perfection. Fishy, weedy smells rode in on bursting waves. I slipped off my saddle shoes and walked. There were only shell crumbs. Everyone else had taken them. I just knew it.

We were close to Disneyland, but my parents claimed they didn't want to fight the long lines, even to shake hands with Mickey. But I knew they didn't want to pay to get tickets.

"Let's drive down to Mexico," Dad said. "We'll eat some tacos and take a picture of some lucky fella taking a siesta."

The official at the border sat on a wicker stool in what looked like a telephone booth. Dad said it was customs. I wondered if the man took siestas in there. He smiled with lots of teeth and reached out the window, patting Dad on the shoulder. Maybe the man in khaki clothes thought Dad was a native. Everyone said Dad's skin was dark enough to be Mexican. His black hair and mustache blended with the folks I'd seen so far. Dad talked a couple of words to him in Spanish. They acted like friends.

We drove through the streets looking for a gas station. The one we stopped at was dirty-white cinderblock. A couple of spotted dogs ran around the pump, barking, slapping their tails against Dad's legs as he lifted our canvas water bag off the hood ornament. He raised his eyebrows at my mother, still sitting in the car. She juggled the baby, trying to get the diaper bag handles unwound from her feet.

As the dogs skidded around the corner, Mother said, "You kids can get out."

I could see piñatas crepe-papering the front window and knew there was more in there than cans of oil. I hurried in front of Tony and Cheri. "Come on you guys."

Sombreros lined the top of the wall like a velvet strip. Caught by the color, I studied the gold-braided cords circling the black brims.

And then I saw it.

Stapled to the wall, behind the cash register, a red can-can fanned out in crinkly layers so fluffy I envisioned my skirt poofing higher than any other girls' in third grade. I saw myself sit down at my desk. I would scoop up the back of my skirt, steady the bulk, and land squarely in the middle of the chair so as not to teeter to either side. Then I would poke the billowing layers under my desk, controlling the springy newness.

The twirliest can-cans I had ever seen were worn by square dancers down at the community center. This one was better than those. No girl in my third grade classroom had ever owned one like this. I would come back with the stiffest, most beautiful red can-can in the whole world. Most can-cans were white or ivory. This one was red pepper and I had to have it.

When Mother came into the station I ran to her, pleading. "Please, can I have that can-can? I won't ask for anything else the whole trip."

She stepped closer to the register, looking at the price tag pinned to the can-can. It was marked in Spanish. "How much?" asked my mother, pointing at the wall.

"Five American dollars," the man replied, his yellowed teeth outlining his mustache as he grinned.

A round woman in a bright yellow dress stepped up beside him, saying only, "Boy, it's hot."

Mother squeezed her hand tighter around her wallet, smiled at the woman, and then shook her head.

My stomach knotted, the netting on the can-can sagged in my mind, as my mother spoke reality in familiar phrases. "We can't afford it."

Without changing her expression, the woman in yellow repeated, "Boy it's hot."

Not ready to give up, the man with the mustache reached up to the edge of the petticoat and patted the layers. "Four dollars-fifty cents for you." His grin didn't budge.

Mother shook her head again and turned away, shifting Cheri to her other hip. "It's time to head for the car, kids."

Dad had entered the station and picked the top oil can from the pyramid stacked in the corner. Pulling his wallet from his back pocket, he moved toward the cash register. I ran to him, begging for the can-can.

"She won't let me have it." Near tears, I softened and touched his hand.

Before Mother said anything, the lady behind the counter looked directly at Dad, her manner unchanged and said, "Boy, it's hot."

Dad nodded at the lady who was really hot, and then called my mother back. "Let her have it," he said, "We're not going to go broke buying a can-can."

"She doesn't need it."

The rows of sombreros faded into the background. I did *need* it. I needed it like a child needs food or a winter coat in Wyoming winds.

Tony had been playing with a box of Mexican jumping beans. "Can I have these?" he asked.

"Not today." Mother said.

Tony shrugged his shoulders and followed Dad outside. Tears were falling down my face. I tried to sniff them back until I got outside, but they fell out. Then all my hopes and sadness washed in rivers down my blouse. My petticoat would not be red. It would remain my limp, one layered, hand-me-down—the one with constant static cling—the one that sparked as I detached it from my legs.

We returned to the station wagon. Dad turned the key, wiped his hand over his dripping forehead and said. "All that woman could say in English was, 'Boy, it's hot.' The tourists taught her that."

I climbed across the back seat and laid on a sleeping bag thrown over lumpy boxes in the rear of the car.

Dad's voice soothed my sobs. "We'll see another can-can down the road."

A few minutes later he whistled a "whew," grinned, looked at Mother and said, "Boy, it's hot."

We never did see another can-can.

"At least you're not coughing," Mother said as she turned around in her seat to look at me."

I didn't want to talk.

Maybe, if I faked a coughing attack, my parents would turn around and take me back to Arizona, and I wouldn't have to face all those girls in my Wyoming class.

"Are you ready to go home?" Dad asked, somehow reading my mind.

"I liked the orange trees and the cactus."

Some of the hurt seeped out as I thought about the photograph of Tony and me in our shorts posing with the palm trees that ringed the celery field in front of our housing complex. When we got home, I would hold up that picture at show and tell. Everyone would wish they could have worn shorts in January.

A smile crept through my dimples.

"I hope the renters didn't tear up our house." Dad started to fuss about going back to all the work—in the house and in the oil patch.

Mother steered him back to the present, asking questions about the next town. "Do you think we can find a cheap motel?"

I flipped over, fidgeting for a more comfortable spot. Grabbing the ironing board leg, I pulled myself halfway up, but sunk back down, twinges sparking my backbone.

I wanted to think about Arizona, not the can-can remaining on the wall.

Except for Elmer, I had liked walking to school and the ten-cent milk carton snacks during reading class. I saved the booklet from the cactus garden we visited. Blooms were peeking between the pokies. Orange groves smelled real good. I still wanted to prove palm trees had coconuts.

Tony liked playing outside all winter and I hadn't once heard Dad talking about his boss in a loud voice. Mother kept repeating, "The women around here say they've never seen anyone take care of clothes like I do. They like my ironing."

But there was still a deep longing for home.

I missed snow angels and ice-skating, stars at night and crisp air—even if it did make me cough. Tony wanted to jump off the haystack—pretending to fly with his handkerchief parachutes. Cheri couldn't pet a kitty in that tenement. Mother missed her cupboards and more room. Dad had his land. He was going to build his own welding shop one day. He even had it stepped off. The strings had probably blown off the stakes.

We went home but I never forgot about that red can-can and boy it WAS hot.

My family wanted to do something special for my fiftieth birthday. The party was at our house. The guests began laughing hysterically when Jan handed me her gift. What was up with this bunch? They had dragged in a couple of black balloons and a box of prunes, but they weren't finished. I slowly unwrapped the box, taped like it was protecting the Hope Diamond.

I smiled. They laughed as a red can-can exploded out of the box. They must have bought it at Denver Tent and Awning. Somehow, I didn't experience the joy I had envisioned as an eight-year-old. I must have whined about that can-can for too many years. Besides, can you picture me behind my desk, trying to tastefully untangle can-can netting?

In Arizona. Mother holding Christie, plusTony, Cheri, and me. Actually it looks like I have a can-can, albeit not poofy enough.

I Think I have Depression

Let me take you back to my sick-bed in 1976, where days after our last baby, Jonathan, was delivered, I began to disconnect from the world. The fog shrouding my mind felt like a candlesnuffer—the perfect tool to extinguish light. My short-circuited brain seemed to scramble signals; when morning came, I remained hiding in bed. An easy decision such as what to have for supper, crippled me, and I would again retreat to my bed.

When I tried to practice the piano Carl had recently bought for me, terror climbed over the keys and played havoc with my focus. Notes on the music danced in and out, my fingers faltering on the keys.

Anger stalked my heart, leaching my happiness.

Others might have shifted into denial, however I wanted a diagnosis—one with a cure. I was willing to spend hours making appointments in low-lit waiting rooms. Steam rose in my self-preservation pressure cooker, forcing me to doctors, psychiatrists, counselors, and even chiropractors.

My primary physician was an OBGYN from the adjacent town—a boomtown overflowing with laborers working in the bulging trona mines. He was overworked, overburdened, and overbooked. One afternoon, notified that he had been called to a delivery, I stubbornly remained five hours in the waiting room to keep my appointment. After dozing off, I became coherent enough to thumb through a stack of brochures on a corner table. There was the answer, clues to my disconnection. The brochure provided a list of symptoms of depression. My pencil checked each box down the list like soldiers raising rifles in syncopation with each check.

I grabbed it as a nurse finally called my name, grasping hope as I sat on the end of the examination table. Exhausted, I held onto the stirrups, trying to pull enough energy to reiterate my symptoms and unveil the brochure—my ammunition the blackened squares.

"I think I have depression," I announced.

"Describe what you're feeling." The doctor said, looking over his half-glasses. I looked for any sign that this man believed me. Skeptical after so many retellings, I didn't really trust any of these guys anymore. I handed him the brochure.

"Well let's see. Let me review your chart first." His finger skimmed cryptic notes: "your baby is four months old, you have been given anti-anxiety meds, putting an end to nursing. You have complained of fatigue, muddle-headedness and excessive anger."

He has been my OBGYN for the last year, I know he's overworked, even missing the delivery of my baby, but still I dreamed that his personal interest in my healing would match the attention he was giving my notes.

"It looks like you've answered yes to all the questions on the brochure: Do you feel worthless or out of control? Have you lost interest in activities that you once enjoyed? Are there changes in your sleep patterns—sleeping more or having difficulty sleeping? Have you ever contemplated suicide? We sure want to get you feeling better."

"What do you think is wrong?" I ask with very little hope that his diagnosis would be right.

"You could have a little depression."

How dare he downplay the symptoms I had just verified? *A little depression*? Is he a doctor or an idiot—if my arm was lacerated and dangling by the stump, I would be immediately treated to stem the bleeding. If I went into diabetic shock, nurses would run for the proper IV's, glucose mixtures and insulin to stop a comma.

"In addition to your anxiety medication, let me put you on an antidepressant—an MAO inhibiter. We'll get this thing under control. It might take a couple of tries with new medication, they're coming up with more all the time."

I shuffled to the car, scooted inside and fell back on the headrest, immediately into a deep, exhausted sleep, a desperate attempt to regain enough strength to drive the 25 minutes home.

Soon after, I began to experience what the psychiatrists label depersonalization. Pinocchio-like arms swung from wooden joints—not belonging to me. Looking at my suspended hands, they seemed to hang over the immensity of space—far from my world. There was so much pain; my denial of even residing in this foreign body consumed my days.

We rolled the baby's crib closer to my side of the bed so I could reach as far as my strength would allow. By swinging my floppy arms over the rails, I could stretch my alien fingers to touch my baby bundle, scoop him up, giving me enough momentum to roll us both back into bed.

My bed became my haven—escaping to sleep.

My depression lasted for years, intermittently turning to psychosis. The doctor suggested I take some classes at the college, or go to work part time at the newspaper office where Carl was editor. Slowly life became bearable and almost pleasant. Postpartum psychosis and chronic major depressive disorders are real, but the passing of years have made life much better. And, of course, there are the medications that didn't exist when it all began. We survived, loved our way through it, and still see the humor in the funny moments.

Even playing softball didn't lift depression.

His World in a Ditch

Jonathan had been experimenting again, the kitchen counter carpeted with his ingredients. I had already picked up a trail of his belonging scattered from the bathtub to his dresser drawers.

I needed some space. "I'm going for a walk," I said. "I just hope that infernal wind has stopped."

"Can I go?" my son asked, the frayed edge of his baseball hat turned sideways over his ear.

I had been picturing nature's organized solitude, but it was such a simple request.

"Let's see how cold it is before we plan any long treks," I said. I poked my nose out the back door, deciding we could brave the chill. Jonathan was right behind me.

My young son packed his wooden sword, pointing it forward to ward off any would-be opponent who came crashing through the ditch bank's dried weeds.

"I never want to grow up." Jonathan announced, like it was his right to detain adulthood. "This is my world."

And as I looked around, it was a kid's world. His bicycle leaned against the corral, camouflaged with wear. His horse pawed at the crusted ground, sending puffs of dirt spraying his own belly. Our unconcerned cat wove through the horse's hooves. The empty swing seat flipped figure eights in the air.

A gust of wind shivered under my collar, lifting the lid off my musing as I told him, "The only place we can get out of the wind is in the ditch. Let's go."

The ditch had been repaired, but we had a few weeks before the water was let down. Sand sat in the bottom, as last year's silt was pushed to far corners. Jonathan hid his sword in a sagebrush and we climbed in, laying on our bellies, facing each other—two runaways in a tube.

Tumbleweeds rolled over our sleeves, dotting our jackets.

A red ant lugged a seed three times his size across the terrain.

"There's another world down here," I said.

"Let's stay for a while." He spoke quietly as he doodled with a stick.

The bond I felt at that moment stretched upwards to meet the light sliding down into our retreat, warming me all over. I wanted to grab rays and shove them into my pockets. I wanted to taste the sand, lapping up a few grains—tangible proof that spiritual awakenings happen in ditches with little boys.

"Let's stay for a while," I repeated.

Subaru to the Rescue

Poor Rambo. Not only did that truck have uneven racing stripes, it was about to get introduced to the hazards of another Bechtold campout. On a whim we decided to load up and take the kids a few miles up the South Fork to camp overnight. The camper was already on the truck bed and even though it was late afternoon, the lake was close. I know it was my idea, anything to start a campfire and roast a marshmallow impaled on the end of a willow branch.

Carl drove the big bad boy. Although I think it was illegal, the boys rode inside the camper; Monika, inside the cab lamented missing the overnighter she had planned with her best friend, Cari.

About six miles off the highway, we turned onto the dirt lane toward the lake. Carl was in one of those moods. The lake had receded further than we had ever seen it. "Let's drive out and see if we can get closer to the edge of the water," he said.

"Carl, that doesn't look good. We'll sink. I don't even think Rambo will make it over that water pool. I won't go."

"I want to go back home," Monika said. "This is uncool. Dad, you're going to get stuck and we'll be out here in the mud and I'll have to listen to Dustin and Jonathan whoop it up all night. Get us back to civilization."

"I'll go out and lock in the hubs. Four wheel drive and Rambo will never fail us."

He didn't stop to ask the boys. They would be all for it anyway.

"We're set," he said as he scooted into the dip in the driver's seat, his shoes billowing little puffs of powdery alkali.

"Why are you wearing your dress shoes?"

"That's what I was wearing when you handed me the marshmallows and the keys to the truck."

"This is crazy! Monika and I don't want to go."

"You'll be okay. I know what I'm doing."

"Okay---FINE," Monika replied.

"Don't go any farther," I yelled. Monika grabbed the dash, right over Rambo's embroidered name.

He put the truck in gear and stepped on the accelerator. Rambo lurched forward, a roaring lion with alkali billowing from each flying paw. Half a yard, half a yard, half a yard onward, into the mouth of the puddle we charged. Then slower, and lower, and slower and lower until poor Rambo sat with his belly on the alkali with his wheels flopping in the soup, spraying something that resembled well-warmed chocolate malt.

Carl wasn't talking at all now. He got out, and inspected the situation. One of the front wheels apparently wasn't up to the axle yet, so he popped the truck into reverse and stomped on the gas again, sending Rambo sideways, sticking the right rear of the truck even further in the mud.

I didn't say a word.

Eventually, he surrendered.

"Let's just sleep in the camper. I'll get us out in the morning."

There went the marshmallows.

"At least we have a bed. It will be fun—another adventure," I said hopefully.

We slid down into the mud as it oozed into our shoes and clung to Monika's three layers of socks.

The same Christmas that I had bought Carl the custom-made dashboard cover, I also bought him mud flaps for Rambo. They weren't my favorite—not Carl's either—little men in sombreros, BACK OFF, printed under each in jumbo sized type. They certainly hadn't done any good in that situation.

Dustin and Jonathan were elated. "Wow, Dad. We thought you would make it," Dustin said. "You always get us out of jams on our scout trips," Jonathan added.

"Everyone just hunker down. Pretend we're down by the lake."

Jonathan laid down in the cab. Dustin climbed into the upper bunk, Carl right behind. "We might have a small problem," he said. "I'm going to roll right out, on top of your mother."

Trouble was, the truck was at such a slant, we were all in misery. Monika and I had to stay in bed by bracing our feet against the wall. "This is killing my feet, honey," I said in the most pitiful voice I could muster.

"You guys try to get some sleep, I'm going to get something to get us out."

"It's almost nine miles home. We can tough it out."

He didn't listen.

About dawn I was awake for the hundredth time. I could hear the sound of a car engine and then chains rattling like the Grim Reaper's. It was Carl with a giant Handyman jack lifting the sunken corner of the truck out of the mud. He had brought timbers, and jacks, and chains. It took a while to stuff enough timber under to even start.

I laid in bed, enjoying the leveling. Monika scowled.

Dustin and Jonathan joined in the fray outside.

Eventually I was summoned to drive the "tow vehicle," our little 4-wheel drive Subaru wagon. "OK," Carl explained. "This is going to be a bit tricky." I could see he had tied a few nylon tow straps together with one end hooked to Rambo and the other to a tow bracket on the front of the little car. (Fairly obvious this was provided to pull the little car out of the mud, and not the other way around.)

Carl had already backed the Subaru up to tighten the tow straps. He explained, "Now you back straight out with the car. I just need a tug. Don't pull too hard. Don't make the wheels spin. And when Rambo comes out, just keep the strap tight. And try not to back into a tree."

Har har, the closest tree was like two miles away. After all, who had gotten us into this mess in the first place?

It was almost too easy. The timbers and boards held, as Carl eased the truck backward and onto firmer ground, sort of like a small cricket pulling a giant beetle across a sea of face powder.

When we made it to "shore," Monika drove the Subaru home and was not seen again for hours.

"Two cars passed me, but wouldn't stop to pick me up," Carl recounted. "My record at hitchhiking is—nil."

"It might have been your shoes," I chuckled (a little). "You must be beat," I said.

"Mostly my feet are killing me. Worst shoes I could possibly have worn for a midnight hike down the pavement and gravel in pitch black."

"Oh. Did I forget to mention? The flashlight in the jockey box was dead."

The batteries are always dead when you have boys around.

There's Hope

Another Wyoming winter wind roars through the canyon, wrapping huge snow drifts around the corners of our house. Both the snow and the temperature continue to fall, as rows of icicles twist off the eaves. Our driveway is impassable—mounds of snow and ice meeting the retaining wall, blocking any access. The dirt road to the highway is invisible, as the wind has blown snow racing across its width until halted by the barriers of timothy grass and weeds.

All three kids have earlier arrived for Christmas Eve—even Jonathan, our college son who lately comes home only to get a box out of storage, or ask for a little cash. I'm content as the raging blizzard whirs around the windows and doors. The heat from the fireplace has caused steam to form on the windows—I wipe it away and call the grandchildren over to sneak a peek at Santa streaking through the sky.

Mom has joined us this holiday.

Dad has been gone for 21 years. I miss him tonight and squeeze my eyes tight for a moment, envisioning him standing at the window, trying to catch Santa *in the act*.

With perfect recall, I see him welding a pipefitting, clamped in the vise on the back of his truck bed. He's wearing his red polka-dotted welding cap; the bill turned backward to ward off stray sparks. The grey welder revs as he strikes his arc. Tiring of the noisy exhaust pipe, he had built a custom-made bird muffler. This fat bird's metal body sported wings—metal plates cut in jags. In his beak he clamped a ball bearing, resembling a perfectly round berry. This bird flapped around the pipe with any wind gust or puff of exhaust. When he turned just right his

This snow cave we built in early April, 1983 -- in our driveway! The snow was much like the storm that kept us all penned in for Christmas. (Left-right,) Dustin, Monika, and Jonathan.

tail feathers covered a perfect pile of bearing Babbitt, a tin and lead alloy that can be heated and formed to look surprisingly like bird droppings.

He told my sister Christie one summer that he felt so good that day at work that he unlaced his work boots, slipped them under the cab, and walked barefoot through the sand. I wonder how many other whimsical birds he would have made if there weren't so many days when he felt bad. Dad was prone to pneumonia, had ¾ of his ulcer-ridden stomach removed, and was one of the first to undergo heart by-pass surgery—all before he was 50. Many winter days he sloshed through the frozen mud down in the hole, struggling through pain and fatigue. Many nights he fell asleep exhausted in his recliner—eyeglasses eschew--one sock on, and the other dangling off the end of his toes. Oil rigs were man-eating drills that made the bosses rich.

He never wanted to be an old man. He died at age 52, missing any stint in the nursing home (where they had an ejection seat that could shoot you straight to heaven). He would chide, "Have you ever seen one of those old people go in there and come out alive?"

My thoughts quickly return to the present as the fireplace tools are accidentally knocked over, hit the hearth, and bounce to the floor. The cat screeches and runs under the couch. The children arrange cookies on Santa's plate and actually ask when it's bedtime. I'm not ready for them to go to bed, but they know Santa won't come when they're awake. I tell them the story of their uncle Dustin setting his alarm clock for 3:00 a.m. so he could wake and catch the old boy coming down the chimney.

"Did he catch him grandma?"

Once again too many gifts and toys erupt from under the tree. The adults want to see each individual gift—savoring the unwrapping. Mother tries to organize some of the bedlam, but gives up and watches as mounds of wrapping paper bury plastic toys, candy boxes, dollies, and plaid flannel shirts.

Mother pops into the bedroom and brings back a large manila envelope—my gift. As I pry open the clips, I think maybe it's a photo, never guessing the treasure that lies inside—a letter from dad. I quickly recognize his sprawling handwriting as I read the first paragraph-

> Dear Dixie and our family,
>
> What a Summer (77) What a Family! Dixie you and I really started something and I don't mind saying there was some fun in the doing. I had to write this down. When I tried to send Willard back up to Tony's house, he just wouldn't go this time. When he seen you and the kids all pull out in the car he just caved in and layed down. I guess we threw too many sticks for him to chase into Yellowtail Lake and made him pull the boat in to shore too many times.

I audibly inhale a sob as I lay the papers in my lap and look toward Mother. "I've sent your sisters and brother a copy of this letter for Christmas this year." She thinks we've seen it before, little realizing the significance of the gift she's given. As I talk to each sibling that day, we echo each other's statements across the miles. "Remember Willard? That crazy lab ate live firecrackers like popcorn. I really miss dad today. Do you think he'll look down on our next 4th of July?"

I carry the pictures of that summer in my heart all day, but wait to finish the letter in the quiet of the night. Laying comfortably on my bed, I continue and, a slide show begins—one where reality *is* that summer and dad's still here and the crazy chaotic Olsen clan have descended on the old home for the 4th of July. The icy snow is forgotten and I'm glad to be trapped in my warm home viewing scenes from that summer, the summer of '77.

...Snakes have always been my favorite fireworks. I love to put two side by side and watch the little black bits fatten and grow as the fire feeds their writhing, crispy fluff. As the wind disconnects them and scatters ashes all over the yard, the fourth of July holiday is officially brought in and blown throughout the neighborhood.

I'm less enchanted with the booby traps my kids find so fascinating. For days surrounding the holiday, I'll deal with stretched strings setting off flashes of burnt paper. They tire of setting the traps on doorknobs and proceed to the gas pedal on my Toyota. I now have to watch for contraband on any moving item, even the toilet handles.

Monika and Dustin have stashed some of their booby traps to try the nerves of unsuspecting family in Wyoming. Each year we travel toward a familiar routine of activities spiced with chaotic, crazy laughter and confusion—our favorite day of the year.

Tony and I are the only ones with children in 1977. Dad worries about the little ones, remembering the hazards of his own childhood. He warns the children of the danger of matches and punks but allows them the freedom of playing on the drain ditch bank littered with plenty of rocks for snake burning. He teasingly thrusts out the joint of his dismembered pointer finger stating, "This is what can happen when fireworks blow up in your hand." They play outside all day collecting grass stains, dirt particles, and fallen red bottle rocket sticks.

Sister Cheri has mentally geared up for the noise level, but is ready to bolt with her boyfriend, Steve, if the confusion becomes

Pyrotechnicians (l-r) Jay Tony, Justin and Jacob Olsen, plus Karl Krivanec. Note the size of the pipes and "bombs."

unbearable. Our little sister, fourteen-year-old Cathy, is easily annoyed with all the antics, but jokes her way through the melee. "Yeah, watch the war break out when all those kids start running through the house."

Before beginning the five-hour trip from college in Idaho, Our other sister, Christie, petitions for safety angels, as she drives the crumbling Buick homeward. A few miles from the house she spots billowing smoke rolling out the engine. She keeps a steady foot on the accelerator and swings into the driveway as Dad rushes out to greet her. He quickly springs the hood, freeing fire and smoke. "Get some water, she made it to the driveway."

We girls spend much of the time recounting silly stories that have us laughing so hard we get weak-kneed, slump, and roll on the floor. This secret society is undeclared, just there. Periodically we blurt out synchronized words marked with the same inflections. At these times we stop for a moment and say, "Ah" as if it still is a bit of a surprise. We get it. Others don't.

The rhythms of the holiday begin as surely as the presence of the American flag leading the parade. The morning of July fourth our caravan drives the thirty minutes to Cody for the Stampede Parade. Unfolding our lawn chairs, we stake a claim along the sidewalk edge and spread blankets spilling into the gutters. Here the children bounce, waiting for flying candy or miniature flags on sticks.

Every year there are way too many horse entries and not enough candy thrown to satisfy the treasure-seeking cousins. At least one child goes berserk as the mountain men load their rifles and blast deafening black powder wads. Every year mother points out the same man making music on the Elks Band Wagon. "There's your Uncle Ike's brother."

Year after year she unabashedly shouts, "Hi Hope—over here Hope"-- to our cousin's wife, Hope, the dog groomer.

I can't help but check her out one more time as she struts down the entire parade route on stiletto heels, wearing a pink ruffled dress and flamboyantly netted hat. She follows her perfectly coffered pink-dyed poodle holding high her dog grooming sign advertising, *There's Hope for your Pooch*.

Mom always says, "She's in good shape."

Dad talks about strange genetics in his wife's family.

Tony chuckles and tips his head in recognition.

Christie feels like now she's home.

Cheri looks ahead.

Cathy muses, "Nothing changes."

Hope Sheets and her "pooch" (above) and Monika lighting bottle rockets at her grandfather's home in Powell.

Dance Moves

I'm going to blab about another secret—only known to a few. Every Friday night in high school there was a dance at the log building and I was there. Even though the "Wa-Watusi" was going out of style, I knew it. "The Freddy" was easy, absolutely loved "The Jerk," and danced "The Hustle."

The first time I saw Carl was at a dance. My girlfriend had scoped him out and told me he was cute. He was leaning against the stage and I asked him to dance. He was from Cody—a tall, skinny, blue-eyed hunk. I led him onto the dance floor.

The secret is, he couldn't dance.

Carl was raised in a church that didn't believe in dancing. And so, he took up playing the guitar—listening to records for hours—memorizing the chords. He started his music career as a bouncer for a local rock band. Soon, he was whaling on stage with them. His band played off and on at what everyone knew as the log building.

A few years after I had met *The Hunk* he was playing the electric guitar on stage at the same log building, stepping on his wah wah pedal screaming through *Light my Fire*. I didn't make the connection to the guy that couldn't dance. These guys were good. They even had strobe lights. I had my favorite dance partners, moving to *Magic Carpet Ride, Spinning Wheel, Twist and Shout.*

Sitting around a table at the college student union three years after our introduction, one of my friends asked me if I knew Carl Bechtold. "He has the most gorgeous eyes, and you keep your hands off him," she said. Well, I had eaten grasshoppers, spied on pickled cow heads, and tried to nurse a cat. My curiosity wasn't going to be curtailed by a little threat.

Days later, I discovered my challenge sitting at a table in the student union. His blonde hair dropped over one eye, mustache and sideburns thicker than any nineteen-year-old I had ever met. But, rumor had it he was done with women. A of couple bad experiences had shut down any desire to date.

I flirted.

A lot.

It took me a month to get him to ask me out. It took two months more to get him to kiss me. One night sitting beside him in his white Ford Fairlane, I noticed him turn and sneak a puff of mouth spray… *and then he kissed me, and then he kissed me, and then he kissed me.*

I had won.

His band became more popular. We were going steady. He didn't care if I danced while he played. I danced "The Grapevine" to *Turn Turn Turn.*

And after we married, some of the old band members joined with a couple of new ones and he played weekends to help with the cost of attending the University of Wyoming. I pretty much gave up dancing.

Until….

We moved to Green River, Wyoming. By then we had Monika and Dustin and I wanted to hang out with the girls once in a while. One of my good friends, DeAnn, mentioned joining a dancing group. I didn't know about all the silk and tassels. She talked me into it.

Belly-dancing.

Yep, I registered, bought the finger cymbals and took the class. Not willing to invest in the costumes until I knew this was the dance for me, I worked out in t-shirts and polyester pants.

The teacher told us that in countries where belly-dancing is a custom, ALL women are considered beautiful, no matter what their belly size. Okay, if any size goes, I was up for it.

Belly dancing involves many more parts than the belly. Coordination, rhythm, muscles—all of it was a lot of work.

Sometimes when Carl worked late and the kids were in bed, I'd close all the drapes, pull out my belly-dancing record, and practice. I was actually good at the camel walk and hip rolls, but I didn't disclose my practice habits to Carl for a few weeks. Maybe I wanted to have the charms dangling from my hips first. I had to have one of those tinkling veils for sure. He knew I was taking the class, but not practicing with the house sealed off.

Of course when I told him of my late-night hidden rehearsals, he wanted me to put on the record right away. I only did a couple camel walk steps and figure-eighted my hips a while. I don't think he told me to get a day job, I'm the one that decided I was a whole lot more comfortable dancing the "Freddy," "Grapevine," or "Wa-Watusi."

The belly-dancing record stayed with me longer than the lessons. I joined the women's softball team instead. Actually, if I tried to belly dance these days, my belly would circle the whole continent and maybe never come back.

Wands, Wires, and Air Waves

I breezed through ticketing and headed for security; purse over one shoulder, C-PAP breathing machine dangling from the other, coat and scarf over one arm, my carry-on rumbling behind. As I slipped my shoes into the bin, that nagging thought that viruses were free to attach to my socks surfaced, but otherwise, I was in travel mode. I passed with flying colors. At the end of the belt, I grabbed my stuff from the bins, plopped my shoes on the floor, tugged on one and hopped around until I could dive into the other. I made it to Gate C in time for the announcement.

"Attention passengers. Due to bad weather, flight number 320 to Chicago has been canceled. We hope to get you out within the hour on the next flight."

Okay, I'll pass the time reading.

I headed for the book stand and set down my gear. Not wanting to leave anything unattended, I stood like a flag pole in front of one shelf and perused. *The Accidental Tourist*, now that's a book to fit the situation. I scooted my stuff between my feet and inched away, a Near Death Experience book in hand.

Back at Gate C, I claimed one of the stiff blue chairs, wondering how many germs were flipping around the cushions, how many weary bums have occupied this unyielding piece of furniture.

In the next couple of hours, two more nonproductive announcements bounced around the blue chairs. Grumbling travelers cursed the snow, the airlines, the idiotic mismanagement.

I stood, stretched my hip sockets, slung my coat over my arm, slipped my purse handle over my shoulder, grabbed my machine and the handle to my carry-on, and headed for a bagel, leaving my scarf to claim the evil chair.

The snack did give me a boost, but needing a break from reading, I loaded all my stuff again and sprinted to the garbage can to dispose of my bagel sack.

The microphone clicked. Yes! It's got to be a boarding call.

"We thank you for your patience. All morning flights going into and out of O'Hare have been cancelled. Please go to baggage claim number one and retrieve your luggage. You'll be booked on the first available flight out."

Hey, it's pushing two o'clock. Let's call the whole thing off.

My arm was hot. My purse heavy. Blisters, raised from bouncing my breathing machine and purse from one shoulder to the other squeaked as I once again pulled my suitcase through the halls. A line as long as the entrance to Disney's "Haunted House" beaded around a ninety degree in the distance.

One of the agents behind the counter screeched, "You people making a connecting flight, form a different line." Her ruby fingernail pointed off into the wild blue yonder. I thought of the witch-infested haunted house.

This line is shorter, I thought. I'm back in business.

For the second time that day I got a ticket and repeated the security ritual. What! The alarm screamed as I went under the arch.

"I went through here this morning and passed the guards."

Nobody smiled.

"Take off your watch, step back, and try again. "

Do they think they've got a criminal here?

The alarm brayed again.

My face flared.

"We need a female check here."

You've got to be kidding.

Her profile was much like any other security person; six foot two inches, approximately 300 pounds, brunette, all business—mean pulsing from her eyes.

Mother used to trip the buzzers with her hip replacement paraphernalia when she f;ew, but I still have my originals. So WHAT's doing this?

She pointed her wand, "Your leg."

I looked at my leg.

"Hold out your leg for the wand."

I lifted my leg.

My purse is going to be stolen from the end of the conveyer belt.

"Okay, now I'll run the wand over the rest of your body."

You'll do what to what?

Wand down one side, wand down the other, triggered the beeper two times.

"Do you really think you're going to find something on me?"

"Everyone is subject. Even the flight attendants are checked."

But, are these flight attendants pushing sixty and already have made it through the bad-boy barricade once today?

The wand traveled around my perimeter, circling like a lit sparkler on the 4th of July. There were no sparkles however, only rapid-fire beeps jetting out the end.

It's got to be my underwire bra. I'm going to laugh.

"I've got to pat you down."

Joke's over.

Her fingertips jabbed under one armpit then under the other one. She squished the wire over my cleavage a couple of times, pushing clear to the bone. I glared at her.

I wonder if these guys don't have enough to do.

"You can go on through. This happens from time to time. We found nothing."

Duh, I knew that. Next time I'm going to demand a search warrant. I grabbed my junk, then stopped at the nearest counter for pain reliever and another bottle of water.

At gate B6 I claimed a blue seat, my new best friend.

The stupid microphone flipped on. "We thank you again for flying with our airline. Your plane will arrive at this gate in approximately two hours."

Or days, I thought.

Four p.m. We were finally in the air. My nerves were ragged. When the cart rolled by I asked for a V8 with a slice of lemon. Taking a deep breath, normalcy was returning, until the voice of doom interrupted. "This is your pilot speaking. We're behind several planes trying to land at O'Hare. We're going to circle to kill some time."

Wrong word choice.

Why don't we just give up and go back home? I hear my bed calling me.

Circling like a big gray vulture got to my stomach. The next announcement got to my nerves. "We are running low on fuel. Your copilot and I have decided to divert to Iowa for fueling. We'll let you know more as details come in."

Dorothy was blown out of Kansas, not Iowa. No place like home.

We sat tight. The fasten seatbelt light was off at least. I felt the need to go, but no way was I chancing that tiny toilet. We had been there a good long time.

Those toilets are overflowing.

I tried not to think about it. I'm glad I didn't buy *The Accidental Tourist.*

After forever, the pilot apologized. "Chicago has opened additional runways. Visibility continues to vacillate, but we're going in." My Near Death Experience lay unopened in the seat pocket.

We'll all be killed.

At least I won't have to carry a CPAP to heaven, and, please, don't let them run their wand over my wires at the Pearly Gates.

At midnight we bumped down the runway. "The airlines will hold your luggage and issue you a new departure ticket for tomorrow. Weather in the windy city is blustery and snowing—ten degrees below zero, Fahrenheit." The hairs on my big toes stood up.

Wonder if they'll pay for a hotel. At least I don't have to go to baggage claim. Oh no, I don't get to go to baggage claim. Well, as long as I have my breathing machine, I can do without everything else. Morning breath and sweaty socks are the least of the troubles I've seen. When I get to that hotel room I'm going to stuff this dad-burned bra in my purse for the flight tomorrow. No wire, no wand.

A stewardess pointed out the line for vouchers. The crowd bolted to get in front. I bolted for the bathroom.

When I got to the place, the lines for ticket vouchers were folded back on themselves so many times, unfolded they might have reached the White House.

Just two people away from the desk, some grumpy attendant plopped the *Closed* sign stand right in front of my feet. "What are we supposed to do?" I asked.

"Go back to your arrival gate and get a ticket voucher. We're on overtime here."

Yep, know what you mean. Those grandma hugs are way overdue.

"Do we at least get a discount on hotel rooms?"

"Not from the airlines. As instructed, go back to your gate."

They're all malcontents. These gate keepers have forgotten that *fly the friendly skies* motto advertised when I was young.

Back at the gate, I asked the lady, "Can I get a hotel discount because of all the delays?"

"We don't give discounts because of weather. You must be new to air travel."

I thought she was going to say "doo doo happens."

She wanted to.

She handed me a card. "The hotels listed here give a percentage off for stranded travelers."

Mental note: This situation sounds common. Why isn't my layover in Denver? Joke is everyone who lives in the West has to fly through Denver. If you die you have to go through Denver.

I fumbled for my cell phone.

"Yes, we do have a room left, but our last courtesy bus left the airport ten minutes ago. You'll have to call a taxi."

My loving, grandmotherly-self had departed and I was a plain, ticked-off mama. I snarled at miss unfriendly, "Can't you at least call me a cab?"

"Not our job. You'll find courtesy phones in the lobby. Go up the stairs to the fourth floor, swing around to your right and look at the walkway, decide if you want to walk on it or carry your stuff another three miles to the train stopping at gate C after it stops at A, B, B1, and Cincinnati; hop on, take three flights of stairs down to the main terminal, turn left and walk around the potted plants growing under the *Welcome to Chicago* sign. Most times taxis are waiting but since it's late you'll have to call one from........blah blah blah."

May your car stall tonight, may your purse dislocate your shoulder, and when you need to go, may every toilet at this so-called airport be frozen up as tight as your airline discounts.

I stifled a tear. "Thanks a lot."

I'm going to report this to Oprah.

My shoulders had lowered at least an inch, bum was asleep, back pinched, and fatigue had invited itself to an overnighter in my eyeballs by the time I found the front.

I called.

Taxi arrived.

I scooted inside.

Don't even think about clicking that meter before you pull away from the curb.

"You staying long in Chicago?"

"No, I'm on my way to visit my grandkids in Minnesota. I missed my connection. I've been trying to get there all day."

"O'Hare gets pounded this time of year. But even when it's nice weather my own grandmother won't visit. She refuses to fly anymore."

After this experience I could understand, but what was her trigger?

"What happened to her?"

"I picked her up right here at this curb. Usually overly perky, she sat and stared like she'd seen a ghost."

Maybe she'd been in a Haunted House line too.

Grandmother finally told me that she should have stayed out of *Victoria's Secret.* I didn't want a discussion about Victoria and changed the subject to her cat. She wouldn't even talk about her tabby, she kept mumbling something really bizarre about "I should have burned my bras when everyone else did."

Bathroom Decor

Carl never piled up toenail chips on the bathtub again. We had to sell the horses, so what fun would the tub scene have been without sliced-hoof accents? I did notice a rather peculiar thing happening in the bathroom again, though. Empty cardboard toilet paper tubes began to pile up in the corner.

I held onto my mouth and waited. Yep, as the days went by, the empty tubes increased until one day, they began resembling some kind of a tower. Neatly stacked I changed my mind about the tower, thinking it might be a layered cake. In the bathroom?

I had to bug him about this latest phenomena. "Dumb question, honey, but what are you building in the bathroom corner?"

"It's a surprise—for you."

"I'm not sure I want to be reminded of all the toilet paper we've gone through."

"You're going to love it."

Hump.

The Eiffel tower climbed the corner, finally reaching tube capacity. Was this his amazing surprise?

I was sick of it, to tell the truth—ready for a wrecking ball. Just when I'd reached the nagging point, I went in and sat on the closed toilet lid. I had to sit, otherwise I might have fallen on the floor. Poking from toilet paper tubes in quite a stunning arrangement, twigs and little branches aped a perfect-looking little tree. Plastic flowers swooped down the cardboard and into plastic greenery. Pinks, reds, yellow—Memorial Day tombstone finery.

I laughed so long, scenes of his other stunts parading in my mind. I did, and do, adore that creative husband of mind. I sat in solitude, soaking in the talent of my budding florist.

I think he was holding onto the designer dream, OR he admired the attention. He was planning more décor. I had purchased one of those metal wall vases—the ones with scrollies on the front, kind of shaped like an upside down dustpan, I pondered on the exact flowers to set off the shower curtain, maybe something with flamingo-colored vines cascading down the wall.

The "dust pan" hung there quite a while—until the day I went into the bathroom again. This time I didn't swoon, but I couldn't take it in.

Carl had saved up dryer lint from several loads and beautifully (okay—not) arranged puffs of it in the wall vase. He'd stretched fine filigrees in grey, a few gum wrappers and jean threads hanging on like spiders.

Hey, folks are selling tumbleweeds for dining room table accents, why couldn't we write a how-to book? Maybe, *Seventeen Ways to Recycle Dryer Lint and Toilet Paper Tubes.*

Where or When?

Mrs. Farley lived two bean fields away. I'd seen her once at a neighborhood picnic, brushing her straggly hair over the dessert table and swatting flies with her purse.

One Friday afternoon, as I was winding down from a long school week, her name was mentioned.

"Mrs. Farley is a lonely woman," Mother said as she sliced a jellyroll. "Her husband passed on last year."

Mother wiped powdered sugar from her hands and turned back to the sink.

"She needs some company. You'll be good for her."

I froze. "What?"

"She's a nice lady. It's just one evening. You can walk down and spend the night." I opened my mouth to protest, but she kept going. "Think what it would be like to be alone day after day."

I didn't really like to be alone either. Mother had a knack for laying on the guilt, smooth as glass candy.

"She's our neighbor; we should really help her out when we can."

You help her out if you like her so much, I thought. Even though I wanted to go to a show with my friends, I knew I couldn't avoid going to Mrs. Farley's. Okay, there's a first time for everything, including babysitting fly-swatting-moldy-oldies.

Dad was spraying weeds along the fence as I set out for her old house. "I hear you're staying overnight with the old lady."

"Mother wants me to go," I said, kicking my shoe over some loose gravel. "Her son's going to pay me."

"From what I hear, that guy's a skinflint. Doubt you'll get much out of him."

I reached down and picked a weed. "I wanted to go to the show tonight."

"You might get a show alright; you know why the old lady needs you down there don't you?" Dad took off his cap and scratched his head. "She's afraid of being alone with her husband's ghost."

I recognized that grin—the one that scooted over his lips when he was teasing, but the tone was set.

"Take care of the old gal," Dad called after me as I took off down the dirt road, squeezing the paper sack Mother had packed with my nightgown.

I paused by an anthill taller than my anklets and watched ants carrying seeds three times their size. Minutes later, I slid into the empty ditch to monitor ladybugs.

Lollygagging further down the road, I braved a glimpse at Wire Hair's clapboard house. It was neglected—brambled with woody shrubs. Peeking into my sack, I checked to see if Mother had remembered my teddy bear.

Just then a pheasant whirred from a cottonwood stand a few yards behind me. Startled out of my gizzard, I wondered if an eleven-year-old girl could up and die of fright.

As I crossed Mrs. Farley's yard, a barn swallow darted at me, apparently an occupant of one of the several nests stuck to the lopsided eaves of her ramshackle house. That swallow probably had a host of nasty friends ready to turn on me.

I wanted to run, but imagined tomorrow's headlines, "Girl Pecked to Death by Half-Crazed Swallows."

I tiptoed to the front porch, ignored the split screen across the old lady's door and knocked.

"It's about time someone came," Wire Hair said as she opened the screechy door.

I stood on the threshold and looked at my shoes.

"My nincompoop son never shows up here," she said.

I looked at her shoes, worn and bunion-bulged.

Maybe her son never showed because of the odor. A mingling of mold, cat pee, and old-lady skin thickened the room.

"Let me look at you," she said, thrusting her head an inch from my eyeballs. Her breath killed any response. Stymied by the smell of her false teeth, a mixture hinting of putty and cat tuna, I was rocked back on my heels.

Wire Hair beckoned me into her front room and motioned me to sit. Straightening the doily on the armchair, I resisted the urge to bolt.

The lamp above my head oozed a dim glow. An ancient cane chair rested in the corner, the caning sagging in the shape of a big-bottomed somebody. My captor moved toward the sofa. *She* had not made the dent in that chair. Wire Hair Farley was shrunken and bony as the insides of a trout.

She nudged a half-naked cat out of her way. Wads of fur had sloughed off its skin. "Cinnamon's got the mange," she muttered, not bothering to brush off her housedress. Little wreaths of cat hair matted Cinnamon's favorite spots. I scratched my nose and spit out a few hairs.

Holding back a sneeze, I tilted my head and caught a good look at the ceiling. It should have come down around her chapped ears long ago. Cracks the size of lightning bolts scarred the plaster. Cobwebs hung like safety nets under circus performers.

"It's amusing to have a smart girl like you visit," she said.

I'll act dumb, I thought to myself. Then I'll never have to come back.

"You ever play cards?" She asked.

I nodded my head. She whipped out a rickety card table from behind the couch and snapped the rubber band on a worn deck of cards.

"A good game of crazy eights makes my blood pump."

"I'm not good at cards," I lied. When it was my turn to change suits, I named one I didn't have in my hand. I figured if I kept up that tactic she'd win in a hurry. It worked.

"You don't have a prayer at learning this game," she said, shaking her head as she rose. "Let's eat. I'm so hungry I could eat shoe strings."

I trailed her to the kitchen.

The gas burners on the stovetop were crusted in grease. They smelled like burnt pinfeathers. I pictured her singeing hens over the flames. Oh please, don't whip out the skillet and start frying up chicken.

She opened the Frigidaire freezer and yanked two TV dinners from its ice-encrusted cavern. "You like chicken?" she asked. Relieved that dinner was sealed, I blurted out, "My favorite."

She grabbed an oven mitt, the thumb burnt clear off. Reaching into the smoking oven, she asked. "Do you say grace?" Our family always said a prayer before meals, but all of a sudden my dimples caved in and in my mind I silently repeated:

Rubba-dub-dub
Thanks for the grub.
Yea… Jesus!

I answered Wire Hair Farley, "Not for TV dinners." My mother had never served a TV dinner in her life, so it really wasn't a lie.

I picked at my food.

She gobbled down everything, even the freezer-burnt corn.

"I like these new-fangled disposable dinners," Mrs. Farley said and tossed the tray into the paper sack she used for trash. "Saves on the mess." Cinnamon thumped off the linoleum counter top, landing between my feet. Dropping my tray into the sack, I resigned myself to more of old Wire Hair's chatter. "We might as well watch some TV," she said and headed back to the sofa.

Watching TV was preferable to the thought I had held in the back of my mind all evening. I just knew she was going to invite me to comb her lovely hair—she seemed to have been so proud of it at the picnic. I suspected cooties back then and they were probably still holed up in her bun.

Cinnamon yowled, waylaying my fear. "Needs out," she said, sidling to the door. "She's got a litter box right in the kitchen, but she likes to prowl."

The box was obvious.

A stream of cold air goose-bumped my legs as she let Cinnamon out.

"One night she dragged a dying bird in here, feathers flying everywhere. How's a body supposed to keep the place clean?"

Birds had died in the house? I wondered if she buried them in beds of cat hair. I shivered and drew my legs into my chest.

"Don't you be putting your feet on the furniture," Mrs. Farley said. "That's Elmer's chair. Don't need him coming back here all out of sorts."

I dropped my legs, my oxfords thudding in unison on the floor. Consequences were coming from beyond, I had dared to plop my shoes on her old man's chair.

But suddenly I had a problem bigger than cooties or cats. I needed to go! I crossed my legs and decided to hold it.

By the time Perry Mason and Della were sorting new evidence, I was wiggling. Old Wire Hair showed no signs of sleepiness. In fact, she had gotten more animated.

"Elmer and me used to do some square dancin' on Friday nights before these new-fangled televisions."

She got up and faked a do-si-do around her partner. I leaned back in my chair, just in case it was Elmer's ghost she was swinging with. I knew by the size of the sag in that chair if it was old Elmer, his swing might catapult her smack into my lap.

Farley fell to the couch, landing with all her limbs unlatched. She sure was wiry for such an old lady.

"I'm going to hit the hay," she said. "You can stay up as late as you want."

I stood up and stretched, nonchalantly asking, "Where's your bathroom?"

"No bathroom in here." She pointed toward the door that Cinnamon had recently exited, "Just the outhouse behind the clothes line."

1960 and no indoor toilet!

"You can use the chamber pot in my room if you can't bring yourself to go outside."

Go outside? I wouldn't be caught dead outside. With my luck, those swallows hovering around the eaves were nocturnal. That chamber pot nonsense was a *no* too, probably hadn't been emptied since Elmer croaked. And who knew what weirdness lurked in her bedroom. Maybe she pinned live moths to her reading lamp.

"That's all right," I said.

She shrugged her shoulders.

"You'll sleep in the spare bedroom. I save it for company."

I gulped and followed her.

Inside the room, a bare light bulb struggled to stay attached to the ceiling. Wire Hair snagged the string and pulled. Sparse light crept around the bed, made up with a quilt pieced from the fattest neckties I had ever seen.

I gingerly set my sack of clothes on the chest of drawers. A satin scarf with the word MOTHER embroidered across the top momentarily comforted me. Then I remembered her good-for-nothing son had probably bought it for her. Why couldn't he have bought her a toilet?

"Don't let the bed bugs bite," she said as she closed the door behind her. Never before had that expression made so much sense. I scratched the back of my neck and took Teddy out of my sack. Lifting him for a hug, I smelled the fur under his neck, hoping for a whiff of home.

Leery about undressing in a strange bedroom, I sat on the bed, my nightgown in hand. A dull ache traveled through my middle, but I hoped that I could sleep through my need to pee.

Turning to divine intervention, I slipped on my nightgown and kneeled by the bed. My predicament seemed like a petty problem in the scope of universal goings on, but I whispered, "Sorry for saying that Rubba-dub-dub prayer at supper. Please make this agony go away and keep Elmer in heaven, where he belongs. Amen."

I resorted to lifting up the covers. I was already on my knees I expected an immediate answer to my problem in the form of an abandoned chamber pot under there. Nothing but cat hair coated the shadows.

I stretched on tiptoes and snagged the light string; complete darkness--blacker than the inside of a crow. Wondering how big bed bugs were, I settled into a sunken spot in the mattress and laid still enough to eventually drift into an eerie sleep.

Nightmares about cats, birds, and disjointed square dancers jangled across my sleep. I dreamed it was Halloween and I had dressed like a clown in a polka-dotted suit and a giant necktie.

Suddenly, I found myself in a strange neighborhood where all the trick-or-treaters screeched like birds. I had to go to the bathroom so bad that when I spotted a lopsided, door-less outhouse, nothing would stop me. Tugging at my zipper, I stepped inside. The tab wouldn't budge.

I woke with my legs in a knot. Creeping out of bed, I swung my hand around for the light string, but gave up and inched my way across the room. I needed to open the window wide enough for my bare bottom to hang over the edge.

When I felt the closet door, I knew I was moving in the right direction. As I slid my fingers down the molding, a filmy net broke loose, gloving my hand with cobwebs.

More accustomed to the darkness, I headed to the wisp of moonlight seeping under the shade. Fly bodies scrunched as my hands rested on the sill. I pushed on the pane. It was painted shut.

I felt my legs tighten harder in denial.

Desperate for any receptacle, I obsessed on finding a shoe in the closet. My urge outweighed the fear of opening the closet door. But if I found Elmer standing inside, drumming his fingers on the coat hangers, I'd have a real excuse for wetting my pants. I opened the door, fell on my knees, and swept the floor with both arms.

Another cobweb caught me by the nose as I rose to get some air. Ripping it off, my arm bumped something solid, sending debris clattering down on my head.

I sat motionless, braced for the next blow. Choking from dust, I coughed and wiped my eyes, realizing I had a good-sized lump above my ear. Rubbing the spot, my elbow bumped into an object jutting from my lap. I ran my hand up the knobby length curving around into the form of a cane. It must have been hooked over the clothes rod. Mrs. Farley probably used it to beat the begeebies out of Elmer during his night stalks.

I didn't need a weapon, what I needed was relief. Maybe I would squat down and go right in the closet. I wrestled with right and wrong in my ethical note cards and decided to go back to bed and wait it out till morning. Earlier, I didn't want any money from the old lady or her son, but things had changed. The agony was worth at least two bucks.

Back in bed, I rubbed Teddy's belly in hypnotic strokes. You don't have to go. You don't have to go. You're getting sleepy. Your eyelids are getting heavy.

The last thing I remembered was a feeling of desperation swelling my imagination with new headlines, "Girl Dies of Ruptured Bladder—Old Woman Accused of Locking Her in Bedroom."

I woke up to the smell of coffee. Looking around, I saw the walking stick lying on the floor and dead fly bodies scattered across the windowsill.

I became aware of a sore spot on my head, and then remembered my predicament. The searing pain of my overloaded bladder seemed gone. I reached under the covers to feel my backside, certain that the bed would be sopped.

It was dry as a biscuit.

Dressing in yesterday's outfit, I pulled at some clingy hair tufts and gathered Teddy into my sack.

"I don't suppose you drink coffee?" Wire Hair asked as I walked into the kitchen. She was doodling on a newspaper.

"No, I'm not thirsty."

Cinnamon stretched on the floor. Two fat flies buzzed around the stove. Mrs. Farley reached for her nearby purse, swatted, but missed both of them.

"How long you want to stay?"

"I have a lot of homework, I better get going."

Mrs. Farley stood and walked toward me, fishing through the contents of the purse. Pulling out a quarter she demanded, "You take this money."

Even though I wasn't in immediate pain, last night's whole charade erupted in my head like a shaken soda pop. It had been creepy, but I had survived. The way this woman lived, she needed every quarter in her fly-swatting purse.

"That's okay. You don't need to pay me."

"I can't let you go home without something."

Mrs. Farley headed for her bedroom. Worried that she might bring me a petrified piece of Miss Havisham's wedding cake, I got up and paced until she returned.

"I got this in one of those Cracker Jack boxes," she said, as she opened her fingers and thrust a miniature magnifying glass at me—a plastic bobble that wouldn't have enlarged a thing.

I smiled at her, relieved it wasn't cake.

I just wanted to go home.

I hesitated. She wasn't a bad old lady. I figured she *was* scared of Elmer's ghost floating down to cause what was left of Cinnamon's hair stand on end. But he hadn't appeared despite my fears. He was probably afraid of her purse.

A car honked out front. Maybe Mother sensed I wanted out of there. "Thanks for the Cracker Jack prize."

Mrs. Farley shooed me out as Cinnamon streaked past, leaving a wad of hair on my pedal pushers.

I turned to wave at her, but she had disappeared.

I glanced at the outhouse on the way out. There was a door, but when a gust of wind rushed past, I feared the whole thing would topple.

"Why didn't you tell me Mrs. Farley didn't have a bathroom?" I asked Mother as I climbed into the station wagon and slammed the door.

"I guess I forgot. An outhouse won't hurt you."

"Just hurry," I said, thoughts of relief gushing like water from a hose. "I haven't gone since I left home yesterday." I was pushing my luck carrying a bladder the size of a football.

In my room I stalled, testing my will power to the absolute limits. I moseyed around straightening some books, putting teddy back on my pillow, swiping the windowsill to check for flies. I was on my own terms—a bathroom of my own. The toilet was pink, a perfect place to think. What would I have done in the morning with a soggy shoe, anyway?

Dad was eating breakfast when I came out. He asked if I'd seen any ghosts up there.

"Yeah," I said. "Elmer was in the mood to polka."

"Can the old gal still cut a mean rug?"

"I don't know about any rug cutting, but I'm not going there again. Mrs. Farley can dance all she wants, all the way to the outhouse."

"What'd I tell you about her skinflint son? How'd that privy smell?"

"I didn't go out there and chamber pots scare me too."

"Next time your mom wants to send you up there, tell her I said you can go to the show."

I got no sympathy from Mother. I was determined she would never send me again. I formulated a plan. My two younger sisters could babysit Mrs. Farley. I figured if I paid them a quarter apiece and Mrs. Farley shelled out, they would double their money. Actually the old gal was pretty okay. She let me stay up as long as I wanted and she didn't make me comb her hair, sic Cinnamon on me, or force me to eat swallow eyeballs.

But, I needed reinforcements. Besides, they wouldn't be scared, they'd have each other for support. I bet Mother wouldn't even bring up the outhouse; she'd repeat the nice-thing-to-do theory and "a whole quarter apiece!"

Note: This whole tale is true—Cross my legs and hope to dry.

Womanhood, Part Two

No amount of finger crossing could stay the inevitable.

The visitor came.

This time I wasn't so scared to tell Mother. I knew it was all up to me anyway. She was never going to even hint about the monthlies. We'd tackled the underwear, or... lack of underwear, and now I owned two J.C. Penney bras. In my mind, the next revelation fit under, "Run for your life."

She was in the kitchen again, rubbing another rag around in circles over the counter. Rain obscured any sunlight and the only noise I heard was background from the television show, "Rin Tin Tin."

"Something happened today at school," I said, ready to get to the point. I really didn't feel very good.

"Did you get a bad grade?"

"No, I found some spots on my underwear."

The rag stopped circling the counter and she hesitated a few seconds before replying, "I have some things in my bedroom you can use until we get to the store."

I was mortified that she might actually show me how some of that paraphernalia worked.

She didn't.

Later I found a little brown sack on my bed. Remembering the names of the implements from THE film—an elastic belt and sanitary napkin, I pulled each out of the sack. I called the pad a "Kotex" in my mind, but hated saying the word aloud. I wondered if it could be cut in half, attached to the elastic, and used for a pair of earmuffs. Once again, Mother's silence meant, figure it out on your own.

The girls in junior high were ruthless about this part of femininity. One day after the bell rang, between classes I heard a rumor rumbling down the hall like a bowling ball. A girl had been walking to class and her "Kotex" had fallen on the floor.

"How do you know?" I asked my friend, Violet.

"Two people saw it happen," she said.

I was creeped out. How could something so private suddenly become so public?

"Did she know? What did she do?"

Violet cupped her hand over her mouth and looked at her feet, embarrassed for our fellow comrade, but willing to gossip. "I heard she stopped, looked, kept right on walking."

The girl had been unnoticed before—one of those that looked like she was born old, her skirts touching her ankle socks, her hairdo outdated by at least two generations. Because of the embarrassing incident, she had now been exposed, suspected of having cooties.

No one had ever seen a cootie, but everyone knew who had them.

Physical changes nudged emotional changes. I can prove it.

My grades led me to believe I was smart, yet when the roster for eighth grade was unveiled, I was not in 8A. I was in 8B. At least I wasn't clear down in 8F. Those guys were doomed. Everyone knew the principal set up the system alphabetically in descending order—the brains in 8A, down to the dummies in 8F.

That B placement rattled the shaky esteem I tenderly carried, like a rag doll whipped between the teeth of a big dog. Self-labeling stuck me in the ranks of the skags—ugly girls with no chance with the boys.

With my peers, I didn't stand a chance, but one of my dad's friends from Utah had a son my age. They visited a couple of times a year. After dinner, the adults talked away. I got Michael and me out of there.

"We've got an owl outside in a big metal cage my dad made. Want to see it?" I asked. I should take that stinky hamburger out to him. Did you know the chili was made with deer hamburger?" I wrinkled my nose pinching it together in a pee-yew symbol. "That's why I picked out the meat and laid it around the rim of my bowl. I can't stand deer meat."

Michael perked up. "Does your dad hunt? Did he find the owl out hunting?" he asked.

He found Mr. Owl out in the oil field and I think that was my uncle's deer. Dad said my uncle gut-shot it. Dad thinks the critter ate sagebrush and cactus needles."

Michael's mind seemed to have wandered down some wooded trail. "My dad took me hunting once. I had to wear an orange vest. My feet were numb." I thought he was going to tell me he didn't like hunting, but he said, "It was fun. My dad let me shoot his rifle."

"Did you actually shoot a deer?" I asked, really curious about why he would like bloody dead deer.

"No, but my dad and I ate some of the heart. We cooked it on a stick."

That grossed me out, but I was listening. I thought he was cute.

He must have been tired of hunt talk. He asked me, "What's your best subject?" both hands stuffed in the pockets of his blue jeans.

"English and Spanish," I said, standing a bit taller.

"I'm pretty good at math," he said.

Math was the worst. I knew my math grades were the reason why I was in 8B. I changed the subject this time.

"Let's go check out the owl. He has the weirdest yellow eyes." I started to lift the tarp off Mr. Owl's cage, but remembered it wasn't quite time for him to wake so we moseyed over to a couple of hay bales beside the corral. Too soon, his little brother came out yelling that they were leaving. "Maybe we can write sometime," Michael said, looking down at his boots.

When he left, I daydreamed about him coming to visit me at school. Everyone would see Michael, his arm leaning on my locker just inches from my face. He would look into my eyes, wait while I stacked my books on his arm, and walk me to class.

The next week I got a lumpy envelope from Michael in the mailbox. Inside, a short note explained.

Dear Cindy,

I kind of liked the chili. Do you want to go steady?

Your friend, Michael

I couldn't breathe—and it wasn't my asthma. A new feeling swirled through my being, like a chiffon scarf tickling my neck.

Shaking the envelope, I dislodged his ring. He wasn't old enough for a class ring, but the black stone was perfect. I twirled it around each finger, mesmerized by its boy-ness. All the girls going steady wrapped the back of their rings with tape to make them fat enough to fit their own finger. We didn't have a piece of masking tape in the house. I looked for my sturdiest necklace, disassembled the gold heart and threaded Michael's ring through the chain.

Knowing how my mother felt about dating before the age of sixteen, I was hesitant to show her the ring. When she saw it dangling from my neck, she reacted as anticipated.

"Michael sent you that? You're not even supposed to date yet."

I thought to myself, if she only knew how much the boys could have cared less about me. "He lives in Utah. I'll never see him."

She turned back to her chores, "Okay, but remember the dating rule."

The next morning I pulled my favorite purple-and-white striped angora sweater from my dresser, dabbed some Evening in Paris perfume behind my ears, and slipped the emblem of acceptance around my neck.

My stomach fluttered as I walked past the row of eighth-grade lockers, anxious for someone to notice, yet scared someone would. After first period, I returned to my locker, rounding the corner just in time to hear one of the cheerleaders. Becky sneered to her sidekick, "Guess who's going steady? Cindy Ol—sen." The disgusted emphasis on the first syllable of my last name mimicked the tone in Grandpa's Moor—man ridicule.

I picked the ring up, tried it on each of my fingers once again, and dropped it inside my sweater.

Mouse Patrol

I had to use a laptop while visiting family for Christmas one year. Eek. All that rolling around on that little pad drove me crazy. Where was my mouse? I kept reaching to click my cell phone lying nearby. It never worked.

Couldn't those computer guys have shaped the mouse into a nice green turtle or a polka dotted ladybug? I hate mice, almost as much as I hate rats. Jan kept rats as pets. Of course the cousins would continually let them out of the cage to roam free. One Sunday the rats were roaming and Mother was visiting. Suddenly as she rose from the couch, she started dancing around. "Ooh, ah, ooh," she hollered as she lifted her skirts and swatted a rat clear across the room.

She abhorred mice also, but living in the country, mice did what they wanted. Besides a few barn cats, she had a stockpile of traps. I remember her setting them in her underwear drawer. She could have started a private cemetery for all those creepy little bodies snapped in those traps.

We four daughters helped her move into assisted living when she was eighty-six. Cleaning her house was quite the adventure. She had been failing for some time and couldn't keep up. The mice had marched into the house army style.

We all threatened to suit up and purchase a gross of snorkels. I know all about that hanta virus.

"We're going in."

Cheri got the biggest surprise. Opening the silverware drawer she yanked her hand back. A mousetrap sat in the middle of the fork slot—set. Later I asked mother if she realized there was a live mousetrap planted in the silverware drawer. She replied, "You have to take the bad with the good."

Huh?

I'm reminded of my continual curiosity of how Mickey Mouse came to be so cute. Everybody loves Mickey. Walt must not have had to deal with them in the sugar bin.

Anyway, we had cats and a few packages of traps on Oleo Acres. I thought we had the critters under control, but when we moved out, I learned the truth. As Carl pulled out the refrigerator, I froze. There, nose-first, a mouse's bum poked straight out from the socket, rigor mortis having set in long ago.

Okay, the macabre nature of the death set me off. I couldn't quit laughing.

"I'm sure glad the buyers didn't see this corpse," I said.

I hate mice.

Mother at assisted living.

Hot Dogs and Sacroiliacs

Tristan and I unloaded hot dogs, marshmallows, and a few carrot sticks onto the log table. It was November and the last time for a picnic up the American Fork canyon. One thing I do love about Utah are the mountains and the National Parks. The leaves were falling, air holding a bit of crisp. This canyon was maybe five miles from our house.

My four-year-old grandson was great company.

"Where's the wood to start the fire?" he asked.

"Just gather a few twigs and put them into the pit. I brought some wood." The matches were hidden in my purse.

The last time we had tried a picnic, I had lost two out of four hot dogs, due to a metal roasting rod the size of a broom handle. Split sideways and hanging on, I had turned the third one over, and it too plopped into the ashes.

This time I had brought the man-sized, all-beef dogs.

"Remember last time all those hot dogs fell in the fire and you said _______ ?" Tristan asked.

"Just open the potato chips, like a good boy," I replied. "Look at those dogs," I said, as I opened the buns and spread catsup along the fold.

"This is the best picnic, ever. Can we come tomorrow?"

"There might be snow tomorrow, little man. We'll come next spring and bring your new baby brother."

"I never wanted a brother," he said. A short ten minutes later Tristan was ready to move on. The breeze was getting a little nippy, so I headed him and a bag of left-overs to the car.

"But, I wanted to go down to the river," he whined. "Please, please, you promised next time we could."

Oh, boy. *Mr. Memory* was right. I had promised. "Okay, put on your jacket and we'll drive down a ways to find the best trail."

A half mile down the road I saw a turn-off with several passenger-less cars parked in a row. There must be a good hiking trail, I thought to myself. The old boys from those cars are fishing.

"Okay, T.," I said, as we pulled in and parked in the lineup. "We'll take a short hike and you can throw some rocks into the river."

He scrambled out of the Suburban and took off. "Wait," I hollered. "I'm locking the doors." I certainly didn't want to drag my red purse down there, so I locked it inside and held the keys in my hand.

Looking over the edge of the river bank, it didn't seem too far. It was a bit steep, but I knew from previous hikes, I just had to dig my heels in and carefully maneuver to the bottom.

"Okay, Tristan, hold my hand and dig your heels in like"...................... They say when an accident happens, sometimes it feels like slow motion.

NOT.

I remember landing on my butt, moving so fast I thought I would roll clear to California, and, seeing a boulder the size of Mount Olympus coming to get me. Splatting my head off that boulder was a death sentence as far as I was concerned. I somersaulted over it and landed backwards, Tristan's legs underneath me, his head a couple of feet from shore.

I laid there a few moments, not connecting the dots.

"Gramma?"

In a dazed panic, I thought, Oh, please, let him be okay.

"Tristan, are you hurt?" I found a pair of big eyeballs looking kind of like someone's I knew.

"We fell down that mountain," Tristan said.

I was stunned, groggy and thankful he (and I) were alive.

"Grandma hurts," I said.

"I'll help you."

It was a good thing I had been working out. Fellow athletes at the gym were surprised at how much weight I could lift for an old lady. A sixty-three-year old gal planking for two minutes?

I had a reputation.

I leaned on my left hand, slowly pushing myself up and out enough to grab a tree root with my other hand. I army-crawled up the slope, Tristan right behind me.

"Gramma, you okay?"

"I'm okay," I lied, tears rolling. I felt blood and touched a gash in the back of my head.

I got up enough energy to sit and lean on a log beside a bunch of pine trees, Tristan right beside me. Lifting his shirt to inspect him, he brushed my hand away. "I'm fine, Gramma. Let's go."

"Just a minute. I have to rest a little."

Reconnoitering wasn't an easy task with a foggy head. I was close to the car, I felt like I could walk, But.................the car keys. Oh, help me.

About that time two bikers pulled over onto the shoulder. "You okay?" one of them asked.

No, I thought

"Gramma fell down that mountain," Tristan said. "I did too."

"I lost my keys in the fall and my car's locked."

The two jumped off their bicycles and searched for the keys for at least thirty minutes. I wondered why they didn't lie me down, brace my neck, slam together a slab stretcher. My bum was killing me. I was shivering and Tristan wanted to go home.

"There's no phone service here," one of them reported. "We'll go back to the station. Do you want us to call your husband?"

No, I thought. But, "yes, please."

They were gone a good twenty minutes, but did come back with a vehicle. They had called Carl and he had told them there was a spare set of keys under the back bumper. One of them drove the Suburban back, the other told us to get in the car and he'd take us home. Tristan wanted no part of that. He wasn't getting in that car with a bunch of strangers.

Strangers or not, we were out of there.

Carl was home when the guy dropped us off. I told him we had decided to take a hike to the river and had taken a tumble down a few feet. He shook his head, naming off body parts I might have injured. He took me to the ER for one x-ray—verifying no broken back, one affirmation—that I seemed coherent, and—one $350 stitch.

Afterward he said, "You're going to bed. Tomorrow we'll drive up after work and find those keys."

The next day we drove up and parked in the exact spot as before. He looked down at the slope covered with autumn leaves. "Good grief," he said.

"I dug my heels in."

"You needed to slide sideways, not on your heels," he said. There's loose gravel under those leaves and it's not a few feet down. It's at least sixty."

Now, that makes a better story, I thought.

I said a silent prayer. He looked under every leaf.

No keys.

Tristan arrived at our house on Monday as scheduled. "Remember that big rock you fell on? That was fun. Can we do it again?"

The following weekend, my friend loaned us her metal detector. Surely we would retrieve those keys. There were two on the ring that were the expensive remote kind.

Not a leaf was left unturned. Carl mumbled a couple of times. Something about how in the world we had come out of there alive. It was starting to snow. I must have hurled those keys over the river and through the woods. "Let's give up," I said.

Carl trudged up the slope and gently rounded the metal detector a few feet from where I thought I had hit the ground first. It was at least the third attempt. "Okay, we're out of here," he said.

One day a few weeks later Tristan said, "Remember that mountain? You hurt your back. Next time let's slide down on our bums."

After two months of intense therapy on my sacroiliac something, something; and staying away from lifting weights or planking—even for two seconds, I still favored one side and was diagnosed with bursitis, to add to my woes.

By the way. Guess what I got for Christmas? A remote car key.

I think I would have rather had a Veg-o-Matic.

Unknown Headstone

I was about seven the year I found out.

Mother always cut fresh lilacs from our backyard bushes and snipped sweet peas from the fence every Memorial Day to decorate family graves. I liked to hold the water-filled quart vases in my lap as we drove to Lovell, (before I knew it was home to 9-ers).

Every year Dad would hop on the topic of Mr. Birdsley, the cemetery caretaker as we neared the cemetery. "I think old man Birdsley is a ghost that shoots out of one of those tombs once in a while to see what's going on," Dad would say.

I wondered if he was still above ground at all. Mr. Birdsley grew a twiggy white beard clear down to his belt. But, he was definitely no fat and jolly Santa type, more like skinny old Ichabod Crane.

Creepy.

"I hope he's here," Dad always said. "Maybe he's doing an inventory of flowerless graves and will haunt the forgotten until next lilac day."

"Now Vern, he's run this graveyard for a very long time and has everything in order," Mother would reply.

"We should stay 'til dark and see how much order escapes these rows," Dad said.

I just hoped old Birdsley was around so I could sneak behind a pine tree and listen. Dad could probably get some ghostly information out of him.

Dad went to find Mr. Birdsley. I watched Mother arrange sprigs of lilacs and sweet peas in those metal vases on either side of my grandma and grandpa's headstone. I noticed her placing some sprigs on the ground close by.

"Why are you doing that," I asked. "There's nobody there."

She bent down again and wiped back the long grass under the flowers. "Look at the plaque."

My fingers pushed aside the tough clumps encroaching on the piece of metal. Using my fingers, I wiped the plaque as best I could. She laid some sweet peas on top of the lilacs.

"Who's Gary?"

"He's your brother," she said.

"What brother? What are you talking about?"

"I had a baby before you were born."

"Why don't I know about it?"

"He only lived three days."

"What happened to him? Did he die?"

"His lungs were weak and the doctors couldn't fix them."

"Did he look like me, or like Tony?" I squeezed my eyes hard, willing my younger brother's face to the brother I had never known.

Mother remained bent over one of the monuments. "He was a nice baby."

I continued, "Do you have a picture of him?"

"We didn't take any pictures."

"Why? How do you remember him?

Mother flowered each grave in sequence, never answering my last question.

She had visited each of the family plots and now shared the last of the sweet peas with the rows in the back. Here my grandparents rested under pine trees, their marble headstones dotted by brown needles continually recycling into the earth. Following Mother, I tried one more question as she tipped the last drops of water into the containers.

"Do you miss him?"

Not looking up, she answered quietly. "It was a long time ago."

As we drove home that day, I daydreamed about what it would have been like to have a big brother. Would he have thought I was a pesky girl or his adorable little sister?

And so I grew up the second oldest child, this brother I had never known, Gary, never mentioned except on Memorial Day. Each year we visited his grave and each year I asked questions, hoping to dig deeper into my mother's memory. She would never volunteer more than the bare facts of his death.

I thought a lot about heaven in those years, knowing from the get-go that my brother was up there and that sometimes he might be looking down on me.

I wondered why Heavenly Father needed him more than we did.

A few years ago on Memorial Day, Carl and I took a long weekend and traveled to Lovell. Not to see 9-ers but to decorate the graves, so familiar to me. There's nothing sure but change and that's for sure. The baby pine tree Mother had planted beside Gary's plaque years before had been removed, even though it had grown over 7 feet tall. The city had banned private planting because of tree roots pushing on coffins.

Reminding me of other pine trees, I pictured our dismembered pine tree on *Oleo Acres*. I hadn't thought about the displaced fairies in years. We have a pine tree in Utah now on a slice of grass we own—still not big enough to spread the boughs and slip inside for a picnic, but my two youngest grandsons are getting old enough to poke bugs and watch for rats.

I'll wait.

Not only was the tree gone, Mr. Birdsley was long gone and Dad's bones were in the grave beside Gary's. I knew Dad was up there just shooting the breeze with Mr. Birdsley. Heavens, they both were probably flitting up and down the rows trying to get a rise out of me.

I stuck my arm through Carl's, wondering how long it would be before Mother was laid beside Dad. Mother did tell me later that while she was in labor her dad had woken up in the middle of the night and said, "Dixie has lost her baby." That was touching, especially since Grandpa was not the spiritual type. I still wondered if Mother had cried, screamed at God, or was afraid to get pregnant with me. She showed me no emotion—Stoic and closed like a casket until resurrection day.

I have felt Dad's spirit around several times. Clear as the day it happened, I recalled him reach out to the family on Jonathan's wedding day.

During the time Carl and I were dating Dad had mentioned several times that Carl looked just like Chuck Conners, *The Rifleman.* Carl couldn't see it, but I definitely saw the resemblance. Chuck Conners was a looker too.

Jonathan was a clone of Carl's at the same age.

As Carl and I walked arm in arm into the reception, I was saying a silent prayer of thanks for keeping our firework-obsessed, overly zealous adventuresome son alive to see his wedding day. At the book signing table, I was still in reminiscing mode. I reached for a pen and suddenly came back full force to reality. There beside the wedding book was an 8x10 black and white glossy of Chuck Conners! Instant tears. "What's up with the picture of Chuck Conners?" I asked the guy behind the table.

"Oh, I've teased Jonathan about how much he looks like him and I brought a photo to prove it."

I felt Dad say, "I'm here. I'm proud of all of you." I know Dad has forgiven me for midnight chases down the Willwood Highway during my high school rebellion stage. He's probably laughing about his "fake" spanking and the poodle skirt. I'm sure he now knows about the stock rack and is glad he's not around to have to weld another piece of iron.

Through all my rebellion Mother never has stayed mad at me long. She threw a hairbrush at me one time in high school, but I deserved much more than that. (She missed.) A few days later I found a new blue satin pillowcase when I laid down for bed. The next morning she told me the ladies had made them at church. "The satin is supposed to help keep your hair less tangled." After I apologize for being lippy, she still says, "Oh, Cindy. You remind me of your dad."

Mother is well into her eighty-seventh year. Last Christmas she stayed with us for five days. I took her shopping. I got her to throw away three worn-out, ill-fitting shirts. Okay, she told me to donate them to charity, but I pitched them. However, she listened to my opinion on our shopping spree.

I also told her whenever she reads my book, not to worry about certain parts. Parts where I whine and complain about feeling poor, unfashionable, being bullied, having to wear cheap shoes, being deprived of my killer red can-can, and stuff. She has no idea of the drain ditch revelation, the 9-ers hanging on the stock rack, or that I'm a lunchmeat thief.

But I know what she'll say—"Cindy, you have been a trial. But that's just the way it was."

And it is.

It's been an amazing adventure.

The End.

CPSIA information can be obtained
at www.ICGtesting.com
Printed in the USA
LVOW13s2207260117
522341LV00013B/943/P

9 781523 866748